Getting Ready
for Benjamin

Curriculum, Cultures, and (Homo)Sexualities Series
Series Editor: James T. Sears

Queering Elementary Education
Edited by William J. Letts IV and James T. Sears

Getting Ready for Benjamin: Preparing Teachers for
Sexual Diversity in the Classroom
Edited by Rita M. Kissen

Troubling Intersections of Race and Sex
Edited by Kevin K. Kumashiro

Forthcoming in the Series
Border Sexualities and Border Families
By Maria Pallotta-Chiarolli

Sexual Orientation and School Policy
By Ian K. Macgillivray

Getting Ready for Benjamin

Preparing Teachers for Sexual Diversity in the Classroom

Edited by Rita M. Kissen

LEARNING
RESOURCES
CENTRE

HAVERING
COLLEGE

ROWMAN & LITTLEFIELD PUBLISHERS, INC.
Lanham • Boulder • New York • Oxford

ROWMAN & LITTLEFIELD PUBLISHERS, INC.

Published in the United States of America
by Rowman & Littlefield Publishers, Inc.
A Member of the Rowman & Littlefield Publishing Group
4720 Boston Way, Lanham, Maryland 20706
www.rowmanlittlefield.com

PO Box 317, Oxford, OX2 9RU, United Kingdom

British Library Cataloguing in Publication Information Available

Library of Congress Cataloging-in-Publication Data

Getting ready for Benjamin : preparing teachers for sexual diversity in
the classroom / edited by Rita M. Kissen.
        p. cm. — (Curriculum, cultures, and (homo) sexualities)
Includes bibliographical references and index.
    ISBN 0-7425-1676-8 (cloth : alk. paper) — ISBN 0-7425-1677-6 (pbk. :
alk. paper)
    1. Homosexuality and education—United States. 2. Teachers—Training
of—United States. 3. Homophobia in higher education—United States.
I. Kissen, Rita M. II. Series.
    LC192.6 .G48 2002
    371.826'64—dc21
                                                                    2002012975

Printed in the United States of America

For Benjamin and Julian
and all those who love them

Contents

Preface

How ought we to go about preparing the first millennial generation of new teachers for an increasingly multicultural society within a world ever more divided along religious, regional, and cultural lines? How do we educate future teachers about the interrelationships of prejudice? About sexual differences? About teaching tolerance, discussing diversity, and deconstructing gender and sexual identities? What concepts and strategies would be helpful to convey to those passing through our professional programs?

Getting Ready for Benjamin addresses these and other questions. It comes at a time when many teachers, parents, and administrators are more sensitive to the needs of queer youth. And it could not come at a better time. There has been no single resource targeted specifically for preservice teachers that places sexual diversity squarely within multicultural education. Some of these essays are poignant, others are complex or provocative—all are essential reading for those who truly want to educate every child.

James T. Sears
Series Editor

Acknowledgments

I am most grateful to the twenty-eight contributors to this book, who shared their insights and experiences and stayed with the project through various delays and postponements. Thank you for believing in me and in our work together.

Jim Sears, editor of the Curriculum, Cultures and (Homo)Sexualities series at Rowman & Littlefield, has offered encouragement and editorial guidance when it mattered most. Thank you, Jim, for your patience, tact, and thoroughness.

April Leo and Gretchen Hanisch helped guide the book through various editorial stages. Thanks also to Christine Gatliffe, who worked with me early on when the book was still a series of essays just coming together.

The Lesbian and Gay Studies Special Interest Group of the American Educational Research Association has supported and encouraged everyone connected with this volume. Thank you all for laughing at my jokes, listening to my voice, and making this fifty-something straight ally feel so at home.

Finally, I am continually nourished by all the members of my extended family, who help me to treasure the past, live in the moment, and look to the future with hope. Most of all, love and gratitude to *mon cher* Norm, my life partner, best friend, and wise advisor on all things editorial and personal.

Introduction

Rita M. Kissen

WHY THIS BOOK?

Nearly eleven years ago I overheard a conversation that became, in a way, the genesis of this book. I had just begun a new job, metamorphosing from English professor to teacher educator because I wanted to work more closely with future teachers. I was climbing the stairs to the fifth floor teacher education office behind two male colleagues who were jockeying for space on the narrow stairway, when one of them remarked playfully to the other, "Get your hands off me, you faggot!"

As an activist and educator for social justice, I am always offended by slurs, but as the parent of a lesbian daughter, I am assaulted somewhere in the solar plexus by the word "faggot." When we reached the office, I took my colleague aside and said as calmly as I could that my daughter and other gay people I knew found that kind of remark very hurtful. Of course he assured me that he had been "only joking," and I said I was sure that was true, but that jokes could hurt too. To all appearances, this was the end of the matter, although it took years before he and I managed anything more than a polite distance.

But it was not the end of the matter. Over the years, I have facilitated diversity workshops, mentored lesbian and gay preservice teachers, and tried to use my position as a heterosexual ally to promote the visibility and safety of my lesbian, gay, bisexual, and transgendered (lgbt)[1] colleagues, students, and partner teachers. Yet I know that heterosexism and homophobia remain almost as embedded in teacher education programs as they were in the minds of my two colleagues eleven years ago. The appalling level of verbal and physical violence against lgbt youth in our schools, the personal and legal battles that these youth and their families have fought and occasionally won, and the challenges faced by lgbt teachers remain virtually invisible in most teacher education programs. When in November 1996 a federal jury ordered the Ashland, Wisconsin, school district to pay nearly $1 million in damages to Jamie Nabozny for the unspeakable anti-gay violence he had suffered as a middle and high school student, few asked how an entire middle and high school staff, from the principal on down, could have condoned repeated acts of homophobic violence perpetrated against a student by other students. And then there was the murder of Matthew Shepard in October 1998, a crime that caught the nation's attention but prompted little media speculation about what Shepard's murderers, Russell Henderson and Aaron McKinney, had learned about gay people in school. To answer this question, one might turn to a 1999 survey by the Gay, Lesbian and Straight Education Network (GLSEN), which found that the average gay student hears twenty-five homophobic remarks in school every day, over one-third of these from faculty or school staff. Not surprisingly, GLSEN also reported that 75 percent of the nation's teachers have received no training about the needs of lgbt students.

RESEARCH ON SEXUAL DIVERSITY IN TEACHER EDUCATION

Most scholarly work on sexual diversity in schools has focused on the vulnerability of lesbian and gay youth and the importance of creating safe classrooms and schools for sexual minority students and teachers (Besner and Spungin 1998; Epstein 1994; Kissen 1993; Letts and Sears 1999; Silin 1995; Walling 1996; Woog 1995), as well as for children in lesbian and gay families (Rubin 1995). Approaches to ending homophobia have included changing conditions in schools: creating gay-straight alliances, mandating that staff development include sexual diversity, encouraging activism by concerned parents and community members, and building solidarity among lesbian and gay teachers through organizations like GLSEN (Casper and Schultz 1999; Garber 1994; Harbeck 1992; *Harvard Educational Review* 1996; Jennings 1994; Khayatt 1992; Kissen 1996a; Kissen 1996b; Mayer, 1990; McConnell-Celi 1993; Rofes 1985; Walling 1996).

Less attention has been paid to influencing the knowledge, attitudes, and beliefs of preservice administrators and teachers about these issues (Butler 1999; Mainey and Cain 1997; Rofes 1995, 1997; Sears 1989, 1992). Although preservice programs have begun to teach teachers how to create classrooms free of racism, sexism, able-ism, and classism, little has been done to integrate sexual diversity into the teacher education curriculum.

THE PUBLIC RESPONSE

Responses to school violence since the Nabozny and Shepard cases reveal the continuing invisibility of homophobia in the public mind. Few newscasts reported that student gunmen in at least five of the major school shootings in the past five years, including Dylan Klebold and Eric Harris in Littleton, Colorado, were said to have been targets of anti-gay harassment (GLSEN 2001). In 1999, the Massachusetts Youth Risk Behavior Survey documented that lgbt youth are nearly three times as likely as their heterosexual peers to have been assaulted, involved in a physical fight, or threatened or injured with a weapon at school (Massachusetts Department of Education 1999; chapter 1). In May 2001, Human Rights Watch, the largest U.S.-based human rights organization, released *Hatred in the Hallways*, an extensive report based on interviews with 140 youth and 130 service providers from seven states. One of the report's most telling findings is the degree to which positive changes for lgbt youth in schools have come from the work of the youth themselves, rather than their teachers or administrators. From California, where youth activists have organized an annual Queer Lobby Day since 1996, to Utah, where students managed to reverse a decision that had abolished all noncurricular clubs in an effort to dismantle the East High School Gay Straight Alliance, to Hartford, Connecticut; Lincoln, Nebraska; Boston, Massachusetts; and a dozen other cities around the country, where youth have organized gay proms—the activism of lgbt youth puts adults to shame.

The Human Rights Watch report also documents the pervasiveness of homophobic harassment (nearly every one of the students interviewed reported verbal harassment based on sexual orientation), as well as its devastating effects on sexual minority youth—depression, alcohol and drug abuse, risky sexual behaviors, homelessness, and suicide—a dismal litany that has been well documented elsewhere (Bochenek and Brown 2001).

Most disheartening is the report's indictment of administrators, teachers, and teacher educators. David Buckel, staff attorney with the Lambda Legal Defense and Education Fund, says administrators typically respond to anti-gay violence in two ways: first, "Boys will be boys . . . [and] a boy should be fighting back as a man," and second, "If you're going to be gay, you have to expect this kind of abuse, because you'll face it for the rest of your life" (Bochenek and Brown 2001). Although the report quotes some closeted gay teachers who were understandably reluctant to make themselves more visible by intervening in homophobic harassment, the vast majority of their straight colleagues were silent as well. As the report puts it, "The most common response to harassment, according to the students we interviewed, is no response" (Bochenek and Brown 2001). One student described how a teacher would walk out of the room when other students were throwing things at him; others were told by their teachers or principals that they deserved to be harassed because they had "chose[n] this lifestyle," or that they were sinners and would go to hell. Some teachers had themselves been perpetrators of anti-gay harassment, such as a substitute teacher who sent threatening handwritten notes to a gay student in his class, or a science teacher who said to a rowdy class, "Stop that! What are you, a bunch of homosexuals?" (Bochenek and Brown 2001).

SEXUAL DIVERSITY AND TEACHER EDUCATION

This anthology grew out of a symposium sponsored by the Lesbian and Gay Studies Special Interest Group at the American Educational Research Association conference in 1999, titled "Over the Rainbow and Under the Multicultural Umbrella." The assumption of that symposium, and the guiding vision behind this book, is that lgbt issues are inextricably interwoven into the basic concerns of preservice education. When we teach about curriculum, for example, our awareness of sexual diversity will affect our understanding of the "hidden," or implicit, curriculum (Apple 1985; Giroux 1977; Kanpol 1988; King 1986). How will we make our students aware of assumptions regarding masculinity, femininity, and sexuality that arise from what is presented, represented, or omitted from curricula and classroom practice? What do we say about homophobia and heterosexism as we prepare them for the administrative hierarchies, school cultures, parents, and community politics they will encounter as teachers? What special challenges in classroom management might face a teacher (straight or gay) who incorporates sexual orientation into a discussion of Tennessee Williams or Willa Cather in a high school literature classroom or responds to a homophobic remark in the hallway or the cafeteria? How should we prepare a teacher for a parent conference with two moms or two dads?

FROM MULTICULTURALISM TO POSTMODERNISM

As they seek to answer these questions, the writers in this book echo arguments that have engaged educators for the past three decades. Chief among them are debates variously framed as "liberal inclusion versus identity politics," "assimilationism versus historical specificity," or "multiculturalism versus social reconstructionism." The question at the heart of all these approaches is the same: How do we promote democratic schooling in a diverse society?

Early efforts to recognize "diversity" and advocate "multiculturalism" in teacher education drew on the "melting pot" theories of the 1950s and 1960s: Diversity and difference were real and valuable, but the ultimate goal was to create a homogeneous society that assumed that everyone was equal. Differences such as race, disability, and socioeconomic status were not to be stigmatized but should remain in the background. According to this way of thinking, lesbian and gay students and teachers (if they showed up at all) were one of many minority groups, presumed to be "just like" their heterosexual peers, "except for" their sexual orientation. This first wave of the current revolution in our thinking about diversity brought the vision and energy of the Civil Rights movement into classrooms and teacher education programs and challenged educators to confront the changing demographics of the student population.

As the multicultural education movement matured, however, members of "minorities" (parents and students of color, poor people, people with disabilities, women, and members of sexual minorities) pointed out that they were not, after all, interchangeable (Banks 1997; Edgerton 1996; Grant 1977; Grant and Sleeter 1989). An African American student in an inner city school whose guidance counselor assumed he was not "college material" and a wheelchair-bound middle class white student trying to survive in a school without ramps might both face challenges connected to their "minority status," but these challenges were very different. Identity did matter, and courses in Black history, women's history, Chicano/a history and even gay and lesbian history proliferated on college campuses. For lesbian and gay teachers and youth, identity politics provided a revolutionary opportunity to celebrate what had heretofore been a source of shame, harassment, or persecution. "Safe Schools" programs promoted the idea that all adults were responsible for the welfare of the lesbian and gay students in their schools; teacher education programs and in-service workshops featured lgbt speakers and videos such as *Before Stonewall* (1986), a powerful history of lesbians and gay men from the 1920s to the Stonewall uprising in 1969. Encouraged by their newfound pride, lesbian and gay teachers founded GLSEN (the Gay, Lesbian and Straight Education Network), and some actually dared to come out in their schools, while students began organizing GSAs (gay-straight alliances) and demanding that they be accorded the same status as any other school club.

Yet even as they celebrated identities that had heretofore been invisible or stigmatized, members of minority groups recognized the diversity within their own communities, along with inequities of power. Social critics and activists suggested that identity was neither fixed nor unitary, but multiple and shifting. A parallel shift taking hold in the lgbt community was embodied most visibly in a new use of the word "queer" to suggest the complex, shifting nature of identities, particularly with regard to sexuality (Britzman 1995; Jagose 1996; Pinar 1996).

Since its first use to convey homosexuality in 1922 (Nichols 2001), "queer" had always been a pejorative slur by which heterosexuals sought to demean homosexuals. But around the mid-1990s, lesbians, gay men, and others who did not identify as "straight" (i.e., conventionally heterosexual) began reclaiming the word to convey their growing awareness that fixed categories like "lesbian" and "gay" did not describe the lived experience of many lesbians and gay men, transgendered people, transsexuals, cross-dressers, and a host of others (some of them heterosexual) who rejected the absolute categories set forth by liberal positivism. Debates over the term continue to rage within the gay community, where some still view it as abusive while others claim it proudly, even defiantly (as in the chant still heard at gay pride marches, "We're here, we're queer, get used to it.").

The idea that identities are always shifting is more than just a theoretical concept for lgbt teachers and students. Will a gay teacher who comes out to his students find that he is now "the gay professor," whose sexual identity obliterates his roles as scholar, teacher, and advisor? Should a closeted high school gym teacher who is criticized by her principal for "getting too close" to her students assume that the principal suspects she is a lesbian? Or is he just giving her some professional feedback based on sound pedagogical observation?

Questions associated with visibility and invisibility are, in fact, at the heart of the queer perspective for lgbt teachers and teacher educators (Sedgwick 1990). The concept of heteronormativity, explored by many writers in this volume, means that heterosexuality is taken for granted (the "norm") in our culture. Silence, then, is never neutral (Patai 1991), and the dominant culture—religious, political, economic, legal—is always sending a message of inferiority to the silenced. A gay teacher who does not mention the fact that he is gay will be asked if he has a girlfriend, but never a boyfriend; a child of gay parents given a note to bring home to "your mother and father" will be forced to explain that she has two moms or two dads. Heteronormativity means that lgbt teachers and students are always either hiding or coming out; there is no "normal" way for them to present themselves in a heterosexist environment.

LOOKING AHEAD

In seeking to make lesbian and gay issues more visible in teacher education, the contributors to this volume find they must painstakingly negotiate the institutionalized obstacles of heterosexism in the curricula and classrooms of their lives. Although they come from four countries and three continents, and write from twice as many points of view, all share the belief that education for sexual diversity is as important as education about all other forms of difference, and that future teachers need to know how to create safe spaces for the Jamie Naboznys and Matthew Shepards of the next generation, along with the children of gay families who are increasingly a part of the classroom landscape. Among those children is my grandson Benjamin, a child with two moms, who will enter first grade in the year 2005. At three years old, Benjamin's gender identity is delightfully fluid: He loves walking around in his mother's hiking boots, building towers with his Lego set, talking to a recycled Barbie from the thrift shop, and driving his choo choo train along the living room floor. This book is meant to help teachers welcome Benjamin, and all his lesbian, gay, bisexual, transgendered, straight, and questioning classmates, into their classrooms and schools.

NOTE

1. Like many heterosexual allies, I refrain from using the term "queer" to describe individuals—as opposed to theories—because I am aware that many in the lgbt community find the term offensive and because I believe it has a different resonance when used by a straight ally than when used by a member of the community.

REFERENCES

Apple, M. 1985. *Education and power.* New York: Routledge.

Banks, J. 1997. *Teaching strategies for ethnic studies.* 6th ed. Boston: Allyn & Bacon.

Besner, H. F., and C. I. Spungin. 1998. *Training professionals who work with gays & lesbians in educational and workplace settings.* Washington, D.C.: Accelerated Development/Taylor & Francis Group.

Bochenek, M. A., and A. W. Brown. 2001. *Hatred in the hallways: Violence against lesbian, gay, bisexual and transgender students.* Human Rights Watch. Available: <www.hrw.org/reports/2001/uslgbt>, or from Human Rights Watch, 350 Fifth Ave., 34th Floor, New York, NY 10118-3299.

Britzman, D. 1995. Is there a queer pedagogy? Or, stop reading straight. *Educational Theory* 45 (2): 151–65.

Butler, K. L. 1999. Preservice teachers' knowledge and attitudes regarding gay men and lesbians. *Journal of Health Education* 30 (2): 125–29.

Casper, V., and S. B. Schultz. 1999. *Gay parents/Straight schools.* New York: Teachers College Press.

Edgerton, S. H. 1996. *Translating the curriculum: Multiculturalism into cultural studies.* New York: Routledge.

Epstein, D., ed. 1994. *Challenging lesbian and gay inequalities in education.* Buckingham, UK: Open University Press.

Garber, L., ed. 1994. *Tilting the tower: Lesbians teaching queer subjects.* New York: Routledge.

Giroux, H. 1977. The politics of the hidden curriculum. *Independent School* 37 (1): 42–43.

GLSEN (Gay Lesbian and Straight Education Network). 2001, March 8. GLSEN statement on reports of anti-gay harassment at Santana H.S. Available: <www.glsen.org/templates/news/record.html?section=13&record=600>.

Grant, C. A. 1977. *Multicultural education: Commitments, issues, and applications.* Washington, D.C.: Association for Supervision and Curriculum Development.

Grant, C. A., and C. Sleeter. 1989. *Turning on learning: Five approaches for multicultural teaching plans for race, class, gender, and disability.* New York: Macmillan.

Harbeck, K., ed. 1992. *Coming out of the classroom closet: Gay and lesbian students, teachers and curricula.* New York: Haworth Press.

Harvard Educational Review. 1996. 66 (2). Special issue, "Lesbian, Gay, Bisexual and Transgender People and Education."

Jagose, A. 1996. *Queer theory: An introduction.* New York: New York University Press.

Jennings, K., ed. 1994. *One teacher in ten: Gay and lesbian educators tell their stories.* Boston: Alyson Publications.

Kanpol, B. 1988. The hidden curriculum as emancipatory and non-emancipatory tools. Paper presented at the meeting of the American Educational Research Association, April, New Orleans, Louisiana.

Khayatt, M. D. 1992. *Lesbian teachers: An invisible presence.* Albany: State University of New York Press.

King, S. 1986. Inquiry into the hidden curriculum. *Journal of Curriculum and Supervision* 2 (1): 82–90.

Kissen, R. 1993. Listening to gay and lesbian teenagers. *Teaching Education* 5 (2): 57–67.

———. 1996a. Forbidden to care: Gay and lesbian teachers. In *Caring in an unjust world: Negotiating borders and barriers in schools,* edited by Deborah Eaker-Rich and Jane Van Galen, 61–84. Albany: State University of New York Press.

———. 1996b. *The last closet: The real lives of lesbian and gay teachers.* Portsmouth, N.H.: Heinemann.

Letts, W., and J. T. Sears, eds. 1999. *Queering elementary education: Advancing the dialogue about sexualities and schooling.* Lanham, Md.: Rowman & Littlefield.

Mainey, D., and R. Cain. 1997. Preservice elementary teachers' attitudes toward gay and lesbian parenting. *Journal of School Health* 67 (6): 236–42.

Massachusetts Department of Education. 1999. *Massachusetts Youth Risk Behavior Survey.* Boston: Massachusetts Department of Education. Available: <www.doe.mass.edu/lss/yrbs99/>.

Mayer, M. 1990. Gay, lesbian and heterosexual teachers: Acceptance of self, acceptance of others, affectional and lifestyle orientation. Unpublished paper.

McConnell-Celi, S., ed. 1993. *The twenty-first century challenge: Lesbians and gays in education—bridging the gap.* Red Bank, N.J.: Lavender Crystal Press.

Nichols, J. 2001. Why queer? *Out in the Mountains* (August). Available: <www.mountainpridemedia.org/oitm/issues/2001/aug2001/view02_why.htm>.

Patai, D. 1991. Minority status and the stigma of "surplus visibility." *The Chronicle of Higher Education* (October 31): A52.

Pinar, W. F., ed. 1996. *Queer theory in education.* Mahwah, N.J.: Lawrence Erlbaum.

Rofes, E. 1985. *Socrates, Plato and guys like me: Confessions of a gay schoolteacher.* Boston: Alyson Publications.

——. 1995. Queers, education schools, and sex panic. Paper presented at the meeting of the American Educational Research Association, April, San Francisco, California.

——. 1997. Gay issues, schools, and the right wing backlash. *Rethinking Schools* 11 (3): 4–6.

Rubin, S. A. 1995. Children who grow up with gay or lesbian parents: How are today's schools meeting this invisible group's needs? Unpublished Paper.

Sears, J. T. 1989. Personal feelings and professional attitudes of prospective teachers toward homosexuality and homosexual studies: Research findings and curriculum recommendations. Paper presented at the meeting of the American Educational Research Association, April, San Francisco.

——. 1991. Helping students understand and accept sexual diversity. *Educational Leadership* 49 (1): 54–56.

——. 1992. Educators, homosexuality, and homosexual students: Are personal feelings related to professional beliefs? In *Coming out of the classroom closet: Gay and lesbian students, teachers, and curricula,* edited by K. M. Harbeck, 29–79. Binghamton, N.Y.: Harrington Park Press.

Sedgwick, E. K. 1990. *The epistemology of the closet.* Berkeley: University of California Press.

Silin, J. 1995. *Sex, death and the education of children: Our passion for ignorance in the age of AIDS.* New York: Teachers College Press.

Walling, D., ed. 1996. *Open lives, safe schools: Addressing gay and lesbian issues in education.* Bloomington, Ind.: Phi Delta Kappa Educational Foundation.

Woog, D. 1995. *School's out: The impact of gay and lesbian issues on America's schools.* Boston: Alyson Publications.

I

SURVEYING THE LANDSCAPE

As they describe the "landscape" of teacher education, the writers in this section present a vivid and varied portrait of the current state of lesbian and gay awareness. Arthur Lipkin's efforts to infuse lgbt concerns into teacher certification programs illustrate the limitations of "generalized tolerance" as well as the tension between the need for visibility and the ultimate goal to "make labels irrelevant." Lipkin's experiences show that even in a progressive state like Massachusetts, with its Governor's Commission on Gay and Lesbian Youth and state-mandated standards for equity competencies that include sexual orientation, there is much work to be done. Part of this work involves shifting the focus from "victimhood" to more positive images of lesbian and gay youth—images that, as he demonstrates, may prove more threatening to heterosexual adults than stories of gay and lesbian despair.

Diana Straut and Mara Sapon-Shevin describe a hands-on approach to classroom practice resting on a keen awareness of the intricacies of visibility and invisibility, especially what they call "hyper visibility," the process by which "those outside the norm [who] assert their identities . . . are perceived as pushy or 'flaunting it.'" Nevertheless, Straut and Sapon-Shevon offer concrete suggestions for infusing lesbian and gay awareness into the preservice curriculum in subject areas ranging from social studies to literature to mathematics and science, along with strategies for gay-affirmative interventions that future teachers can use in their own classrooms.

The next two chapters, by Michael Gard and Deborah Berrill and Wayne Martino, analyze the social constructions of masculinity and femininity that limit the lives of preservice teachers and the children they teach. As an Australian sensitive to the particular meanings attached to "sport" in the British tradition, Gard deconstructs the world of physical education, with its "scientized" view of the body and its devaluation of pleasure. Unspoken rules about the kinds of physical activity appropriate for males and females, he points out, reinforce the knowledge and assumptions students already bring to the classroom and serve to perpetuate rigid definitions of male and female directly connected to homophobia. Similarly, Berrill and Martino's interviews with male teacher candidates reveal the crippling effects of sexist masculinity on young men grappling with fears of social labels such as "pedophilia" or "deviancy" if they violate homophobic norms of behavior.

Delores Liston and Jane Page, in their essay on student teachers' perceptions of homophobia in the schools, and Cris Mayo, in her account of the shortcomings of "civility," give us glimpses of a particularly southern landscape. Liston and Page document the prevalence of homophobic slurs and teacher inaction, as seen through the eyes of their student teachers, while Mayo's deconstruction of southern "civility" echoes the critique of "generalized tolerance" found earlier in part I. Like Straut and Sapon-Shevin, Mayo identifies paradoxes of visibility and invisibility, but unlike them, she takes a more confrontational stance in challenging students and others in the community. Mayo also points out how the separation between the public and the private serves to perpetuate lesbian and gay invisibility, as naming one's sexuality becomes a form of bad manners in a particularly southern system of values.

Finally, Allison Young and Michael Middleton conclude the section with a critical look at the "geography" of education textbooks. Examining text and pictures in a variety of adolescence and lifespan texts, they note that lesbian and gay lives, when they appear at all, are usually described in opposition to or in contrast to "normal" heterosexual development, or as part of a discussion of pathology. Reflecting on the lgbt presence in these textbooks, the authors echo the tension (noted earlier in this section), between presenting lgbt people as "normal" and asserting that "lgbt people have a unique identity."

Although they vary in tone and approach, all the essays in this section remind us that teacher education programs have a long way to go in addressing lesbian and gay concerns, but they remind us too of our power as educators to change the landscape within which our students learn to be teachers.

The Challenges of Gay Topics in Teacher Education: Politics, Content, and Pedagogy

Arthur Lipkin

We as teachers have a responsibility to bring the world our students will have to confront—are already confronting—into our classrooms. Anything less than that is professionally and morally irresponsible.

—Hoffman, *"Teaching Torch Song: Gay Literature in the Classroom"*

INTRODUCTION

The above exhortation, urging schoolteachers to integrate gay and lesbian topics into their curricula, could have been directed just as keenly to the professors who had taught them. Most would agree that any teacher education program that does not prepare its students for the demands of a diverse classroom is failing them. Yet when it comes to readying educators to deal effectively with lesbian, gay, bisexual, and transgendered (lgbt) students, there is virtual silence—few public demands and little reform of undergraduate and graduate curricula. The plight of gay and lesbian adolescents, which is at last being afforded some attention in secondary schools, demands that such short-comings in teacher education be rectified. Although gay studies are burgeoning at some universities, little of substance has seeped into education syllabi. The number of courses devoted exclusively or even substantially to the topic of gay issues in education is miniscule (Rofes 1995; Rofes 1997). Granted, such instruction is no less important in departments of social work, psychology, medicine, government, and law. Yet it appears to me that resistance is strongest in education programs, and those who lobby for inclusion are few. Openly lgbt education faculty and students are scarce. Among those preparing for work in elementary and high schools, the old slanders about predation and youth recruitment may inhibit self-disclosure and advocacy.

The limited mention of homosexuality that does appear in introductory history, psychology, and sociology texts is sometimes inaccurate and distorted (Phillips 1991)[1]. Evidence that some prospective teachers are both homophobic and uninformed (Butler 1994; Sears 1989) renders these omissions and falsehoods inexcusable. Education students must have sufficient study to master method and content, as well as their own discomfort, to help make lgbt experiences part of a K–12 school's multicultural vision.

Education schools are rightly accused of slighting multiculturalism overall. When such content is included it is often an add-on of dubious value, more a feint than a conscientious effort to integrate such issues into a range of undergraduate and graduate curricula. Many education students are left to perceive "diversity sessions" as just another requirement to be gotten through (Ladson-Billings 1999). Refashioning teacher education to meet broader diversity goals will meet opposition both within the academy and without, especially during a time of conservative backlash against all multicultural education (Cochran-Smith 2000).

My experience in Massachusetts has been instructive. For six years (1993–1998) I taught a half-semester module on gay and lesbian issues in education at the Harvard Graduate School of Education.[2] For two years (1996–1997) I conducted trainings with college and university education departments to help them meet new teacher certification standards that were inclusive of gay and lesbian youth needs.[3] In addition, I taught the module once in two suburban Boston school systems and twice in a state college summer program and taught a semester course for two years at the Harvard Extension School.

THE POLITICS

In 1994 the Massachusetts State Board of Education added "sexual orientation" to the equity competencies of its teacher certification standards, requiring mastery of "effective strategies within the classroom and other school settings to address discrimination based on each student's race, sex, religion, socioeconomic class, or disability." Because of this one explicit mention, sexual orientation was easily interpolated into other related provisions regarding equity for all students, namely regard for freedom of expression, nurturing of self-esteem, attention to unique developmental and cultural needs, and awareness of diverse family backgrounds.

At the urging of the Governor's Commission on Gay and Lesbian Youth, this emendation was followed by the establishment of the Project for the Integration of Gay & Lesbian Youth Issues in School Personnel Certification

Programs, which I led. We invited the state's nearly seventy education departments, both college and graduate level, to attend or host one three-hour training that would include explication of laws and regulations, development and counseling issues for lgbt youth, lgbt family concerns, and antiharassment strategies.

Over the two-year life of this initiative about half of the departments accepted our invitation—a good response rate, we concluded. As for the rest, many faculty are inattentive to current gay-focused research in child development and other disciplines and unaware of the subject's relevance to their mission. Some are politically fearful or lack the pedagogical means to deal with gay topics in their own classrooms. Some may have assumed the board's action was a political gesture to appease gay activists and would not be enforced.

A number of faculty members who did participate questioned how they could seriously prepare students to teach tolerance in their school placements when their colleges were themselves oppressive, homophobic places. They steered the discussion toward strategizing ways to make their campuses safer for gays and lesbians. Although I acknowledged the urgency of their situation, my contract with the DOE did not permit rerouting the whole session. Two years later the Safe Colleges program began to address those questions directly.

Inertia was perhaps the greatest obstacle to the long-lasting reform we tried to inspire. We hoped that our brief trainings would be held at faculty meetings and lead to long-term collaboration and curriculum reform. Instead we were almost always invited to present to education classes directly. Moreover, the professors who set up such appearances did not indicate that they would be revising their syllabi or their teaching, despite being pleased by their students' energetic and mostly positive engagement with the topic. A few seemed happy just to have us back every year. Although their "leave it to the experts" attitude was flattering, it held no promise for lasting institutional change. What would happen when state funding for our sessions ceased, as it did two years later? Would their departments sponsor similar sessions or actively recruit permanent faculty with lgbt expertise to fill the void?

Of course we should not judge education faculties too harshly for paying little attention to sexual diversity. They have been under enormous pressure from state and federal authorities to ready teachers for a world of high-stakes student testing, where "basic" skills–building has cast non-Western cultures and other minority concerns into the shadows. For the last several years, Massachusetts has also been in a panic over the high failure rate on its new teacher test, where I daresay gay issues are notable by their absence.

As if these discouragements were not enough, in 2000 the Massachusetts State Board of Education revised its diversity-friendly teacher certification standards under the direction of a new deputy commissioner, the author of *Losing Our Language: How Multicultural Classroom Instruction Is Undermining Our Children's Ability to Read, Write, and Reason* (Stotsky 1999). The draft of the new equity provisions eliminates all multiculturally specific criteria, substituting language that stresses academic rigor and collective citizenship, for example, "[The certifiable teacher] encourages all students to believe that effort is a key to high achievement and works to promote high achievement in all students." "Helps all students to understand American civic culture, its underlying ideals, founding political principles and political institutions and to see themselves as members of a local, state, and national civic community" (Massachusetts Department of Education 1999b).

Then, in addition to gutting these provisions by which we had justified our two-year teacher certification interventions, the state board also revised the regulations flowing from the Student Rights Law, which the legislature had amended in 1993 to include sexual orientation protections. The board has always had to spell out the "regs" stemming from this law. Before 2000 the Student Rights regs mandated a curriculum reflecting the racial, gender, and sexual diversity of the student body. It also required new books and materials, in the aggregate, to depict minorities "in a broad variety of positive roles."

The new regulations set no content standard for curricula. The "student rights" argument, which bolstered our case for teachers to be trained in gay issues, was reduced to a generic call for tolerance without reference to representation: "All public school systems shall, through their curricula, encourage respect for the human and civil rights of all individuals regardless of race, color, sex, religion, national origin or sexual orientation" (Massachusetts Department of Education 2000). One could fulfill this requirement with a weak "respect everyone" curriculum that would not touch on the specific experience of any marginalized group or analyze the similarities and differences among racism, sexism, religious intolerance, heterosexism, able-ism, and so forth.

As if to add insult to evisceration, the board inserted the following provision: "Teachers shall review all instructional and educational materials for simplistic and demeaning generalizations, lacking intellectual merit, on the basis of race, color, sex, religion, national origin or sexual orientation. Appropriate activities, discussions and/or supplementary materials shall be used to provide balance and context for any such stereotypes depicted in such materials." The new language begs the question: What simplistic and demeaning generalizations have "intellectual merit?" And why are such expressions to be remedied by context and balance rather than reasoned refutation? An earlier rejected draft was much better: "Appropriate activities, discussions and/or supplementary materials shall be used to counteract any such stereotypes depicted by such materials." Still, neither of these provisions addresses the tactic of erasure. These regulations might well lead to curricula that avoid stereotypes by omitting certain groups entirely.

The board's insidious rationale was clarified in a statement by one of its members: "The Board has a responsibility to balance the rights of all students. The language we approved does that. . . . The language is a reasonable accommodation among the demands of competing groups." She then added that the board has a responsibility to parents not to undermine the "traditional rules" that they teach their children at home (Schaefer 1999).

For nearly twenty years, while the regulations applied to race, gender, religion, and national origin, *but not to sexual orientation*, the board made no concessions toward validating home-taught bigotry in the schools. The members' reactionary political intent (or cowardice) could not be clearer. And in its heterosexist backsliding, the board has also undermined whatever curricular progress has been made on behalf of other minorities.

CONTENT

The college and university departments we visited who wanted to include gay topics in their syllabi had a limited notion of what they should teach. For many, sensitivity and consciousness-raising would have been the beginning and end of their enterprise. Although of course important, motivation and comfort are not adequate preparation for teachers. I am mindful of the good-hearted English teacher who agreed to use a lesbian short story and discussion questions I had devised. When the tenth-graders asked, as adolescents always do, what causes lesbianism, he replied, "I'm not sure about women, but I think gay men have domineering mothers and weak fathers." Those who readied him for his classroom must share the blame for this teacher's inadequate response.

Well-meant exhortations for tolerance will never be sufficient to prepare teachers for their encounter with lgbt topics, students, and families. As Gloria Ladson-Billings writes in her powerful argument for training teachers to meet the needs of African American students, "Our understanding of the commonalties of oppression cannot wash out the particularities and specifics of each experience" (Ladson-Billings 2000, 207). Those who would substitute hazy diversity platitudes for substantive lessons on minority experiences claim that multicultural curricula balkanize our schools. We must reject that argument. Knowing the other's life leads to lasting empathy and tolerance at least as much as Brotherhood Week cheerleading.

TEACHING PRESERVICE TEACHERS

Education students need both extensive information on lgbt topics and practical methods for dealing with homosexuality in schools. College and graduate courses should teach them to

- understand the significance of lgbt issues in education;
- teach more comprehensively about the human experience through the integration of lgbt subject matter into the core of learning in a variety of disciplines;
- promote the psychological and physical health and intellectual development of all students;
- reduce bigotry, self-hatred, and violence by increasing tolerance for sexuality differences;
- aid communication between lgbt youth and their families and schools;
- facilitate the integration of lgbt families into the school community;
- nurture the well-being of faculty, staff, and administrators of all sexual orientations; and
- collaborate with the greater community in achieving these ends.

Thanks to the recent growth of gay-related research and publishing, there is no shortage of articles, books, and films to nourish the scholarly appetite for both general introductory and specialized courses with some or all of the objectives listed above.

In addition to readings, I have depended on guest speakers: parents, teens, teachers, and administrators. Parents of lgbt children have not failed to be engaging. My students are especially moved by the personal stories of love and acceptance offered by working class parents, perhaps because many students, even subconsciously, equate tolerance with education and articulateness. There is an unforgettable poignancy in one such father's pain, not over his son's coming out, but over the young man's confession that he had packed a bag just in case his parents threw him out of the house. Lgbt youth, for their part, have offered testimony of both torture and survival. (When students are not available, I have used video excerpts from Joan Jubela's *Homoteens* and from Pam Walton's *Gay Youth*.) Students always have many questions and much praise for both parents and young people. They often take time at the end of the class to thank them personally. Clearly they have been moved.

Lgbt teachers and ally administrators have also captivated my students. Teachers who have come out at the elementary school seem even more galvanizing than their secondary school colleagues. Their apparent courage and the details of their students' responses are both well received. Also popular are high school principals who "get it" and have acted to create safe schools for lgbt people. I am lucky to know two, who have visited my classes. One (who actually enrolled in the class one semester) is an older man of scholarly mien from a small school in a wealthy suburb. The other, younger and burly with a Boston accent, was principal of a larger school in a less affluent community. Although both had fine accomplishments to detail and both impressed the class, the younger man had a greater impact, again because of expectations. His stereotypical principal's demeanor could lead one to anticipate a white male homophobic ex-jock. Instead the students discovered a thoughtful, compassionate, and articulate man who had supported important and lasting anti-homophobia reforms.

Prospective teachers should also learn that improving the welfare of lgbt students and families, although worthy in itself, is not our only goal. Although many of our students eventually understood the importance of stopping gay and lesbian suicide and bashing, few saw on their own how anti-homophobia education can lessen self-destruction and violence more universally. We had to make explicit that becoming comfortable with the range of human sexual feeling and gender expression helps relieve straight-identified students from the pressures and damage of a narrow, inflexible heterosexuality.

Eli Newberger, William Pollack, and others have bravely documented the havoc that ensues when young boys are taught to banish emotion (except anger), to avoid empathy, and to deny pain in their quest for masculinity (Newberger 1999; Pollack and Schuster 2000; Kindlon and Thompson 1999). Many become obsessed with ridding themselves of any emotions or behaviors that appear feminine. They are a source of shame that has been called "the primary or ultimate cause of all violence, whether toward others or toward the self" (Gilligan 1996). Adolescent boys' aversion to affective and effective communication even seems to make their verbal test scores go down (Brawer 1999). Moreover, Carol Gilligan has documented how adolescent girls are led to abandon authentic same-gender relations to compete for men's attentions (Gilligan 1982).

Sexism is more often acknowledged as the cause of calamities in girls' lives than heterosexism/homophobia is seen as the enforcer of crippling and dangerous gender regulations for both males and females. Our students examined why young women's sexuality is often questioned if they are strong in self-expression or athletics and honest in their assessment of gender injustice (Griffin 1998; Pharr 1988), and why masculinity is suspect if boys express emotions, admit weakness, eschew violence, or exhibit nurturance. As a result, rather than accommodating to this underlying homophobia, our students appear ready and eager to take it on in their schools' anti-bullying, anti-violence, and gender equity programs.

A number of role-plays have helped make these lessons real. One of the most evocative is set in the teachers' lounge where a female girls' field hockey coach reveals to her colleagues that one of her players has just come out to her. The coach is "still reeling from the confidence and apparently baffled as to why she was chosen for this disclosure." A second effective role-play concerns a student, home for Thanksgiving with his or her "roommate," coming out to an extended family.

Queer theory also has great appeal for inclusion in our syllabi. It has the capacity to rouse education students with the notion that sexual identities, as well as those based on race and gender, are founded on socially constructed labels that are culturally determined and therefore arbitrary. With a bow to genetic and environmental randomness and our struggle to comprehend and control the world by naming, queer theory challenges us to reevaluate the significance of our accidental and chosen differences. Prospective educators must learn to approach lgbt youth and youth of color in a manner that respects their reactive coming together for safety and affirmation with the perhaps greater imperative to make irrelevant the labels that seem to unite them. Such a course may require a greater leap of imagination and faith than any young person in a racist, sexist, and heterosexist culture can summon. Yet it should eventually be tried, at least intellectually, in the relative security of a classroom, optimally under the guidance of a diverse group of teachers and other adults who have taken the step themselves.

Our introduction of queer theory is not meant to strip away the solidarity and celebration that can be part of the minority experience, nor is it intended to render students naïve and vulnerable. The trick for the teacher is to respect and conserve the unique experience and survival skills of all stigmatized groups, while at the same time suggesting a new vision for a sublimely different world. Moreover, minority youth are not the only beneficiaries of such deconstruction. By delegitimizing the categories of "homosexual" and "black," we call into question the usefulness of "heterosexual" and "white" in determining who any of us is. When teacher education adopts these strategies to eliminate bigotry and self-hatred, all people's intellectual, ethical, and psychosexual development is enhanced.

Our readings and discussion about identity "deconstruction" have been energizing and precarious. The confronting of widely accepted and seldom questioned categories of difference is liberating for some students and threatening to others. For example, those who are recently out or are for some other reason deeply invested in "being lgbt" may be put off by a theory that removes the keystone of their self-concept. At the same time, the palpable heterosexism most of us lgbt people face challenges me to juggle a pragmatic and a postmodern stance in my own discourse. I try to draw a distinction between the exigencies of immediate activism and the ideal future in which desire would not lead to a sexuality label or its compulsory scripts. I think my students have granted me and themselves some leeway.

There have been other transforming lgbt topics for our students. For example, critiquing the "science" of homosexual causation has raised questions of scientific objectivity and political subtext that students were able to apply to race and intelligence tracts or treatises on gender role essentialism. Assessing the state of gay and lesbian families and parenting has helped prospective teachers reexamine the lore about the "natural" family and effective childrearing.

PEDAGOGY

The erasure of gay and lesbian topics across the curriculum (Tierney 1993; D'Augelli 1992) prompts my fear that if students do not grapple with these issues in separate courses and modules, they will find them nowhere else. Such has been the case at Harvard, where, according to student reports, these subjects get little or no attention beyond our module. I have therefore felt obliged to cover in a sixteen-hour module every topic that students might encounter in their careers. Our petitions to the Learning and Teaching Department to lengthen the module to a semester course were never approved, and in 1999 even the eight-week module was dropped, despite positive student reviews. I then moved to the Human Development and Psychology Department, where the reception seemed more generous until the module was canceled just after having been approved in 2000. Because I am reluctant to drop the school reform and curricular components of the module, a joint course between the two departments would be ideal.[4] Yet, despite student demand (four doctoral candidates are writing on lgbt issues), neither course nor module seems to appeal to either department just now.

Colleagues and administrators are known to suspect lgbt faculty teaching lgbt content of having a political rather than a properly academic vision and purpose (Freedman 1994). Indeed, I was told that when my module was first proposed at a senior faculty meeting, one member challenged the idea on the grounds that it had more to do with politics than with scholarship. That, despite an unassailable reading list and a research paper final. (This year a lesbian student petitioning her department chair for more lgbt course content was told he knew of no good developmental research on such issues.)

Although my proposal was ultimately accepted, my suggested title— "Gay and Lesbian Issues in Education"—was deemed too broad. Any course with that comprehensive a name could not possibly be thorough, they said. It became instead "Staff and Curriculum Development for Anti-Homophobia Education." However, since I was certain this module would be my students' only exposure to lgbt topics, I was loath to drop anything. Although the title changed, the syllabus remained intact, a heavy load for few credits yet important rewards.

Sexuality and sexual identity (indeed all facets of identity) are challenging topics in any classroom (Nieb 1994). The intersections and competing claims of gender, race, class, ethnicity, and religion are difficult to navigate (Barbules and Rice 1991; Gonzáles 1994; Tierney 1992; Berg et al. 1994). Trying to help students communicate across differences or just recognize their own positions is arduous, some would say nearly impossible (Barbules and Rice 1991). The dynamics of including homosexuality in teacher education are perhaps the most delicate, even beyond religious and political considerations. Surely it takes time to build the trust required for self-exposure and honest dialogue (Ellsworth 1993). The perception, for example, that one is ranking oppressions or inappropriately analogizing among them can be pernicious. Yet it is imperative to link racism, sexism, anti-Semitism, and heterosexism in our anti-oppression courses.

My position as a white, middle class teacher adds to the precariousness. Because I am privileged by race, class, and classroom role, I sometimes became a target for students' frustration and anger. Particularly vexing in the first two years of the module were accusations from several students of color when I ventured analogies to race. Categorical as I was in rejecting the equation or ranking of racism and homophobia, any mention of the shared characteristics among these oppressions was difficult for me as a white person to make. Over the succeeding years, I believe I refined my effort to distinguish between racism and heterosexism both as oppressive systems and lived experience. The racial composition of my class remained relatively constant, but the discourse became less negatively charged. Perhaps I got better at framing the issues, more subtle, or more tentative. The students, in any case, grew more open to the possibilities and less contentious, though no less passionate.

It is important to persist in working out such differences. Otherwise, the result could be bruised students shutting down and trying to avoid such topics in their schools and communities. These classroom discomforts are ultimately a small price to pay, if they help prepare students more effectively for teaching diversity and collaborating with all minorities in school reform.

My nonprivileged sexuality can be problematic as well for both straight and gay students (Mittler and Blumenthal 1994; Barale 1994). Like any other teacher, I am occasionally drawn to use my own experience as illustration, but as a gay teacher of gay topics, I must be careful not to rely too often on my own lens. Although all university presentations are colored by the instructor's perspective, those of us in minority studies are held to a higher standard of objectivity. So I walk the line consciously: I want to evoke the empathy of my heterosexual students for lgbt people through personal anecdote and gentle persuasion but not turn them off with too much of my story or too much emotionality about the subject.

There are also potential hazards in my relationships with lgbt students. First, they may have unreasonably high expectations of me and of the course. I must be a paragon, a model minority person. I must have explicit instructions for fixing problems in the schools. Perhaps more difficult, I must help them resolve the personal struggles they have had as lgbt people growing up. As much as I want my lgbt students to be forthcoming about their lives, I do not want them to use our classroom as a therapy session. If they are angry about the degradations they have suffered along the way, their resentments and frustrations might be directed at me. If I make a strong argument for teachers to come out in their workplaces, those who are struggling to come out or stay in may feel I am being personally critical.

In the effort to win support for lgbt youth among prospective and veteran teachers, I struggle with our habitual reliance on victimization statistics. The litany of lgbt student ills has become familiar to some youth specialists: harassment, physical attack, low self-esteem, suicidality, substance abuse, HIV, and pregnancy.

I concede the effectiveness of such recitations in eliciting the sympathy of the government officials with power and money, but I fear we may be harming our cause through overreliance on these tactics. First the right-wing assaults on the currency of victimhood in our culture give me pause. Then I wonder if there is also danger to lgbt youth in focusing too much on their suffering and high-risk behaviors.

At a Harvard symposium on diversity in schools, Lilia Bartolome asserted that achieving equity for poor students and students of color is jeopardized when they are portrayed as "culturally deprived" (2000). The same observation must be made regarding lgbt youth. And although concern about their welfare is still warranted, we now have an opportunity to give equal weight to the affirming aspects of the lgbt school experience: the proliferation of gay-straight alliances in the schools; the loud and proud claims of lgbt teens for space and respect; the courage of gender-transgressors, even in the elementary schools; and the increased visibility of lgbt families, particularly the legal victories of lesbian parents. These manifestations of progress, most of which are attributable to gay activism, are sufficiently documented that they must become a part of academic examination.

In my classes and trainings I do present the alarming Youth Risk Behavior Survey (Massachusetts Department of Education 1999a) statistics, but I have recently begun to emphasize that despite their disproportionate risk compared with their heterosexual peers, the majority of lgbt youth are still getting through school healthy. In just the last year I have been able to spotlight emerging research on their resiliency (Klipp 2001). Yet I am still certain that many in my classes are more taken with victims than successes. For lgbt adults, risk statistics may call due attention to their own suffering. For general audiences, accustomed to television talk-show tales of woe, disaster seems persuasive.

Several years ago a trainer for GLSEN/Boston (the Gay, Lesbian, and Straight Education Network) commented that he was having unexpected difficulty using the documentary film *Gay Youth* (Walton 1988) in his Safe Schools workshops. His teacher audiences responded with sympathy and resolve after viewing the first segment of the film, a suicide story with wrenching self-hating diary excerpts and clips of a grieving and regretful mother. But he was distressed over the educators' irritated and defensive reaction to the second segment of the film, the portrait of an articulate lesbian making plans to attend her high school prom with a female companion. His analysis of their feelings: gay despair? Fine. Lesbians at the prom? You're going too far.

When our victim strategy succeeds in cultivating sympathy among potential teacher allies, it is easy to get stuck in that approach. Nevertheless, we must find ways to help teachers move on from pity to empathy and affirmation. This task demands that we understand the developmental process of moving from discomfort, misunderstanding, and sometimes panic and hostility to ease, understanding, acceptance, and appreciation. We have carefully planned the content and timing of our students' exposure to these topics.

In the end, after all the theorizing and focus on the research literature, I must observe that one of the most popular components of our module was the final paper. Students always balked when we asked them to observe and evaluate a school-based anti-homophobia project using criteria drawn from our readings and discussions. It may well have been easier for them to retreat to the library, but I wanted them to get out and see firsthand what was going on in schools that had undertaken such programs, to see what was working and what was not, and to try to understand why. With our help in identifying sites, they attended gay-straight alliance meetings, sat at the back of classes, examined curriculum units, and went on field trips. They interviewed teachers, administrators, students, and Safe Schools personnel at the Department of Education. Many appended notes to their final papers or wrote in their course evaluations that this last project made lgbt issues in education more compelling for them than any reading, lecture, role-play, or panel had done.

Few teacher education programs are lucky enough to have the field opportunities that we have in Massachusetts, yet some resources can be found nearly everywhere. School-based gay-straight alliances are spreading across the country. Community-based lgbt youth groups have sprung up as well. Parents, Families and Friends of Lesbians and Gays (PFLAG) chapters abound. More school assemblies are including lgbt speakers. More teachers are broaching lgbt subjects in their instruction. More are coming out. To judge merely by controversies highlighted daily in U.S. newspapers, every state is grappling with lgbt student rights and with the expansion of diversity education to incorporate lgbt concerns. It remains only for teacher educators to embrace the topic in their curricula and to facilitate their students' entry into the field for observation. What they see may thrill or disappoint them. In either event, our courses should provide knowledge, perspective, strategies, and motivation to work for equity for all young people and their families—and their teachers and administrators as well.

NOTES

1. A perhaps extreme example: A student at a Massachusetts public college complained to me a few years ago that both her sociology text and her professor made clear the only place for the topic of homosexuality was in the context of pathologies.

2. After the first year I was joined by Catherine Roberts, an Ed.D. candidate at Harvard, as co-teacher.

3. Again, with Catherine Roberts.

4. We proposed just such a joint semester course in 1999 and again in 2001. The first proposal was greeted enthusiastically by one department chair, virtually ignored by his counterpart, and then apparently forgotten by both. New chairs in 2001 have not decided differently thus far. To be fair, there is little opportunity at the Graduate School of Education, one of the poorest and most crowded at Harvard, to expand course offerings in any area.

REFERENCES

Barale, M. 1994. The romance of class and queers: Academic erotic zones. In *Tilting the tower,* edited by L. Garber, 16–24. New York: Routledge.

Barbules, N. C., and S. Rice. 1991. Dialogue across differences: Continuing the conversation. *Harvard Educational Review* 61 (4): 393–416.

Bartolome, L. 2000. *Panel on diversity.* Cambridge, Mass.: Graduate School of Education, Harvard University.

Berg, A., et al. 1994. Breaking the silence: Sexual preference in the composition classroom. In *Tilting the tower,* edited by L. Garber, 108–16. New York: Routledge.

Brawer, B. 1999. Quoted in Boys found to trail girls considerably in English. *Boston Globe*, November 12, 12.

Butler, K. L. 1994. Prospective teachers' knowledge, attitudes, and behavior regarding gay men and lesbians. ERIC Document #ED379251.

Cochran-Smith, M. 2000. Teacher education at the turn of the century. *Journal of Teacher Education* 5 (3): 163–65.

D'Augelli, A. R. 1992. Teaching lesbian/gay development: From oppression to exceptionality. In *Coming out of the classroom: Gay and lesbian students, teachers, and curricula,* edited by K. Harbeck, 213–27. New York: Harrington Park Press.

Ellsworth, E. 1993. Why doesn't this feel empowering? Working through the repressive myths of critical pedagogy. In *Teaching for change: Addressing issues of difference in the college classroom,* edited by K. Geismar and G. Nicoleau, 43–70. Harvard Education Review Reprint Series 25. Cambridge, Mass.: Harvard Education Publishing Group.

Freedman, E. 1994. Small-group pedagogy: Consciousness-raising in conservative times. In *Tilting the tower,* edited by L. Garber, 36–50. New York: Routledge.

Gilligan, C. 1982. *In a different voice: Psychological theory and women's development*. Cambridge, Mass.: Harvard University Press.

Gilligan, J. 1996. *Violence: Our deadly epidemic and its causes*. New York: Putnam.

Gonzáles, M. C. 1994. Cultural conflict: Introducing the queer in Mexican-American literature classes. In *Tilting the tower,* edited by L. Garber, 41–46. New York: Routledge.

Griffin, P. 1998. *Strong women, deep closets: Lesbians and homophobia in sport*. Champaign, Ill.: Human Kinetics.

Hoffman, M. 1994. Teaching torch song: Gay literature in the classroom. *Rethinking Schools* 8 (4): 16–17.

Jubela, J., director. 1993. *Homoteens.* [Video.] (Available from Frameline Distribution, 346 Ninth St., San Francisco, CA 94103-3809.)

Kindlon, D., and M. Thompson, with T. Barker. 1999. *Raising Cain: Protecting the emotional life of boys.* New York: Ballantine.

Klipp, G. M. 2001. ReSallying qids: Resilience of queer youth in school. Ph.D. diss., University of Michigan, Ann Arbor.

Ladson-Billings, G. J. 1999. Preparing teachers for diverse student populations: A critical race theory perspective. In *Review of Research in Education #24*, edited by A. Iran-Nejad and P. D. Pearson. Washington, D.C.: American Educational Research Association.

———. 2000. Fighting for our lives: Preparing teachers to teach African-American students. *Journal of Teacher Education* 51 (3): 206–14.

Massachusetts Department of Education. 1999a. Massachusetts youth risk behavior survey. Boston: Massachusetts Department of Education. Available: <www.doe.mass.edu/lss/yrbs99>.

Massachusetts Department of Education. 1999b. 603, Code of Massachusetts Regulations, Draft. Available: <www.doe.mass.edu/lawsregs>.

———. 2000. 603 Code of Massachusetts Regulations, Draft. Access to Equal Educational Opportunity Section 26.05: Curricula.

Mittler, M. L., and A. Blumenthal. 1994. On being a change agent: Teacher as text, homophobia as context. In *Tilting the tower,* edited by L. Garber, 3–10. New York: Routledge.

Newberger, E. H. 1999. *The men they will become: The nature and nurture of male character.* Reading, Mass.: Perseus Books.

Nieb, C. D. 1994. Collaborating with Clio: Teaching lesbian history. In *Tilting the tower,* edited by L. Garber, 63–69. New York: Routledge.

Pharr, S. 1988. *Homophobia: A weapon of sexism.* Little Rock, Ark.: Chardon Press.

Phillips, S. R. 1991. The hegemony of heterosexuality: A study of introductory texts. *Teaching Sociology* 19: 454–63.

Pollack, W. S., with T. Shuster. 2000. *Real boys' voices.* New York: Random House.

Rofes, E. 1995. Queers, education schools, and sex panic. Paper presented at the meeting of the American Educational Research Association, April, San Francisco, California.

———. 1997. Gay issues, schools, and the right wing backlash. *Rethinking Schools* 11 (3): 4–6.

Schaefer, R. 1999. Quoted in Anger mounts over board's actions on gay issues. *Bay Windows,* May 6.

Sears, J. T. 1989. Personal feelings and professional attitudes of prospective teachers toward homosexuality and homosexual students: Research findings and curriculum recommendations. Paper presented at the meeting of American Educational Research Association, April, San Francisco, California.

Stotsky, S. 1999. *Losing our language: How multicultural classroom instruction is undermining our children's ability to read, write, and reason.* New York: Free Press.

Tierney, W. G. 1992. Building academic communities of difference. *Change* 24: 41–46.

———. 1993. *Building communities of difference: Higher education in the 21st century.* Westport, Conn.: Bergin & Garvey.

Walton, P., director. 1988. *Gay youth: An educational video for the nineties.* [Video.] (Available from Wolfe Video, P.O. Box 64, New Almaden, CA 95042.)

2

"But No One in the Class Is Gay": Countering Invisibility and Creating Allies in Teacher Education Programs

Diana Straut and Mara Sapon-Shevin

Undeterred by alarming statistics about violent homophobic aggression in schools, lesbian, gay, bisexual, and transgendered (lgbt) students have realized recent achievements to indicate they're here, they're proud, and they aren't going away. The formation of gay-straight alliances, same-sex prom dates, and growing numbers of gay lesbian parent teacher student organizations are among the harbingers of victory for lgbt students.

The visibility accompanying these gains in recognition has been both a victory and a liability. On the one hand, lgbt students are realizing small victories, finding opportunities to participate or come out in communities of support. On the other hand, however, their gains in recognition and voice have been accompanied by increasing acts of violence and aggression. By being vocal and visible, lgbt students have become an easier target for their homophobic classmates. In a recent *Newsweek* special report, Cornell psychology professor Ritch Savin-Williams pointed out, "Kids who are out are the class president, the star athlete. Same-sex couples at proms aren't even a weirdo thing anymore. [But] there's an interesting dichotomy today. It's really bad for some, but many gay kids are doing well" (quoted in Peyser and Lorch 2000, 55). If it's "really bad" for some students, or even one student, then schools are not the safe havens for learning that they claim they are striving to be.

Just about every stakeholder in education (political leaders, teachers, administrators, parents, and community members) proclaims to be an advocate of safe schools. The paradox of these public proclamations is that while many will say they want schools to be safe for kids, they will overlook, if not deny, that addressing homophobia is a critical element in making schools safe. The discourse about the Columbine massacre in Littleton, Colorado, is illustrative. Although everyone decries the violence and searches for explanations of why it happened (the media, bad families, the easy availability of weapons), the evidence that both boys had been gay-bashed in their school is rarely part of the conversation.

With such silence surrounding homophobia in schools, how can teachers find support for confronting these issues in the classroom?

Sears (1992) found that eight out of ten preservice teachers held negative attitudes toward homosexuality. It seems safe to speculate that little, if anything, in teacher preparation programs has prepared teachers to confront issues related to their own or their students' sexual identities. Nor are practicing teachers offered much support. A 1998 Back to School Report by the Gay, Lesbian, and Straight Education Network (GLSEN) found that over 75 percent of the nation's largest school districts offered no training for staff on issues facing gay youth.

If professional support isn't offered in the field, preservice preparation programs may provide the best opening for preparing teachers to face homophobia in schools. All teachers (teacher education faculty and practicing teachers) must (1) organize and structure their classrooms to create safe, nurturing communities in which students' identities (including sexual identities) or characteristics cease to be fodder for jokes or harassment; and (2) be prepared to respond to acts of aggression and intolerance when they occur.

The universities and colleges where teachers are educated are natural places where teachers could learn to confront heterosexist curricula and homophobic acts. However, in spite of an espoused commitment to the free and open exchange of ideas, teacher preparation programs have not openly challenged norms of sexual identity in schools.

BARRIERS TO INCLUSION

If the inclusion of lgbt issues in teacher education is so critical and central to our job of preparing teachers, why, then, is it so challenging? What stands in the way of including lgbt issues in every aspect of our pedagogical and curricular practice?

We have identified four barriers to inclusion, both for the faculty who prepare future teachers and for the teachers themselves: assumptions, invisibility of the hegemonic norm, counterhegemonic practices, and curricular gaps. Examining each of these can help us to unpack the challenge of doing this work well and can point us toward possible solutions and alternatives.

Assumptions

Faculty often assume that all of the students who sit before them in their teacher education classes are heterosexual, and that assumption pervades many levels of discourse and decision making. Similarly, students may also assume that they "know" their classmates' sexual orientation and may conduct themselves based on that faulty assumption. In one of our classes, a group of students were conducting a "community builder" designed to model a way that teachers could help students bond and get to know one another better. The activity involved having each student say "I love you" to another student and try to make him or her laugh. As soon as the activity was announced, one male student shouted, "I'm not saying that to another guy." Everyone laughed. As the activity proceeded, one male student approached another male student, and mimicking an effeminate, limp-wristed, lisping tone, said "I love you, baby." Everyone again laughed. During the debriefing of the activity, none of the students mentioned the enactment of sexual roles as problematic. When the graduate assistant expressed her discomfort with the roles, she was dismissed. The faculty member then interjected, "I'm uncomfortable with what I saw. It seemed like people were making fun of gay men by enacting a very stereotypical role." A male student answered back, "What makes you think he was pretending to be gay? Not every gay man is effeminate and not every effeminate man is gay." The professor conceded that this was true, but again questioned the intention of the person doing the "imitation," the way it might affect class members who were in fact lgbt, and the implications for students' acceptance of diversity in an elementary classroom. At the break time, the student who had done the imitation approached the faculty member and said, "I'm sorry if I hurt your feelings." The faculty member explained that it wasn't about personal feelings but about creating a classroom environment that feels safe and nurturing to all students. "Oh," said the student, "it's okay. We all know each other and we know that no one in here is gay." "Really?" queried the professor. "Yes," responded the student with great assurance. The professor persisted, "You know the sexual histories of all thirty-five people in this room well enough to say that? And would it be okay to do that even if there were no one in the room who were gay or lesbian?" The student nodded sheepishly and said, "I guess I see your point."

The anecdote raises issues both about student assumptions and about the challenges of bringing these issues to the forefront. How do we convey that this isn't about "hurt feelings" but is, rather, a pedagogical concern related to classroom climate? What if the faculty member *hadn't* raised a concern with the group? What meaning might students have made about their own construction of otherness?

The Invisibility of the Hegemonic Norm

There are two aspects to this barrier: first, the power of the hegemonic norm to inscribe a dominant worldview that everyone is heterosexual, all women students have boyfriends and want to get married, all students were brought up in heterosexual families and have heterosexual parents and siblings, and so forth. The other is the invisibility of that norm: Not only is it assumed, but we are unconscious about making that assumption. We base curricular, pedagogical, and interactional choices on the assumption of compulsory heterosexuality, and we do not even perceive that we have made a choice.

This norm manifests itself as part of both the formal and the hidden curriculum. In the formal curriculum, teachers make choices about what students will read, what assignments they will do, and what they will be asked to implement in their practicum teaching settings. When selecting readings for a course, how frequently do faculty consider the content and the author's sexual orientation? Is there a conscious choice to include articles by out gay or lesbian writers? Do the readings on "classroom management" and "classroom climate" or "diversity" include references to lgbt students, or are they limited to other kinds of classroom differences? When guest speakers come to class, do they ever address gay and lesbian student issues, or are the speakers themselves ever out gays or lesbians discussing their own histories in the field of education? For each of the above, would students even notice the absence of lgbt issues?

Preservice teachers make similar decisions in their practicum classrooms. What do they discuss? What do they assign students to read? What curricular lens do they bring to their discussions?

The hegemonic norm is also powerful at the informal, or hidden, curriculum level. Faculty members refer to families and relationships of both preservice teachers and the children they will instruct and assume heterosexuality and nuclear families as normative. An instructor talks about the importance of working with students' parents and continually refers to "Mom and Dad": "When you bring Mom and Dad in for a conference," or "When a student's parents are divorcing . . . ." Or a faculty member assigns students a project to construct their family trees or interview "maternal and paternal" grandparents. Even the most casual references become part of the backdrop of heterosexual hegemony that pervades the classroom. A professor discussing marriage and family says, "Let's take Sally here. Sally—what kind of qualities would you be looking for in a husband?" Sally, who is a lesbian, feels silenced and invisible. Even the details that a faculty member shares about his or her own life can reinforce norms and limit other discussions. If a class begins with students sharing what they did over the weekend, and the faculty member includes her story of going away for the weekend with her husband or having her in-laws over to decorate the Christmas tree, then it may be difficult for students in same-sex relationships to feel that their own story is welcome. Similarly, if norms of confidentiality and safety have not been established in the classroom, students may be extremely reluctant to out themselves or their families or to share information that they perceive as dangerous to them as college students or future teachers.

Counterhegemonic Practices Seem Dangerous or Too Noticeable

Because of assumptions by both faculty and students, breaking from the heterosexual hegemonic norms set within the classroom may seem dangerous or overly prominent. Patai (1991) has discussed the concept of "surplus visibility": When those outside the norm assert their identities, they are perceived as pushy or "flaunting it." Although no one would pay any particular notice to a heterosexual couple walking into class holding hands, a lesbian couple who entered class arm in arm might be accused of "flaunting their homosexuality." The military policy of "Don't ask, don't tell" illustrates this secrecy and invisibility as normative orientation. In other words, there is no "normal" visibility for members of oppressed or minority groups; there is only invisibility or hyper-visibility: "Why do those African Americans have to wear Kente cloth on their graduation robes?" "Why does the Jewish faculty member have to keep referring to his religion?"

There is little a faculty member can do to include lgbt issues in the classroom that will be perceived as casual or normal. For many, the choices are the total neglect and invisibility of these issues or the accusation that they are "promoting homosexuality" or the "homosexual agenda" or "forcing lgbt issues down students' throats." In making professional presentations about diversity, one of the authors often makes iterative lists of student differences that must be taken into account in planning for students' instruction, including differences in race, ethnicity, religion, family background, ability, and sexual orientation. Although sexual orientation is raised as part of a long list of diversities, there are those who attend to that particular difference with concern and distress and query why the presenter would include that or what point she was trying to make.

Curricular Gaps

Even for those faculty willing and even eager to include lgbt issues in the curriculum, there are often no explicit places to do so. In many programs, the only references to homosexuality occur within the one session on AIDS that is part of the compulsory health education module. But what about the social studies methods course? Or the class on classroom management? Do faculty who teach math methods conceptualize their goals to include sexual orientation? Does the language arts methods course include information on using stories about lgbt families in the reading curriculum? Does the "Working with Parents" course include information about students from gay and lesbian families? Does the course on child development include a section on sexual orientation, on the different ways children experience their sexual identities, and on how teachers can support them in this process?

Because there are prominent gaps in our teacher education programs, when something is done, it is often the result of an individual faculty member's commitment to the issue. Could we organize teacher education programs to include lgbt issues within every aspect of the program? Can we avoid adding a "Sexual Orientation Issues in the Classroom" course as something discrete and apart from the everyday work of teaching and curriculum and preparing teachers for diverse, heterogeneous classrooms and communities?

CONFRONTING HOMOPHOBIA IN THE PRESERVICE CURRICULUM: OUR VISION FOR TEACHER EDUCATION

Although most teacher education programs address race, gender, and class, few feature specific coursework devoted to sexual orientation. Those who hope to prepare teachers to create safe, nurturing learning environments in diverse schools can no longer neglect the importance of addressing these issues within all aspects of the teacher education program. What would it "look like" if preservice teacher educators were successfully preparing teachers to confront homophobia? What are our goals for educators?

Applying a model adapted from Sapon-Shevin's book *Because We Can Change the World* (1999), we propose three goals in teaching for social justice: knowledge, courage, and skills.

Knowledge

What is the core knowledge for future teachers? At a minimum, they need to know correct terminology. What is the appropriate context for use of the word *queer*? What do the words *lesbian, gay, bisexual,* and *transgendered* mean? Teachers also need to know foundational information about lgbt people living in society, including demographic facts about the number of people who identify as lgbt, the number of children in their school who have gay parents, and information about the invisibility or visibility of gays (military policies and discrimination laws, for example). Teachers need accurate information about AIDS, not because it's a gay disease, but because homophobia and misinformation are often linked to discussions about it.

The idea that students can learn the "truth" about sexual orientation is problematic, however. There is little agreement about how each of us develops or accepts a sexual identity or about the fixed nature of such an identity. And there is little value in reducing a deeply personal and political issue to facts and statistics. At the very least, faculty can help preserve teachers become fully informed teachers who can approach the issues from multiple perspectives. This requires that faculty create an environment in which students at the university are able to question, listen, and learn.

Courage

Future teachers need to understand the importance of preventing or confronting homophobia and need the courage to act when they witness hurtful acts or misinformation. We want to position our teachers to take a powerful stand against existing norms and entrenched assumptions linked to the oppression of people for any reason, including sexual identity. This goal requires helping teachers take risks and creating an environment in which everyone will ask questions when he or she is uncertain. Teachers need to know that developing competence is an ongoing process; although they may lack confidence in their own ability to "do it right," they will nonetheless have the courage to seize teachable moments. They will know that this is important work, worth doing, even if they can't predict the outcome of a tense discussion or be assured that it will go smoothly.

Skills

Even when teachers might not be comfortable explicitly integrating lesbian, gay, bisexual, and transgendered themes into the curriculum, they can at least help students develop skills for discussing painful or misunderstood topics. When teachers witness any act of intolerance, they should be prepared to respond skillfully.

A preservice teacher in our program once asked, "What would I say if a student said, 'So and so is gay,' or, 'So and so's father is gay?' I'm not going to get into it because I could upset the parents." Even if the questions aren't so explicit, all teachers will face students who name call and make innuendoes about sexual identity. Teachers should be comfortable fostering a critical and caring classroom culture. This means continually helping students identify their own assumptions, broadening their horizons by asking questions, stimulating respectful dialogue about issues beyond students' immediate experiences, and guiding students to consider the voices of those who have been silenced. Eradicating homophobia in schools requires confronting both subtle and explicit acts of intolerance.

The ability to manage discussion about uncomfortable or unfamiliar issues is nurtured through modeling in the preservice program. When faculty encourage respectful dialogue in preservice courses, students will observe ways to thoughtfully offer (and openly hear) differing points of view. One faculty member in a preservice program diffused a potentially volatile situation in a discussion about the murder of Matthew Shepard. A student in the class, known for her strong Christian beliefs, raised her hand and said, "I wouldn't bring this up because it's just not relevant to the kids' lives. Little kids in a classroom in New York don't connect to something in Wyoming." The faculty member initiated a discussion about that point of view, using prompts such as, "Are there local events in the kids' lives that might help them make a bridge to what is happening in other parts of the United States?" When the student eventually revealed that she was uncomfortable with homosexuality, the other students in the class suggested, "Maybe you would just handle it as, somebody was killed because he believed something that was different from what the men who killed him believed. For kids in the city, that happens almost every day." The students in the class respected their colleague's hesitation to confront the Matthew Shepard case in the elementary classroom and we were still able to participate in a discussion that raised differing points of view.

The inclusion of sexual orientation means excluding other issues equally important to students in our programs. Suggesting support for same-sex relationships, for interracial dating, or for evolution theories may conflict with some students' religious beliefs. Students sitting in the class may come from cultures where homosexuality is a crime punishable by death. How do we reconcile individual students' religious or cultural beliefs with the integration of lgbt issues? Ideally, conflicting points of view will be raised in a way that builds understanding and respect for difference. Even if students can't reconcile the conflicts between their own beliefs and a classmate's, friend's, or colleague's sexual orientation, they will ultimately come to respect and protect multiple perspectives in a dialogue.

TOWARD AN INCLUSIVE PRESERVICE CURRICULUM

Apart from these general approaches, where in the required content courses could university faculty explore gender identity and sexual orientation? Most elementary education students take methods courses in the major content areas—math, science, language arts, and social studies—and most will have some exposure to integrating the visual or performing arts in the elementary curriculum. Many programs also include "garden variety" instructional methods courses, which include cooperative learning, teaching to multiple intelligences, and differentiated instruction for a wide range of abilities. At the secondary education level, the preservice curriculum centers around a student's chosen field of study, with methods courses incorporated across the content curriculum. Opportunities for the integration of issues relating to sexual orientation lie within both methods and content courses.

Math and Science

Teachers can be attentive to hegemonic language in math or science story problems. Story problems need not promote one sexuality or family structure over another. Rather, they can avoid nuances that suggest a norm and can actively challenge pervasive stereotypes. Rather than "'Mary and Sue are baking cookies for the school bake sale," the story might say, "Dan and Mark are baking cookies."

When problem solving, students can use authentic data that include gender or sexual orientation. In a sample lesson used with preservice teachers, a high school math teacher had students use general crime statistics to solve problems. Consider the power of using hate crime statistics for the same activity. Likewise, math and science teachers can show students statistics about gender discrepancies (who gets called on in class, who enters the professions, who makes more money) to generate discussions that might challenge societal norms.

The portrayal of mathematicians and scientists is another area where faculty can help teachers view materials with a critical eye. Biographies about women in math or science often portray the women in gendered ways that send powerful messages about how girls or boys should act. In a critique of biographies about Marie Curie, Wendy Saul (1986) points out that Curie's history is often distorted to focus on her relationship with her husband. She writes, "Most of the biographies described the Curies' courtship as contributing to rather than taking away from, their scientific studies; however, there is a definite implication that for every deserving human being, there is a perfect complementary partner waiting somewhere" (104). In the Curie example, the message is that there is an opposite sex partner to support women in science. Helping preservice teachers identify subtle messages contained in the everyday language of math and science is a small but important step.

English Language Arts

A purposeful selection of literature can provide a space for the discussion of sexual orientation. *Am I Blue: Coming Out from the Silence* (Bauer 1994) is an excellent collection of sixteen original stories for young people on gay and lesbian themes. These stories can be used to help teachers to think about the diversity of the students they will teach. Stories about relationships between people of all sexual orientations open discussions of how we come to interact with and develop feelings for another person. However, university faculty must be prepared to face their own uncertainties when raising previously ignored subjects in the classroom. In an article in *English Education* (Hynds and Appleman 1997), Hynds discusses her own shift in thinking about the book choices she used in an adolescent literature course for aspiring English teachers. In a discussion of the M. E. Kerr novel *Deliver Us from Evie* (1994), a student, Vic, revealed that he had been living with the guilt of not supporting a classmate he suspected was gay. The boy later committed suicide. Hynds writes:

> This incident stands out in my mind, not just because of the heart-wrenching story that Vic shared or the courageous and straightforward way he conveyed it. That moment reminds me that, like Vic, I have made the decision to step out on that shaky tightrope and take a political stance in a way I never envisioned when I began my career as a teacher educator. (1997, 280)

There is tremendous value in simply raising preservice teachers' awareness of the "hidden curriculum"—that is, how their choices of materials, decisions about what to include or exclude in their classroom, and subtle use of language in the content areas promotes a message of what represents the "norm."

Visual and Performing Arts

Preservice teacher educators can follow the lead of museum educators, who suggest the following guidelines: If the sexuality of the art or artist is directly related to the work then it is relevant when discussing the context in which the work was created and/or the sexual content in the work. For example, encountering Michelangelo's paintings in the Sistine Chapel does not require knowledge of his sexual orientation. Such knowledge does not illuminate the intent or the content. However, there are many artists whose sexuality has an impact on their art. The National Art Education Association offers resources for helping teachers address sexual and cultural diversity in art and in the classroom (Check and Lampela 1999). Observance of the national "Day without Art," organized by the arts community to bring attention to the impact of

HIV, allows for a discussion of contributions and losses of gay people in arts and other communities.

Music provides many opportunities to explore sexual identity. In a chapter entitled "Using Music to Teach Against Homophobia," Sapon-Shevin (1999) discusses four categories of songs: (1) those that address gender roles and overtly challenge expectations of how girls and boys should behave; (2) songs written for adults that deconstruct issues of sexuality, sexual preference, and relationships; (3) consciousness-raising songs useful to foster discussion of lgbt issues with upper elementary and older students; and (4) children's songs meant to be sung by children that address sexual orientation.

Visual and performing arts provide a context for helping children explore ways of being and knowing that are often not represented in text-based materials.

Social Studies

Given its growing commitment to teaching about groups who have been underrepresented or ignored, the social studies curriculum is a natural place for including sexual identity. The National Council for the Social Studies (NCSS) and many state standards promote the exploration of themes such as territory, conflict resolution, equal rights, human dignity, and migration. Within each of these is the opportunity to address homophobia. The riots at Stonewall (civil rights movements), the settlement of the San Francisco Castro district (migration), and the Supreme Court decision upholding the right of the Boy Scouts of America to ban homosexual leaders (current events) will fit seamlessly into existing thematic units. Resources like *Becoming Visible: A Reader in Gay and Lesbian History* (Jennings 1994) have helped high school and college teachers present homosexual traditions from a historical perspective. Even without explicit attention to sexual orientation, teachers can present the theme of identity in almost any social studies topic. A thorough study of the Holocaust reveals hatred that cut across race, religion, ability, and sexual orientation. A discussion of The Universal Declaration of Human Rights, a document prepared in response to the massive abuse of human rights during World War II, presents an opportunity to connect past to present. A discussion among preservice teachers about societies where human rights abuses still exist, or about how the basic values of the document are upheld or ignored in contemporary society, opens the possibility for a discussion about homophobia.

Simulation can also help preservice teachers confront inclusion and exclusion in the social studies curriculum. Dan McNamara, a social studies teacher at New Rochelle High School in New York, has developed an exercise in which students act as the editorial board for a high school textbook publisher. The question before the board is whether information about Emperor Hadrian's romantic relationship with another man—Antinous—should be included in the next edition of a global history text. Through the debate about the text, students come to articulate their own "criteria"' for and barriers to including such an issue.

A goal of good social studies instruction is to cultivate a citizenry: to help students understand what it means to live in a democracy and work for social change. This goal can't be attained when "one segment of the population is ignored or vilified in our schools" (Colleary 1999). Education faculty must help their students teach social studies from multiple perspectives, bringing in silenced voices and helping students understand diverse points of view.

Faculty can initiate activities that transcend distinct curricula, helping teachers see themselves as change agents and suggesting that students formulate personal platforms of their beliefs. Faculty can ask students to keep track of teachable moments involving diversity issues in the field—even if the moment was missed. There are many ways that faculty in any content area can explicitly raise lgbt issues in the preservice classroom.

CONCLUSION

We do not suggest that lgbt issues be "add-ons" to the already full preservice teacher preparation curriculum. Rather, we suggest that lgbt issues be infused and confronted in the same way that we need to teach about racism, anti-Semitism, or other acts of exclusion that have occurred throughout history.

It is virtually certain that we have in our classes students who themselves are lgbt or who have lgbt family members or close friends. It is equally certain that our students will work with children and parents who are themselves lgbt. None of us can claim that "no one in the class is gay."

Many teacher preparation programs across the United States are currently revising their programs to meet state-mandated changes in certification. It is imperative that those of us who work with preservice teachers examine the alignment of our mission and our curriculum. The discussion must begin among the faculty: Do our students have the knowledge, courage, and skills to counter invisibility and create allies? Have we availed ourselves of every possible curricular opportunity to teach about lgbt issues? Are we adequately preparing our students to recognize heterosexism in their own practice? As university faculty, it is our place and our responsibility to address these difficult questions. Otherwise, we face the more difficult question, "How are we colluding with the norms and silences that perpetuate intolerance?"

NOTE

Both authors contributed equally to this manuscript.

REFERENCES

Bauer, M. D. 1994. *Am I blue: Coming out from the silence.* New York: Harper-Collins.

Check, E., and L. Lampella. 1999. Teaching more of the story: Sexual and cultural diversity in art and the classroom. NAEA Advisory (Summer). Reston, Va: National Art Education Association.

Colleary, K. 1999. How teachers understand gay and lesbian content in the elementary social studies curriculum. In *Queering elementary education: Advancing the dialogue about sexualities and schooling,* edited by W. Letts and J. T. Sears, 151–61. Lanham, Md.: Rowman & Littlefield.

Ervin, K., and L. Varner. 1999. Gay, lesbian PTSA forms in Seattle area. *The Seattle Times,* September 2.

Hynds, S., and D. Appleman. 1997. Walking our talk: Between response and responsibility in the literature classroom. *English Education* 29 (4): 272–94.

Jennings, K. 1994. *Becoming visible: A reader in gay and lesbian history for high school and college students.* Boston: Alyson Publications.

Patai, D. 1991. Minority status and the stigma of "surplus visibility." *The Chronicle of Higher Education* (October 31): A52.

Peyser, M., and D. Lorch. 2000. High school controversial. *Newsweek,* March 20, 55.

Reed, J. 2000. Suddenly, Republicans are crazy about everybody. *Newsweek Web Exclusive,* August 2. Available: <www.msnbc.com>.

Sapon-Shevin, M. 1999. *Because we can change the world.* Needham Heights, Mass.: Allyn & Bacon.

Saul, W. 1986. Living proof: What Helen Keller, Marilyn Monroe, and Marie Curie have in common. *School Library Journal* (October): 103–6.

Sears, J. T. 1992. Educators, homosexuality, and homosexual students: Are personal feelings related to professional beliefs? In *Coming out of the classroom closet: Gay and lesbian students, teachers, and curricula,* edited by K. M. Harbeck, 29–79. Binghamton, N.Y.: Harrington Park Press.

Service Members Legal Defense Network. 1999. Fifth annual report on "Don't ask, don't tell, don't pursue." Washington, D.C., March. Available: <www.sldn.org>.

3

What Do We Do in Physical Education?

Michael Gard

At a social function not so long ago, someone asked me what I did for a living. I said that I taught physical education to students who were studying to become primary and secondary school teachers.

"How interesting," they replied. "And do you teach all of them?"

I paused.

"All sports, I mean."

Most physical educators have had experiences of this kind. Naturally, we feel aggrieved to learn that people think that sport is all we do. Normally, we console each other with something like, "Don't people realize that there is so much more to it? We're health and exercise specialists!"

However, far from a mere irritation, this simple question, "What do you do?" haunts physical education. It exposes the difficulties many of us within the discipline have had convincing others of its value for children. It is also a politically significant question if one remembers that the place of physical education as a distinct and officially supported part of school curricula remains less than secure. Working in the highly politicized English context, physical education scholars like Penney and Evans (1999) and Talbot (1997) have described the struggle to maintain physical education's status as a core and compulsory component of that country's national secondary curriculum. It is clear from this work that some decision makers feel that physical education should be, at best, an option or, at worst, dispensed with. Furthermore, the most common rationale for diminishing or eliminating physical education is that it represents an unnecessary duplication of extracurricular sport.

The assumption that physical education is simply a collection of sports also troubles physical educators because it is uncomfortably close to the truth of what happens in many schools. Despite the presence of curriculum documents stipulating that physical education should encompass a broad range of activities and pursue a wide range of educational outcomes, in practice, competitive team sports still dominate school programs.

It is with some trepidation, then, that I propose to discuss physical education teacher education (PETE) programs and how they might help "prepare" undergraduates for sexual diversity. This trepidation comes not from misgivings about the importance of confronting sexism and homophobia within physical education, although I do acknowledge that some of my colleagues will see this as dangerous terrain, far removed from our "core" business. Rather, I am concerned that it will be seen as an unwanted complication to an already long-running and, at times, bitter debate about what we do in physical education and why we do it. With this in mind, my intention in this chapter is to show that although sexual diversity, or a lack of it, is scarcely part of the discourse of official physical education, it is *central* to the way physical education is currently experienced by students and taught by teachers.

SCIENTIZED PHYSICAL EDUCATION

There has in recent years been increasing academic and popular comment about the fatness, fitness, and general skill and activity levels of Western children. In general, it is claimed that today's children are less active and more overweight than previous generations. Although not everyone in physical education is convinced of the validity of these claims (e.g., see Kirk 1996; Gard and Wright 2001), physical education has increasingly seen itself as playing a legitimate role in this area of public health and, in the process, has aligned itself with what Crawford (1980) has called "healthism." That is, many, perhaps a majority, within the physical education profession see themselves as pseudoscientists, engaged in a quasi-medical enterprise to improve public health through the promotion of regular physical activity and "sound" dietary habits. Tinning has described the influence of "healthism" as a "regulative discourse in physical education" which rests on the following assumptions:

> that health is a self evident good; that individuals are responsible for their own health; that the body can be considered as analogous to a machine; and that exercise equates with fitness which in turn equates with health. (1991, 8)

As a result, despite mounting evidence that the health benefits of exercise and the risks associated with being overweight have been grossly exaggerated (Atrens 2000), physical educators cling to their medico-scientific mission. It is hardly surprising, then, that we find university PETE programs dominated by courses in the quantitative "human movement sciences" (such as anatomy and physiology) and that academic staff and students tend to see these subjects as the most relevant and important for learning to teach physical education (Abernethy et al. 1997; Green 1998; McKay et al. 1990; Pronger 1995; Swan 1993).

It seems safe to conclude that this situation is partly the product of a general desire within the profession to be recognized as a respectable and legitimate academic discipline (Tinning 1991). But the move toward a rational, scientized physical education, primarily concerned with the sporting skills and cardiovascular fitness of children, must also be seen in the context of wider power and gender relations. In Australia, Wright (1996a) has shown how "what we do" in physical education has been shaped by struggles between different gendered knowledge and movement traditions. In short, she argues that there are many forms that physical education might take, and that the current dominance of the sports skill and fitness approach is a manifestation of a particular "masculine tradition." This tradition is marked by the way it values rational, quantifiable, scientistic knowledge about physical activity over other forms of knowledge, along with an instrumental approach to physical activity itself.

The "masculine tradition" has much in common with the discursive underpinnings of "healthism." First, in both cases, physical activity is seen as a means to an end: to be fit and to be healthy.[1] Second, the acquisition of skill and fitness for sport and being healthy are both seen to rest on clearly articulated scientific principles that can be applied in any context.

Third, both are infused with powerful moral imperatives. On the one hand, the "masculine tradition" is tightly linked with the "games ethic" (Chandler 1996; Kirk 1998), which historians of sport associate with the emergence of rational, codified sports from elite English boys' schools during the second half of the nineteenth century. Here, rough, vigorous, organized games (such as rugby football) were felt to be essential proving grounds for the "character" of young bourgeois males, while boys who avoided games were considered morally weak and (hetero)sexually suspect. And as a large and growing contemporary literature illustrates, participation in competitive sports remains a powerful signifier of male heterosexuality (Connell 1995; Gard and Meyenn 2000; Martino 1999; Parker 1996a, 1996b). "Healthism," on the other hand, focuses on the responsibility of individuals for their own health and fitness. Therefore, people who are overweight or disinclined to exercise are constructed as lazy and lacking self-discipline.

In short, an appreciation of "healthism" and the "masculine tradition" is central to understanding physical educators' almost missionary zeal and belief that sport and exercise produce "good," "healthy" people. And while generalizations about the teaching practice of Australian, let alone Western, school and university physical educators are extremely dangerous, it appears that the moral and scientific efficacy of sport and physical fitness remains virtually unquestioned.

CONTEXTUALIZING PHYSICAL ACTIVITY

It is not within the scope of this chapter to assess the degree to which participation in sport improves a person's "character," or whether vigorous exercise improves "health." Suffice it to say that all attempts to test the former claim have found very little supporting evidence (for a summary see Horne et al. 1999), and the latter claim remains deeply controversial. However, research into the day-to-day practice of physical education in schools does suggest that we can be more definite in two other respects.

First, it is clear that whatever physical educators may say about the value of doing vigorous activity, in practice, children do not actually do very much exercise during physical education classes (Simons-Morton et al. 1993). Physical education classes tend to be too few and too short, and children tend to spend a considerable percentage of what class time there is changing their clothes, waiting, listening, talking, watching, and then changing their clothes again (Tinning et al. 1993). It is equally clear from the research that, for similar reasons, physical education instruction results in extremely modest improvement in children's motor skills (Graham et al. 1991). Many physical educators will concede this point but insist that physical education exposes children to a wider range of activities than they would otherwise have the opportunity to experience. By broadening children's movement horizons, so the argument goes, we increase the number of ways in which people might *choose* to be physically active in later life.[2] An important problem with this line of reasoning is that it uncritically assumes that more exercise equals better health and longer life. But it also ignores the consistent and, I would suggest, unsurprising findings of research into the sociology of leisure that people's exercise habits change in unpredictable and context-specific ways throughout their lives (see Horne et al. 1999 for a review). In fact, there is little evidence to support the claim that people who lead "sedentary" lives do so because they are ignorant of the alternatives.

Second, a substantial body of qualitative research indicates that physical education is neither meaningful nor enjoyable for a significant number of students (Carlson 1995; Portman 1995; Tinning et al. 1993). This finding should also come as no surprise since both the "masculine tradition" and "healthism" cohere around overlapping (although not identical) versions of the ideal "good," "healthy" student; he or she is muscular or slim (depending on gender), athletic, self-disciplined, enthusiastic, and inclined to view exercise in instrumental terms. Students who do not fit this profile are often labeled by teachers and other class members as lazy, uncooperative, incompetent, and as obstacles to the smooth running of the class (Wright 1997).

The picture of physical education that emerges from these two areas of research is of a vast gap between its rhetoric and its practice. The faith of physical educators in the intrinsic value of sport and exercise has allowed them to ignore other knowledge about the social contexts in which these activities take place and the meanings they have for different people.

This is ironic. I have often been told by undergraduates, teachers, parents, and other academics that focusing on issues such as sexism, homophobia, racism, and elitism in physical education "sounds fine in theory" but could never work in practice. But it is precisely the "theory" of improving motor skill, fitness, health, and "character" in physical education classes that appears to have little purchase on the world of "practice." Rather, it is the social interactions that take place, including the construction of knowledge about gender, sexuality, race, and class, which are the "flesh and blood" experiences of people in school and university physical education programs. In effect, what I am being told is that this knowledge about the practice of physical education has no relevance to the practice of physical education.

To illustrate this point more fully, I turn now to research into some of the ways in which sport and physical education have been implicated in the maintenance of oppressive gender regimes in schools and universities. Once again, my point here is not to discourage anti-sexist and anti-homophobic pedagogies but to illustrate how they will sit uneasily alongside dominant approaches to physical education.

PRACTICING TO BE BOYS AND GIRLS

Perhaps the area in which "healthism" and the "masculine tradition" are most problematic is their refusal to see people as socially located. They ask us to accept that all people should have roughly the same aspirations with respect to exercise and the health of their bodies (although they might choose to achieve these aspirations in slightly different ways). Consequently, an understanding of the physiological functioning of the human body, rather than the social contexts in which these bodies function, is considered the discipline's core knowledge. But, of course, bodies have social meaning, particularly with respect to gender and sexuality. And it is physical education's focus on the body that makes it a significant site for the construction of gendered identities.

In school environments where "gay" and "lesbian" circulate as terms of abuse, the ways students hold, move, and deploy their bodies are important signifiers of acceptable or unacceptable gendered identities (Hasbrook 1999; Messner 1999; Renold 1997; Skelton 2000). It is clear that many female students know that showing too much interest in sport or exercise during physical education (unless it is explicitly connected to controlling their body weight, as in aerobics) risks being labeled "butch," unfeminine, or lesbian, particularly if their prowess rivals that of the boys (Burns 1993; Clarke 1998; Delamont 1998; Griffin and Genasci 1990; Scraton 1990). Conversely, a lack of proficiency or interest in sport and exercise remains one of the most common sources of homophobic abuse directed against boys in schools (Connell 1995; Fitzclarence and Hickey 1998; Ingham and Dewar 1999; Parker 1996a). Other research has shown that students can clearly explain the gendered meanings they associate with various forms of physical activity (Humberstone 1990; Martino 1999; Wright 1996b). My own research with my colleague Robert Meyenn suggests that many boys "know" that dancing is not an acceptable activity for boys since it is associated with females and gay men, and that avoidance of rough contact sports like rugby can also indicate that a boy is "gay" (Gard and Meyenn 2000). Parker (1996b, 145) has also argued that physical education is a key site for the enactment of homophobic violence in schools. He suggests that this is precisely because physical education's subject matter relates to sport and the body, and because physical education happens outside of the classroom, thus providing more "spacious" and "informal" settings in which abuse can occur.

The important point here is obviously not that students think that participation in physical activity reveals the "truth" of a person's sexual preferences. It is that "gay" and "lesbian" operate as terms of abuse and, as such, set limits on what can happen during physical education. Fear of sexist and homophobic abuse sets limits on the range of activities students will be prepared to try; the degree of enthusiasm they will be prepared to exhibit for certain activities; and, I suggest, the pleasure children derive from physical activity at school. It is generally not "okay" to be gay in any part of school life, but in physical education students know that the way they walk, run, jump, throw, kick, and catch, the very subject matter itself, will be read and interpreted by others, and that their claims to "normality" will be judged against the capacities and movements of their bodies.

Although research into the culture of university physical education courses[3] has been much less systematic, it appears that "gender work" is also an important part of learning to become a physical education teacher. Authors such as Flintoff (1991, 1994), Skelton (1993), Brown (1998), and Wright (1998) have shown that, although sexual diversity may not be a significant part of the official curriculum, being "cool", "sporty," and "straight" is an ever-present concern of many of the people taking these courses. Flintoff (1994) and Brown (1998) argue that homophobic humor and abuse are deployed by both male and female students to regulate what kind of knowledge is seen as "important," what kind of physical activity is "appropriate," and, in more straightforward terms, what kind of people feel comfortable and accepted in these courses. Using an Australian example, Brown (1998) shows that male students are often incited to use homophobic words and actions to be accepted by the most powerful male peer groups. Like me, Flintoff (1994) has been interested in the ways in which aggressively heterosexual male (and sometimes female) students ridicule PETE dance classes, as well as those who find these classes rewarding. This is not a trivial point and, in my view, it needs to be stated plainly. What this research suggests is that some forms of physical activity are rejected by certain students because these activities threaten their claims to heterosexual "normality." In the course of this rejection, however, they also make these forms of physical activity unacceptable for *other* students, through fear of being labeled gay or lesbian.

I want to stress, however, that these research findings should not be read as indicating that PETE undergraduates are "bad" people. But as in schools, the language and valued forms of behavior in PETE courses are structured by socially regulated gender regimes. This means that they are neither natural nor inevitable, but no less real or powerful as a consequence.

In short, "doing" physical education in schools and universities involves negotiating complex webs of meaning. These meanings will be inflected by local factors but, at the same time, are not easily captured by pointing to isolated examples. But school and university students and teachers *do* have sophisticated knowledge about what is signified by a slim, muscular body, proficiency at sport, and participation in particular forms of physical activity. And although they do not only relate to questions of gender and sexuality, no analysis of why people do or do not participate in physical activity is complete without an appreciation of this gendered and sexualized knowledge.

WHAT ABOUT PLEASURE?

Thus far, I have tried to develop two lines of argument. On the one hand, I claim that the "theory" of physical education is dominated by instrumental, scientistic knowledge about the body. On the other, I suggest that this theory appears to float free of the kinds of knowledge that students and teachers operate with when they "do" physical education. How might we connect these two analyses? What investments are at stake?

I have already alluded to one such investment. At each level of knowledge production, whether in schools or universities, gendered identities are at stake. Performing an unambiguously "straight" masculinity, for example, may involve establishing one's credentials as a (pseudo?) scientist in the academy, or as a "hard man" on the school sports field.

But there is another connection. It is also noticeable that neither "health-ism" nor the "masculine tradition" is concerned with what we might call the spontaneous or immediate bodily pleasure of physical activity. Both discursive formations stress that, first and foremost, physical activity has certain effects on one's "character" and on one's body, but that these are always deferred. Of course, physical educators are fond of emphasizing the importance of exercise being "fun," especially for children. But wherein does the "fun" lie? I would argue that the choice of the word "fun" indicates a desire to sanitize and trivialize the bodily experience of physical activity, while also transferring the value of the experience away from the mover and into the activity itself. Therefore we are told that "games are fun" rather than that "they feel good." Indeed, the word "fun" seems to sit far more comfortably within the dominant desexualized and idealized view of childhood innocence than the more libidinous notion of "bodily pleasure."

This point resonates with current theories of the gendered body and, in particular, masculinities. For example, it has been argued that masculine orientations to bodily practices such as sex and sport are characterized by an obfuscation of pleasure through language (Tieffer 1987) and the deployment of the body as an instrument or weapon (Connell 1990; Messner 1992; Young and White 1999). Thus, in sex and in sport, men tend to talk about "work" and their "performance," but never the bodily pleasure they derive. It is also apparent that "healthism" and the "masculine tradition" stipulate that we should be serious about our exercise and feel at least some pain ("no pain, no gain"; "there is no finishing line"). Rather than seeing the body as something to be enjoyed and as an integral part of one's identity, masculine discourses emphasize a sharp distinction between body and self, coupled with a desire to transcend or conquer the body.

In making this point, I want to be clear that my main concern is with the experiences of children in schools. As an adult who exercises regularly and frets about putting on weight, I still experience the ache of tired muscles and the drip of sweat on my face and body as exquisite bodily pleasures, ones that I return to again and again. The instrumental and the pleasurable *can* coexist. However, this pleasure is only possible for me because of its location within a wider social economy, in which certain ways of being white, middle class, able bodied, adult, heterosexual, male, and a Western consumer (among many other things) have shaped my desires. And while the aspirations, desires, and pleasures of children will also be socially produced, my point is simply that we need to be extremely circumspect in assuming that our pleasures will be their pleasures.

Of course, this raises difficult questions, such as "What is pleasure?" and "How do we know what children find pleasurable?", questions I will not even attempt to answer here. But research into what students do in physical education shows that children are expected to engage in forms of physical activity that many *do not* enjoy. For example, many primary schools in Australia begin their days with massed aerobics-style activities. The explicit purpose is to help children lose or "control" their body weight. The practice of fitness testing in physical education continues to be widespread despite obvious flaws in the efficacy of these tests and research showing that children neither understand nor enjoy them (Hopple and Graham 1995). Despite the fact that many children either are not interested in, or are anxious about, participating in competitive sports, many physical educators still pursue "sport for all" agendas, assuming that *all* children will share their "love" of sport. This situation is only explicable as long as one accepts that deriving pleasure is subordinate to the long term goals of cardiovascular fitness, weight control, and building "character" (whatever that may mean).

In physical education, the subordination of pleasure (as opposed to fun) to longer term goals such as skill development, fitness, and weight control has other obvious effects. First, as I have suggested already, adults will tend to organize games and activities for children that closely resemble adults' games and activities. The rationale for this seems to be that because many adults play sport, jog, or go to aerobics in an attempt to control their weight, children should do likewise. Second, the practice and training for children's games tends to be highly structured, repetitive, and decontextualized (that is, very similar to the training adults do). My experience is that children almost always find these activities boring. But for many physical educators, unstructured, children-centered activities are seen as "a waste of time." Third, winning becomes central. Teachers and coaches will often say that they tell children that fun and enjoyment are the most important things. But the activities that the children are actually doing, the training and the games themselves, are designed to produce winners and losers, and children understand this very well. After all, the games they do at school look very similar to the ones they see on television, where there is absolutely no doubt that winning is the most important thing.

Returning to the main focus of this chapter, the subordination of pleasure also means that physical educators are able to ignore the very social nature of physical education classes. Students who treat physical education classes as chances to prove that they are not gay by succeeding in the "traditional" games that are played, and by disparaging the lack of prowess of others, will tend to be the ones who are "successful" and described as "enjoying physical education." In practice, this means that only the pleasures of certain students will be satisfied. Thus, physical education, along with other heteronormative institutions, can be seen as congealed around a set of practices in which only certain kinds of pleasures are allowed. Physical education stipulates that children use and relate to their bodies in particular ways and not others. And as I have argued throughout this chapter, many children already possess complex gendered and sexualized knowledge about the body every time they enter a physical education class. It is not surprising that many choose to use their bodies in ways that, rather than bringing them pleasure, simply serve to avoid homophobic suspicion.

WHAT TO DO?

My work as a teacher educator has convinced me that there are no "silver bullets" to address the concerns I have outlined here. I believe that change needs to be pursued on a number of fronts, and that, although educational transformation for ourselves and our students occasionally arrives as glorious moments of realization, more often it is gradual, slow, and even tedious. Therefore, based on my own work and that of other teacher educators, I offer the following suggestions.

First, I wholeheartedly believe that part of the business of finding a meaningful space for sociologically informed knowledge about physical education involves engaging with the science of exercise and health. Although this project is in its early stages, we are on the verge of a (probably) quiet revolution in the state of our knowledge about exercise, body shape, and health. Although I contend that the problems in this body of knowledge have, for some time, been obvious to those who have cared to look—particularly the conflation of fitness and health and the demonization of body fat—they are now more obvious than ever. In the next few years we will begin to hear such heretical claims as, "It is better to be fat and physically active than thin and inactive," emanating from the mouths of sport scientists. The realization that scientific knowledge about the body is unstable and ideologically located has come as a great shock to many of my students. I have no doubt that this has helped some of them listen to and think about non-medico-scientific rationales for physical education.

Second, as important as it is for students to read research into sexism and homophobia in physical education, much of the deconstructive work in teacher education courses must be done by the students themselves. Like the children in our schools, our undergraduates have a great deal of knowledge about how gender and sexuality are negotiated in their particular social contexts; they can talk very clearly about what is "cool" or "gay" and what particular forms of physical activity *mean*. I have had "success"[4] where I have asked students to *make sense* (that is, "What is going on here?") of video footage of professional sport and the image-based and linguistic conventions of other sports media. Television and print advertisements in which various forms of physical activity and notions of gender and sexuality are interwoven (and it is amazing how common such advertisements are when one actually looks for them) have also served as valuable stimuli. Having asked students to consider why these advertisements "work" (that is, what meanings are implied so that viewers get the advertisers' intended messages), I have asked students to construct their own linguistic or image-based juxtapositions that do not "work." This exercise in particular has been extremely effective in allowing students to explore and describe the tight and yet rarely articulated links between the institutions of sport and heterosexuality. Of course, the discussions that flow out of this kind of exercise need to be sensitively and carefully managed so that no students are put at undue emotional risk, and this leads to my third suggestion.

Teacher educators need to articulate a rationale for physical education in which notions of sexual diversity and social justice are central. In other words, moments when discussions move to sexuality and homophobia, as in my previous example, should not come as a surprise to students. They may not want to discuss these issues, and they may not agree with our points of view, but they should not be left wondering why (on earth!) their studies have moved to this terrain. In Australia, linking physical education with sexuality, gender equity, and social justice has, at least in one respect, become easier in recent years as most states have moved to integrate physical education with subject material in "health" (usually defined broadly and equated with words such as "well-being") and what is sometimes called "personal development" (a term that explicitly deals with care and respect for the self and others). In other countries, a growing recognition of the importance of holistic notions of health is reflected in physical education curricula in many parts of the world. In other words, ample scope exists for making a sound and, perhaps more important, officially sanctioned case for linking sport, physical activity, and questions of sexism and homophobia.

Finally, returning to my notion of pleasure, we need to validate forms of physical activity that are playful, spontaneous, and incidental. For too long physical educators have tended to argue that only organized, purposeful, rule-bound activities could deliver "health" and "character" benefits. In my view, we need to acknowledge unambiguously the impoverished nature of this vision and to speak clearly and often (rather than begrudgingly and occasionally) about the value of physical activity that would not normally be considered the stuff of physical education. I also think that it wouldn't hurt if we talked about our own pleasure in physical activity, whatever form it takes, and, in our teaching and our research, if we told stories about pleasure, rather than just about "hard work" and "goal setting." You never know, the people we are trying to influence might actually choose to join in.

CONCLUSION

Pronger has argued that the scientization of physical education, particularly in universities, has affected the way PETE students view knowledge and the human body. Seeing the body as an object involves overcoming our emotional responses and devaluing the

> total way that the body appears in the full emotional, intellectual, and cultural complexity of our human engagement in the life and death of the body. The distinction between the narrowness of the scientific gaze and what is seen in the fullness of human perception is lost. (1995, 436)

The narrowness of the way in which physical educators have asked us to experience and understand physical activity is the focus of this chapter. My concern is with a deeper appreciation and understanding of the ways in which we experience physical activity (its pleasure, its pains) and of the social meanings (particularly, although not limited to, one's gender and sexuality) it conveys. Focusing on the notion of bodily pleasure that is immediate and non-instrumental may be one way of bringing children and their experiences out of the margins of PETE knowledge.

We cannot simply add "an appreciation or acceptance of sexual diversity" (or whatever words we might choose) to our list of objectives in PETE. As I have tried to show, objectives of this kind simply do not fit comfortably within the heavily scientized and technocratic bodies of knowledge that currently dominate PETE university courses. Therefore, in thinking about an explicitly anti-sexist and anti-homophobic approach to PETE, we must engage with the ways knowledge is constructed, taught, and assessed in PETE courses. Among other things, this may mean helping students to see scientific knowledge about the human body as unstable, partial, and highly political.

The challenge for physical education teacher educators is not simply to raise questions of sexual diversity in their classes, although this will be an important beginning. It is also to help students see questions of social justice as consistent with the overall intellectual underpinnings and aims of physical education. In terms of teacher preparation, this means engaging with the politics of knowledge. It means asking, once again, what is central and what is peripheral to our work as teachers.

NOTES

1. In fact, a central critique of "healthism" has been the tendency of its proponents to confuse and conflate the terms "fitness" and "health." Despite considerable research into exercise and health, the amount and the intensity of physical activity required to achieve health benefits remains unknown. However, there is strong evidence to suggest that a high level of cardiovascular fitness does not have significant health benefits.

2. Notice here that participation in exercise is seen as simply one of a number of health decisions that we make. As such, physical education is responsible for helping people to make more "informed" health decisions (in this case about the type of exercise they might choose) rather than helping students to make sense of the social contexts in which health decisions are made and the ways in which these contexts can constrain a person's choices.

3. I am aware that many of what I refer to here as physical education undergraduates undertake university courses that may not bear the title "physical education." This is currently the case at my own institution, which offers degrees in "human movement studies."

4. Of course, what represents "success" in teacher education is not a straightforward matter. In this case, I take "success" to mean class experiences that "felt good," where discussions among my students were lively and thoughtful and where students later talked about thinking differently about these issues.

REFERENCES

Abernethy, P., D. MacDonald, and K. Bramich. 1997. Undergraduate subject relevance: A human movement studies case study. *The ACHPER Healthy Lifestyles Journal* 44 (4): 5–10.

Atrens, D. M. 2000. *The power of pleasure: Why indulgence is good for you, and other palatable truths.* Sydney, Aust.: Duffy & Snellgrove.

Brown, L. 1998. "Boys' training": The inner sanctum. In *Where the boys are: Masculinity, sport and education,* edited by C. Hickey, L. Fitzclarence, and R. Matthews, 83–96. Geelong, Aust.: Deakin Centre for Education and Change.

Burns, R. 1993. Health, fitness and female subjectivity: What is happening in school health and physical education? In *Feminism and education,* edited by L. Yates. Melbourne, Aust.: La Trobe University Press.

Carlson, T. B. 1995. We hate gym: Student alienation from physical education. *Journal of Teaching in Physical Education* 14 (4): 467–77.

Chandler, T. J. L. 1996. The structuring of manliness and the development of rugby football at the public schools and Oxbridge, 1830–1880. In *Making men: Rugby and masculine identity,* edited by T. J. L. Chandler, and J. Nauright, 13–31. London: Frank Cass.

Clarke, G. 1998. Queering the pitch and coming out to play: Lesbians in physical education and sport. *Sport, Education and Society* 3 (2): 145–60.

Connell, R. W. 1990. An iron man: The body and some contradictions of hegemonic masculinity. In *Sport, men, and the gender order: Critical feminist perspectives,* edited by M. A. Messner and D. F. Sabo, 83–95. Champaign, Ill.: Human Kinetics.

———. 1995. *Masculinities*. St. Leonards N.S.W., Aust.: Allen and Unwin.

Crawford, R. 1980. Healthism and the medicalisation of everyday life. *International Journal of Health Services* 10 (3): 365–89.

Delamont, S. 1998. "You need the leotard": Revisiting the first PE lesson. *Sport, Education and Society* 3 (1): 5–17.

Fitzclarence, L., and C. Hickey. 1998. Learning to rationalize abusive behaviour through football. In *Where the boys are: Masculinity, sport and education,* edited by C. Hickey, L. Fitzclarence, and R. Matthews, 67–81. Geelong, Aust.: Deakin Centre for Education and Change.

Flintoff, A. 1991. Dance, masculinity and teacher education. *The British Journal of Physical Education* (Winter): 31–35.

———. 1994. Sexism and homophobia in physical education: The challenge for teacher educators. *Physical Education Review* 17 (2): 97–105.

Gard, M., and R. Meyenn. 2000. Boys, bodies, pleasure and pain: Interrogating contact sports in schools. *Sport, Education and Society* 5 (1): 19–34.

Gard, M., and J. Wright. 2001. Managing uncertainty: Obesity discourses and physical education in a risk society. *Studies in Philosophy and Education* 20 (6): 535–49.

Graham, G, M. Metzler, and G. Webster. 1991. Specialist and classroom teacher effectiveness in children's physical education. *Journal of Teaching in Physical Education* 10 (4): 321–426.

Green, K. 1998. Philosophies, ideologies and the practice of physical education. *Sport, Education and Society* 3 (2): 125–43.

Griffin, P., and J. Genasci. 1990. Addressing homophobia in physical education: Responsibilities for teachers and researchers. In *Sport, men, and the gender order: Critical feminist perspectives,* edited by M. A. Messner and D. F. Sabo, 211–21. Champaign, Ill.: Human Kinetics.

Hasbrook, C. A. 1999. Young children's social constructions of physicality and gender. In *Inside sport,* edited by J. Coakley and P. Donnelly, 7–16. London: Routledge.

Hopple, C., and G. Graham. 1995. What children think, feel, and know about physical fitness testing. *Journal of Teaching in Physical Education* 14 (4): 408–17.

Horne, J., A. Tomlinson, and G. Whannel. 1999. *Understanding sport: An introduction to the sociological and cultural analysis of sport.* London: E & F.N. Spon.

Humberstone, B. 1990. Warriors or wimps? Creating alternative forms of physical education. In *Sport, men, and the gender order: Critical feminist perspectives,* edited by M. A. Messner and D. F. Sabo, 201–10. Champaign, Ill.: Human Kinetics.

Ingham, A. G., and A. Dewar. 1999. Through the eyes of youth: "Deep play" in Pee-Wee ice hockey. In *Inside sports,* edited by J. Coakley and P. Donnelly, 17–27. London: Routledge.

Kirk, D. 1996. The crisis in school physical education: An argument against the tide. *The ACHPER Healthy Lifestyles Journal* 43 (4): 25–27.

———. 1998. *Schooling bodies: School practice and public discourse 1880–1950.* London: Leicester University Press.

Martino, W. 1999. "Cool Boys," "Party Animals," "Squids" and "Poofters": Interrogating the dynamics and politics of adolescent masculinities in school. *British Journal of Sociology of Education* 20 (2): 239–63.

McKay, J., J. M. Gore, and D. Kirk. 1990. Beyond the limits of technocratic physical education. *Quest* 42 (1): 52–76.

Messner, M. A. 1992. *Power at play: Sports and the problem of masculinity.* Boston: Beacon Press.

———. 1999. Becoming 100 percent straight. In *Inside sports,* edited by J. Coakley and P. Donnelly, 104–10. London: Routledge.

Parker, A. 1996a. Sporting masculinities: Gender relations and the body. In *Understanding masculinities: Social relations and cultural arenas,* edited by M. Mac An Ghaill, 126–38. Buckingham, UK: Open University Press.

———. 1996b. The construction of masculinity within boys' physical education. *Gender and Education* 8 (2): 141–57.

Penney, D., and J. Evans. 1999. *Politics, policy, and practice in physical education.* London: Routledge.

Portman, P. A. 1995. Who is having fun in physical education classes? Experiences of sixth-grade students in elementary and middle schools. *Journal of Teaching in Physical Education* 14 (4): 445–53.

Pronger, B. 1995. Rendering the body: The implicit lessons of gross anatomy. *Quest* 47 (4): 427–46.

Renold, E. 1997. "All they've got in their brains is football": Sport, masculinity and the gendered practices of playground relations. *Sport, Education and Society* 2 (1): 5–23.

Scraton, S. 1990. *Gender and physical education.* Geelong, Aust.: Deakin University Press.

Simons-Morton, B. G., W. G. Taylor, S. A. Snider, and I. W. Huang. 1993. The physical activity of fifth-grade students during physical education. *American Journal of Public Health* 83 (2): 262–64.

Skelton, A. 1993. On becoming a male physical education teacher: The informal culture of students and the construction of hegemonic masculinity. *Gender and Education* 5 (3): 289–303.

Skelton, C. 2000. "A passion for football": Dominant masculinities and primary schooling. *Sport, Education and Society* 5 (1): 1–18.

Swan, P. A. 1993. "This is really important, you need to know this": Hierarchies of subject knowledge within physical education teacher education and student intention. Ph.D. diss., Deakin University, Geelong, Australia.

Talbot, M. 1997. Physical education and the national curriculum: Some political issues. In *Sport and leisure: Connections and controversies,* edited by G. Mcfee and A. Tomlinson, 37–68. Aachen, Germany: Meyer & Meyer Verlag.

Tieffer, L. 1987. In pursuit of the perfect penis: The medicalization of male sexuality. In *Changing men,* edited by M. Kimmel. Newbury Park, Calif.: Sage.

Tinning, R. 1991. Health Oriented Physical Education (HOPE): The case of physical education and the promotion of healthy lifestyles. *The ACHPER National Journal* 134: 4–10.

Tinning, R., D. Kirk, and J. Evans. 1993. *Learning to teach physical education.* Englewood Cliffs, N.J.: Prentice Hall.

Wright, J. 1996a. Mapping the discourses of physical education: Articulating a female tradition. *Journal of Curriculum Studies* 28 (3): 331–51.

———. 1996b. The construction of complementarity in physical education. *Gender and Education* 8 (1): 61–79.

———. 1997. The construction of gendered contexts in single sex and co-educational physical education lessons. *Sport, education and society* 2 (1): 55–72.

———. 1998. Reconstructing gender in sport and physical education. In *Where the boys are: Masculinity, sport and education,* edited by C. Hickey, L. Fitzclarence, and R. Matthews, 13–26. Geelong, Aust.: Deakin Centre for Education and Change.

Young, K., and P. White. 1999. Threats to sport careers: Elite athletes talk about injury and pain. In *Inside sports,* edited by J. Coakley and P. Donnelly. London: Routledge.

4

"Pedophiles and Deviants": Exploring Issues of Sexuality, Masculinity, and Normalization in the Lives of Male Teacher Candidates

Deborah P. Berrill and Wayne Martino

INTRODUCTION

In this chapter we explore the ways that sexuality and masculinity affect the lives of male teacher education candidates in Australia and Canada. We write as teacher educators, as a female and a male, as straight and gay persons with a particular interest in feminist and queer theories. Our study is based on a collaborative research project involving interviews with Australian and Canadian teacher candidates about their self-perceptions as male teachers. Here we focus on how the links between sexuality and masculinity lead these men, regardless of their sexual orientation, to place themselves under a particular kind of self-surveillance to avoid the attributions of pedophile and deviant (see Foucault 1978). Both in Australia and Canada, male teacher candidates grappled with normalized constructions of sexuality and masculinity as they sought to fashion subjectivities that neither questioned their integrity nor rendered them deviant.

We use the voices of five men to highlight how normalization and gender regimes affect the lives of male teacher candidates, and we advocate for incorporating an understanding of queer issues into preservice teacher education programs (Britzman 1995; Epstein and Johnson 1998; Letts and Sears 1999; Martino and Berrill in press; Pinar 1998). In other words, following Pinar (1998) and Britzman (1995), we believe that educators need to move beyond an assimilationist politics—which asserts that "gay people are just like everybody else"—to a pedagogical position in teacher education institutions that draws attention to the historically specific practices of normalization in teacher candidates' lives. This must necessarily involve, we argue, deconstructing the binary logic driving the "heterosexist normalization that essentializes so many students we teach" (Pinar 1998, 44).

We believe this focus is warranted given the debates about the need for more male role models in boys' education that have been raging for some time now in the popular press across three continents: North America, the United Kingdom, and Australia. (For discussion about debates regarding boys' education, see Martino and Meyenn in press; Epstein and Johnson 1998; Lingard and Douglas 1999; Mills 2000; Roulston and Mills 2000). Some of these debates are grounded in heterosexist and essentialist discourses and raise issues about the perception of teaching as a nurturing profession, which seems to be at odds with a normalized construct of masculinity (Frank 1987). This was one of the issues that emerged in our research and is reported on in this chapter. We found that the perception of certain teacher behaviors as gendered led many male teacher candidates to question their ability to form relationships with students, for fear of being perceived as sexually suspect (Epstein 1997; Epstein and Johnson 1998). What follows is an examination of these issues in an attempt to explicate what the implications of this research might be for teacher educators.

"MALES WHO ARE CLOSE TO CHILDREN ARE GAYS OR PEDOPHILES"

Many of the teacher candidates we interviewed talked at length about their fears of being perceived as sexually suspect because they related to students in nurturing or friendly ways. They felt that a pastoral pedagogy was necessary and effective in enhancing students' learning but were wary of developing such relationships with their students. This fear was related to transgressing what we understood to be the perceived limits of acceptable hegemonic heterosexual masculinity (Frank 1987). For example, Peter, a prospective high school English teacher in Australia who identifies as straight, perceives English as a feminized curriculum site (Martino 1997) and, in part, links the tendency for male English teachers to be more distant than female teachers in their relationships with students to this phenomenon. In this regard, he also associates such teacher behavior with the need to fashion a normalized construct of masculinity (see Mills 2000; Roulston and Mills 2000):

> *Peter:* I always assumed that English teachers are mainly female . . . and then it turns out there is a lot more male English teachers out there. . . . Some of these male teachers I've seen are great, but I've seen the issues that they've had with not relating to, they don't appear to have like a mother's instinct . . . a relationship. They can't establish a relationship with the students . . . easily. They seem to be a little bit more scientific, a little bit more distant from the students. I think that's an issue, I think being a male teacher I want to try and get closer

to students but it's going to be problematic there with parents. Females are allowed to go off and be close to students, male teachers aren't allowed to be.

Interviewer: Why do you think that is?

Peter: I think when it comes down to it traditionally [it's] mothers and kids always, that's one reason, and the other reason I feel is the whole gay scene is a big question and the whole issue of pedophiles, like males who are close to children are gays or pedophiles . . . people are scared, of gays . . . and people are scared of pedophiles and I can understand that one. But then when they assume that people are this because of certain qualities or characteristics, I think that's really wrong. That's one issue I'm going to have to try and deal with when I'm in the school system, being a male teacher, teaching English, who wants to understand students, students' lives, their relationships outside. Just sort of understand what's going on in their life. . . . I think being a male teacher one of the biggest problems is with men, getting close to them, you've got to be gay or a pedophile. Like that's what you can be classified as, or you're not normal, you're not like us, you're not like us men, you're a bit different.

Peter acknowledges how the gendered dimensions of curriculum, such as the feminized pedagogical site of English, require a particular kind of relationship with students. In the case of English, this relationship appears at odds with dominant constructions of masculinity and leads men to regulate their behavior in very specific ways. This conflict appears significantly in his comment about men not "appear[ing] to have a mother's instinct" and in their tendency to be a "little more scientific." However, although he raises important questions about feminized and masculinized learning sites in schools and how they may affect teachers' tendencies to regulate their behaviors in specific ways, Peter makes a qualifying statement that females "are allowed to go off and be close to students," whereas males are not. He refers to the ways in which male teachers regulate their behavior and alludes to practices of normalization organized around the problematic association of gay sexuality with deviancy and, hence, pedophilia (see Sears 1998; Mac an Ghaill in press; Martino and Berrill in press).

Anthony, thirty-three years old, self-identifying as straight, and studying to be an elementary school teacher in an Australian university, also emphasizes that certain teacher behaviors and modes of relating to students are not permissible for male teacher candidates:

Anthony: I know that as a male in a classroom there's going to be things like I'm not allowed to leave the door shut like this if I've got a student. They're the recommendations that they give to male teachers. Touching or signs of affection aren't allowed, not so much allowed but they're not condoned I suppose. All those sort of things. So a female on the other hand could, they could like give a little boy a hug if they've cut their finger, but as a male there's certain taboos that you feel you shouldn't really cross.

Interviewer: Why do you think those taboos exist?

Anthony: Because we have media, sensationalizing the Catholic priest stories, the pedophile stories, so there's all these things about, well especially about male teachers getting themselves into trouble, or males in a position of responsibility taking advantage of younger people in their care.

Once again certain nurturing behaviors, like being affectionate or touching, are unacceptable for men because they are associated with femininity. However, Anthony also accentuates the role of the media as a public form of surveillance that leads men to self-regulate and police their teaching practices for fear of being labeled pedophiles (see Epstein and Johnson 1998). To behave in ways that are non-stereotypical for men poses concerns for these teacher candidates, who believe that their integrity may well be brought into question if such behavior is considered deviant. Anthony further highlights the symbolic and cultural significance of male sexuality and phallic masculinity as a threat to young children:

Anthony: Well it doesn't seem to apply to women because female teachers don't have a penis that they can rape and get little boys to suck on, or whatever. Females don't have that evil entity so to speak. I know it sounds a bit harsh but what I'm trying to say is that men have been caught out, there have been men that have committed these crimes and I think you might hear the occasional, once a year or something, of a teacher having seduced one of the younger teenage students or something. You hear those sort of stories.

In this regard, questions of safety and what might constitute a dangerous pedagogical relationship with students in their care are uppermost in many male teacher candidates' minds (Martino and Berrill in press):

Interviewer: And it's about then protecting yourself, is it, for you?

Anthony: I think you're protecting yourself in terms of you don't want to expose yourself to people saying you're a pervert, or you're a pedophile or whatever. You ought to be able to carry yourself with dignity and be respected I suppose. I remember at pracs if we were walking out into the playground it's okay to hold kids' hands as they walk out, but like when you're sitting down telling a little story you don't want them sitting on your lap and climbing all over you. Even though that's normal for me and my son, in the family, but in a classroom situation it's not.

Interviewer: So this idea of being a pedophile or being a pervert seems to be a very powerful kind of discourse then.

Anthony: I don't mean for it to sound extremist, I don't really feel as extreme. For instance it's not something I fear when I walk into the classroom. I feel it's just something in the back of my [mind]. Just stop a tick there, the kids are getting too close so let's sit down here, come and sit down here, not on top of me, that sort of thing. It's a very fine line that you have to walk between being too affectionate and not affectionate enough. It's a shame that you can't, I certainly don't think I can really be myself in that sort of classroom context.

Interviewer: So the issue is about the line then?

Anthony: Yes, it's like where is that line. Because you don't know where the line is. . . . So you're sort of waving in and out, sort of sometimes testing, sometimes just stopping not prepared to go any further.

The risk of being constructed as a pervert drives Anthony's need to regulate and police what he believes is and is not permissible in his dealings with young children. The tension involved in such working on the self is evident when he refers to the "very fine line that you have to walk between being too affectionate and not affectionate enough."

Being perceived as a sexual threat appeared to be much more of an issue for those men training to be elementary school teachers. For example, Joel, an Australian elementary teacher candidate who identifies as straight, talks at length about the need for male teachers to ensure that they are respected. He links this need, once again, to the public surveillance of male teachers in relation to their perceived capacity for sexual violence.

Joel: I think we're going to have to work hard to be respected in our own right and not just looked at as a potential threat to children. Because here's all that issue about child abuse, all that sort of thing, it's pretty bad.

Interviewer: You mentioned the whole idea of men being seen as sexual abusers or male teachers.

Joel: Well all you need is one person, I mean there was, I can't even remember the name of the town, but some respected male teacher there was found to be . . . abusing children, his students . . . one bad example like that and the media blows it into a thousand versions and suddenly every male teacher is stereotyped. . . .

Epstein (1997) has demonstrated that these men's fears about the power and public surveillance of teachers by the media are well founded, particularly in relation to sexuality (see also Epstein and Johnson 1998). However, what is significant is that Joel elaborates on how such associations of sexual violence and perversity are linked to a particular conception of male sexuality. It is also interesting that he perceives the high school physical education teacher, who may often come into physical contact with students, to be in a vulnerable position similar to that of elementary male school teachers:

Joel: [W]ith small children it's quite different. . . . Most secondary teaching is at a distance anyway. It's not like hands on like primary school can be. But say PE or something like that, I can imagine there's all sorts of issues. . . . Before kids learn any better, like that there's something wrong with touching people, or you're you and there's a personal space around you . . . they need to . . . be guided by the shoulder to show where to go or they need to be, I don't know, ruffled on the head or whatever, as an expression of "good on you" or whatever. And even as a primary school teacher you do have to do things like physical education where . . . you're going to have to show kids how to do a roll, and you have to guide them with your hands because it's the safe way to do it. I mean junior primary as well, I mean cleaning up young kids if that's the case. . . . I don't know how to handle that. . . . I don't know, in terms of litigation and things like that I'd want to even involve myself in that sort of thing. Like say especially . . . a young boy . . . made a mess in their pants. . . . I don't know how to handle that. . . . The temptation would be to go ask a female teacher to help you with that task, like for them to do it, and once again it's this thing of females not seen as threatening for some reason. I think it's the mother image maybe as well. It's something that certainly we haven't been given any answers to. . . . I guess people see [males] as having a sexual drive that can be destructive in a way, something like that. . . . I've never really explored these issues before but maybe it's the fact that male sexuality is penetrative whereas female's isn't. . . . Like a woman can't hurt someone sexually whereas a man can. I don't know. . . . Even way back Egyptian eunuchs used to look after the Queen because they couldn't do [any] harm.

Joel explores the issues of bodily contact with students in teaching physical education in both elementary and secondary schools to stress the role of sexuality and normalization for men in this context. He carries this further when he mentions his fear of litigation in the everyday business of teaching very young children. For instance, he mentions potentially dangerous situations for male teachers such as attending to a child who has "made a mess in [his] pants." He believes that female teachers would be able to deal with this situation because of their cultural status as (potential) mothers and, hence nurturers, which, by implication, leads them to avoid the anxiety-ridden attributions of pedophile and sexual pervert. This in turn is linked, for Joel, to "the fact that male sexuality [in the dominant culture] is penetrative whereas female's isn't" and raises for him the whole question of men's predisposition to sexual violence. Through his reference to the Egyptian eunuchs, he suggests that there may be an historical basis for the heteronormative assumption that the only safe male teacher is a castrated one.

"THEY'D BE WORRIED MOSTLY BECAUSE I'M A MALE BUT ALSO MAYBE BECAUSE I'M GAY AS WELL"

For gay teacher candidates the situation was compounded by the association of gay sexuality with pedophilia. Rob, an elementary Canadian teacher candidate who identifies as gay, emphasizes that any bodily contact with children may pose a major problem for male student teachers:

> *Rob:* I can sort of predict some problems in that area because like nowadays you're not supposed to touch children at all. . . . I can see how that might get me in trouble some day because I've always been like a huggy kind of person, very affectionate and warm. For me reinforcing a child's behavior is more than just saying "good job," or whatever, because I'd usually pat them on the head or give them a tap on the arm or something like that. Now of course this can be construed as sexual and it's being hammered into our head basically not to do those types of things.

While Rob has to deal with the risk of being perceived as a sexual threat for engaging in what is considered potentially transgressive behavior for men, he also has to contend with the anxiety-provoking decision of whether to reveal his gay identity as a teacher:

> *Rob:* I don't know, I just worry that the parents would be really upset and take their children out of my classroom. I don't think that would be fair to the children at all because I think I'd have a lot to give to the children, a lot to teach them. I think the fear of, ridiculous as it is, like a fear like conversion or whatever. Just my influence on the children may make them lean towards more . . . like a gay way of life or something like that. I don't know . . . and again the sexual part of it as well I think. That they'd be worried just because I'm, mostly because I'm a male but also maybe because I'm gay as well that there'd be problems with sexual abuse and things like that.

Although Rob realizes that discourses of recruitment are "ridiculous," he is aware of the potential dangers of coming out as a gay teacher in schools. Several teacher candidates qualified their concerns with similar statements, suggesting the extent to which they felt that they were possibly overreacting or perhaps even paranoid. For example, Anthony claims that he doesn't want to "sound too extremist" in discussing the links between masculinity and sexual perversity. Unfortunately, as Squirrell (1989) confirms in her study of gay and lesbian school teachers, these male teacher candidates have reason to be concerned.

Ari, a Canadian secondary teacher candidate who identifies as gay, describes the binary logic that sets *normal* heterosexual behavior against *deviant* homosexual practices:

> *Ari:* I think there is a connection between male heterosexual behavior and the stereotype of masculinity, because male heterosexual behavior . . . is very much connected to the whole idea of dominance . . . looking for a female . . . to go after, like sort of create the progeny. . . . Because I guess for many looking at a

heterosexual standpoint, being a homosexual you are going against the whole idea of producing any offspring. Because I guess looking at a Darwin point of view, we are seen as that sort of anomaly or mutant in that we can't reproduce and produce offspring.

Ari explores the connection of stereotypical masculine behavior with an essentialist biological interpretation. Within this frame of reference, he articulates the normative assumption that links heterosexual male dominance to the survival of the species through the reproduction of offspring. From this pseudo-Darwinian point of view, nonheterosexual men, because they do not biologically reproduce within their relationships, are constructed as anomalies or mutants—as deviants. This assumption, then, offers Ari an explanation for why stereotypical heterosexual behaviors may have become normalized:

> *Ari:* Because I think it all goes back on the idea of what is normal, and normal being the template on what we should create for our future. Because I think . . . many people in society would consider . . . that being heterosexual is normal and that's the way we should raise our kids. I guess since homosexuality is still a controversial issue, and is it something biological or is it something more environmentally produced, and that can be very confusing for our children. . . . And then there's that risk of a student being affected in the negative way and that might distract them from their education.

Ari recognizes the allure of "the normal," both for the wider community and for secondary school students. From his point of view, things that are not "normal" can be distracting for students, interfering with their learning. He also links this need for the "normal" to the need for gay men to separate their private and public lives within institutions like schools where compulsory heterosexuality is the norm:

> *Ari:* Heterosexuality today in many schools and society is seen as normal and therefore this connecting that normal sphere with the public sphere in teaching is seen as beneficial. . . . Since this is normal it is not a distraction, it will not negatively affect their learning. . . . But for heterosexuality I don't think it's as separate a sphere when it comes to teaching as if a teacher were a nonheterosexual.

Given the association of gay men with deviancy and the capacity to threaten students' learning, Ari believes that he must disconnect himself from his private role in the public domain of teaching students in schools and avoid being designated as the deviant homosexual other. Thus he must fashion himself first and foremost as a *normal* male in his role as teacher in a site where deviating from the heterosexual norm risks attributions of pedophilia:

> *Ari:* When I'm teaching I try to present myself as normal, in the normal masculine stereotypical behavior. I guess then you'd have to explore like what the stereotypical masculine behavior is and for me a lot of it is the very stoic, lack of emotion, almost dominant personality. When I present myself in front of the classroom and teach that's I guess the type of person I portray, a very dominant person, because I do have that authority in that position. The lack of emotion. . . . I do present myself as a very stoic person. I guess that's how I feel that those are parts of the stereotypical masculine behavior that maybe subconsciously I exhibit when I'm teaching.

Ari is conscious of his self-fashioning practices and of the ways they enable him to avoid attributions of deviancy. He feels that these practices are, in turn, conducive to effective teaching and learning. What we wish to emphasize here are the very heteronormative and homophobic regimes that drive these teacher candidates to engage in such self-fashioning practices in the first place. Their words also raise questions about those males who might easily be identified as gay on the basis of "effeminate" behavior or tone or voice and who may not be able to engage in such self-fashioning practices (see Martino 2000).

IMPLICATIONS

Based on our research with male teacher candidates in Australia and Canada, we believe that it is essential for teacher education to address sexuality, masculinity, and normalization. Given the role that practices of normalization play in male teachers' regulation and policing of their teaching behavior, it is imperative that queer theoretical perspectives be incorporated into teacher education programs. This will involve, as Carlson (1998, 108) suggests, providing students with the critical tools for interrogating the binary logics that inform the social construction of identities in contemporary culture. Moreover, as Britzman (1995) states, "the production of normalcy" needs to be explicitly placed on the teacher education agenda and to be problematized. This process, she argues, must also involve the need to "conceptualize strategies that confound . . . the logic of institutional laws and the social practices that sustain these laws as normal and natural" (157). Although it is important to stress that as teacher educators we cannot transform the homophobic and heterosexist cultures of schools, what we can do is provide our students with a theoretical framework for understanding how they have been formed and how they fashion themselves as particular kinds of individuals.

Queer theory provides possibilities and frames for conducting such discussions with teacher education candidates around the power relations that inform the social construction of identity categories (see Carlson 1998). Queer theory can be used to facilitate discussions with teacher candidates about the impact of sexuality and normalization on their lives as teachers.

CONCLUSION

In this chapter our aim has been to highlight how sexuality, masculinity, and normalization affect, in significant ways, the lives of male teacher candidates. Through the voices of these men, we have emphasized the way a normalized construct of masculinity forces male teacher candidates both to police their relationships with students and to engage in particular self-fashioning practices for fear of being labeled pedophiles or sexual deviants. One of the important issues that needs to be addressed involves exploring with teacher candidates how certain teaching behaviors and practices are gendered and how this links to the way males are traditionally expected to behave. In addition, we need to make explicit how such practices themselves are inextricably tied to the normalization of sexuality and, hence, to the particular role that homophobia and heterosexism play in the policing, regulation, and fashioning of teacher identities. By explicitly addressing these issues with teacher candidates within a queer theoretical framework, we believe we can name and discuss the political effects of heteronormative constructions of masculinity. Teacher candidates can then use this framework to make sense of their own experiences and to explore their pedagogical practices.

NOTE

This research with male teacher candidates in Australia and Canada was funded by the Australian Research Council.

REFERENCES

Britzman, D. 1995. Is there a queer pedagogy? Or stop reading straight. *Educational Theory* 45 (2): 151–65.
Carlson, D. 1998. Who am I? Gay identity and a democratic politics of the self. In *Queer theory in education,* edited by W. F. Pinar. Mahwah, N.J.: Lawrence Erlbaum Associates.

Epstein, D. 1997. What is in a ban? In *Border patrols: Policing the boundaries of heterosexuality,* edited by D. L. Steinberg, D. Epstein, and R. Johnson. London: Cassell.

Epstein, D., and R. Johnson. 1998. *Schooling sexualities.* Buckingham, UK: Open University Press.

Foucault, M. 1978. *The history of sexuality vol. 1.* New York: Vintage.

Frank, B. 1987. Hegemonic heterosexual masculinity. *Studies in Political Economy* 24 (Autumn): 159–70.

Letts, W. J., and J. T. Sears, eds., 1999. *Queering elementary education: Advancing the dialogue about sexualities and schooling.* Lanham, Md.: Rowman & Littlefield.

Lingard, B., and P. Douglas. 1999. *Men engaging feminisms: Pro-feminism, backlashes and schooling.* Buckingham, UK: Open University Press.

Mac an Ghaill, M. In press. The significance of teaching boys. In *What about the boys? Issues of masculinity and schooling,* edited by W. Martino and B. Meyenn. Buckingham, UK: Open University Press.

Martino, W. 1997. The costs of gendered behaviour: Exploring boys' underachievement and under-representation in subject English. In *Gender equity: A framework for Australian schools.* Canberra, Aust.: Gender Equity Taskforce.

———. 2000. Policing masculinities: Investigating the role of homophobia and heteronormativity in the lives of adolescent school boys. *The Journal of Men's Studies* 8 (2, Winter): 213–36.

Martino, W., and D. P. Berrill. In press. Dangerous pedagogies: Exploring issues of sexuality and masculinity in male teacher candidates' lives. In *Masculinities and schooling: International practices and perspectives,* edited by K. Davison and B. Frank. Halifax, N.S.: Fernwood.

Martino, W., and B. Meyenn. In press. *What about the boys? Issues of masculinity and schooling.* Buckingham, UK: Open University Press.

Mills, M. 2000. Issues in implementing boys' programs in schools: Male teachers and empowerment. *Gender and Education* 12 (2): 221–38.

Pinar, W. F., ed. 1998. *Queer theory in education.* Mahwah, N.J.: Lawrence Erlbaum Associates.

Roulston, K., and M. Mills. 2000. Male teachers in feminized learning areas: Marching to the beat of the men's movement drums? *Oxford Review of Education* 26 (2): 221–37.

Sears, J. T. 1998. A generational and theoretical analysis of culture and male (homo)sexuality. In *Queer theory in education,* edited by W. F. Pinar. Mahwah, N.J.: Lawrence Erlbaum Associates.

Squirrell, G. 1989. In passing . . . teachers and sexual orientation. In *Teachers, gender and careers,* edited by S. Acker. New York: The Falmer Press.

5

Homophobia in the Schools: Student Teachers' Perceptions and Preparation to Respond

Jane A. Page and Delores D. Liston

OBJECTIVES

As the death by crucifixion of Matthew Shepard in Wyoming has so painfully reminded us all, homophobia is a pervasive problem in our society and consequently in our schools. This death in a relatively remote location may at first seem to have no direct bearing on southeast Georgia. However, it serves to remind us of the symbolic violence (Bourdieu 1991) perpetrated against lesbian, gay, bisexual, and transgendered (lgbt) people on a regular basis. Although racism, sexism, and xenophobia supposedly have become anathema within our culture, the isolation and rejection of lgbt identity remains one of the more generally "acceptable" prejudices. Few speak out directly on behalf of lgbt youth and adults.

Homophobia must become at least as much anathema as racism, sexism, and xenophobia. Although the school is not the only institution that can address homophobia directly, it is the one within which we, as teacher educators, have some influence. Recognizing this need, the researchers in this study directed their attention to teacher preparation programs in one university in southeast Georgia to evaluate the present state of homophobia in this region.

The object of this study was to develop an understanding of the perceptions of student teachers in the concluding phase of their teacher preparation program in a university in rural southern Georgia. How do these preservice teachers perceive the presence of homophobia in the schools where they student taught? And how do they evaluate their preparation to deal with homophobia as teachers? A secondary objective of this research study is to determine whether significant differences in perceptions exist among groups of student teachers categorized on the basis of background variables.

PERSPECTIVE/LITERATURE REVIEW

"We don't have any gay students at our school" was the response of a high school counselor here in rural south Georgia when she was asked what the counselor's office was doing to assist gay students. Her response epitomizes the challenge we face in confronting local schools and their teachers. The challenge, of course, is not limited to rural school systems. After surveying forty-two of the nation's largest public school districts, the Gay, Lesbian and Straight Education Network (GLSEN) gave sixteen districts a grade of F and three a grade of D for their failure to protect students and teachers from discrimination and harassment. Only eight districts earned grades of A or A−.

Why the need for such report cards and research studies on homophobia? GLSEN surveys show that on average, lgbt high school students hear anti-gay epithets twenty-five times a day. A more distressing statistic is that 97 percent of the time teachers hearing these epithets fail to respond. Although almost all of the students in the GLSEN study (99.4 percent) reported hearing these remarks from other students, over one-third reported also hearing homophobic remarks from faculty or school staff. The majority of lgbt youth (69 percent) reported experiencing some form of harassment or violence, and a plurality (41.7 percent) did not feel safe in their schools because of others' homophobic behavior (GLSEN 1999). This symbolic violence often leads to physical violence. In surveys of lesbian, gay, and bisexual people, 21 to 27 percent revealed that they have been pelted with objects, 13 to 38 percent have been chased or followed and 9 to 24 percent have been physically assaulted (Campaign to End Homophobia 1990). The U.S. Department of Health and Human Services reports that gay and lesbian youths are two to three times more likely to attempt suicide than their heterosexual peers, and they account for 30 percent of all completed suicides among youths (Besner and Spungin 1995, 49).

Although some school systems have begun to provide teacher training to combat homophobia, virtually nothing is done in many teacher education programs around the country (Koerner and Hulsebosch 1996; Wickens 1993). Further, although some colleges and universities boast an emphasis on diversity and multicultural education, that emphasis rarely includes sexual orientation and gender identity (Pohan and Bailey 1998; Mathison 1998). Allison Young and Michael Middleton (1999) found in their recent studies that institutions in which a "champion" had stepped forward to bring lgbt issues to the forefront were much more likely to raise these issues "in a significant way" (15). Without such a champion, lgbt concerns remain invisible (Harris 1997).

Among the first steps in preparing preservice teachers to deal with homophobia in the schools is assessing the attitudes of preservice teachers themselves. To date, only a few studies have been conducted in this area. The earliest of these studies were completed in 1980 and 1982 (Baker 1980; Fisher 1982). Their findings suggest that the preservice teacher population holds more negative attitudes than the general population, and that negative attitudes toward homosexuality correlate with lower socioeconomic status, lower levels of educational attainment, and more rural areas of the country.

More recent studies corroborate these early findings. For example, James Sears (1989, 1992) found that "in comparison with other populations, these prospective teachers held much more negative feelings. They were five times more likely to be classified as 'high grade homophobics' than a group of college students surveyed a decade ago" (Sears 1992, 53). Sears also found that although where a student was in his or her education program did not affect his or her attitudes toward homosexuality, the grade level at which the preservice teacher planned to teach did affect the findings. He found that elementary preservice teachers held much more negative attitudes than did their secondary and middle school counterparts.

Kelvin Seifert (1988) provides one explanation for the high rates of homophobic attitudes at the elementary education level. Although lgbt issues are not the focus of his article, Seifert explores the ways in which traditional gender roles affect early childhood education and reinforce a traditional culture: "Men in this field present certain paradoxes which can be understood most parsimoniously as an incompatibility between the cultural expectations of early education and the biographies of individual men" (Seifert 1988, 69). His analysis of the culture of early childhood education as an extension of parenting, a role more strongly encouraged in females, helps explain homophobic attitudes in this population. More recently, MacGillivray (2000) presented an exploration of "the culture of heteronormativity and heterosexism" that sheds further light on the impact of heterosexual privilege on educational equity for lgbtq (queer/questioning) students. This analysis reminds teacher educators that denial of full participation in culture and education is a breach of our cultural ideals of democracy and social justice.

Preservice teachers who were exposed to homosexuality in high school, especially through lgbt friends, exhibit less homophobia and more accepting attitudes (Sears 1992). This finding has been confirmed repeatedly in other studies (Maddux 1988; Maney and Cain 1997).

Karen Butler's recent studies (1999) of the attitudes and knowledge of preservice teachers regarding gay men and lesbians also corroborate Sears's earlier finding that, "those who have more factual knowledge about gay men and lesbians are likely to hold more positive attitudes and exhibit more positive behaviors as educators" (Butler 1994, 15).

As noted above, elementary preservice teachers appear to be more homophobic than their peers preparing to teach at other grade levels. Thus, some recent studies have looked directly at the dynamics of preservice elementary education. For example, Karen Butler and T. Jean Byrne (1992) argue that the attitudes and behaviors of elementary school teachers are especially important for the development of healthy attitudes in future generations. Their findings show that "the more gay friends, relatives, and acquaintances one has, the more positive the attitudes" (Butler and Byrne 1992, 357). They argue that "reducing homophobia must begin at the personal level" and that interventions planned to reduce homophobia must address both the cognitive and affective aspects of homophobia.

Maney and Cain (1997) also focus on preservice elementary teachers' attitudes toward lgbt issues. Their study uses gay and lesbian parenting to ferret out differences in preservice teachers' attitudes toward gay men and lesbians. Their findings show that these preservice teachers are "very comfortable" interacting with gay and lesbian parents as long as the issues involve filling out forms or explaining school policy or curriculum relative to the child. However, a higher percentage report being "very uncomfortable" discussing homosexuality or asking the parents about their family unit. Overall, their study indicates lower levels of homophobia among the population sampled than earlier studies. Nonetheless, over 50 percent of the respondents feel that "male homosexuality represents a lifestyle that should be condemned" (Maney and Cain, 1997, 240). Clearly, this degree of hostility against lgbt parents indicates that elementary education programs need to address homophobia.

METHODS AND DATA SOURCES

The student teaching semester is usually the culminating experience for undergraduate teacher education majors. Although field experiences are usually included in other preservice courses, the student teaching experience is generally the first time the preservice teacher is totally immersed in a K–12 setting for an extended period. This extended period provides student teachers with opportunities to observe and practice what they have learned in their programs.

The researchers chose the end of the student teaching experience as the time to collect data for this study. At this point in preservice teacher development, we felt we would best be able to discover what our students were perceiving about homophobia in the schools, since they had recently been immersed in the classroom. And, since they were finishing their programs, we would also be able to evaluate how well they had been prepared to deal with homophobia in the schools.

An informed consent letter and survey was provided to all 175 student teachers at a southern university as they signed in for their final seminar on campus, May 6, 2000. Sixty-eight percent (119) of these students chose to participate by completing the surveys and returning them to a box in the front of the room. The student teachers were provided with the following definition and description of homophobia on the survey:

> Homophobia is the fear of feelings of love for members of one's own sex and therefore the hatred of those feelings in others. Homophobia refers to the many ways in which people are oppressed on the basis of sexual orientation. Sometimes homophobia is intentional, where there is a clear intent to hurt lesbian, gay, and bisexual people. Homophobia can also be unintentional, where there is no desire to hurt anyone, but where people are unaware of the consequences of their actions. (Campaign to End Homophobia 1990, 20)

The survey asked about homophobic remarks heard in schools and about how teachers and others intervened (or did not). These questions were based on the ones GLSEN used with high school students (1999). The anonymous survey also sought opinions about the level of homophobia in the schools and the education (both intentional and unintentional) of students regarding sexual orientation. An important question for teacher educators asked student teachers about their own preparation for addressing homophobia. Some demographic background information was solicited for analysis and comparison purposes.

Data were analyzed using frequency statistics and one way analysis of variance. Results were also analyzed in light of GLSEN's findings in the survey of lgbt students.

RESULTS AND ANALYSIS

Student teachers were asked whether they had heard words such as "faggot," "dyke," or "queer" from students, and how frequently they had heard these remarks in their classes, in the hallways, and on school grounds. About one-third (32.8 percent) of the student teachers indicated that they frequently or sometimes heard these remarks. This compares with 90.4 percent of lgbt youth in the GLSEN study. As in the GLSEN study, hallways and classrooms were the most were the most common places for hearing the remarks. A slight majority of the students (51.2 percent) indicated that adults seldom or never intervened when homophobic remarks were made, a finding similar to the GLSEN study. A majority (62.2 percent) agreed that teachers and school administrators were more likely to intervene in other kinds of harassment than in homophobic harassment. However, 60.6 percent of these student teachers said that they themselves had attempted to intervene in these situations. Fewer than 10 percent of the student teachers observed any proactive attempts to address homophobia through the curriculum in the school. When asked where students received the greatest amount of information about sexual orientation, "other students" was cited as the first choice by over a third of the student teachers, followed closely by "television." Parents were cited as the major source by 21.2 percent of participants. Only 2.7 percent believed students received this information from teachers and only 1.8 percent thought they received it from churches or other faith communities.

The student teachers were asked whether they received preparation in their teacher education courses for dealing with homophobia. Only 11.9 percent responded affirmatively. When asked whether teacher education programs should increase awareness of and preparation for homophobia in the schools, 66.1 percent responded affirmatively despite the fact that most student teachers (62.3 percent) did not regard homophobia as a problem in the schools. Yet a majority (57 percent) agreed that lesbian, gay, bisexual, and transgendered youth have good reasons for indicating that they do not feel safe in schools, and a majority (64.9 percent) agreed that straight individuals are victims of this homophobia.

There were no significant differences among groups categorized on the basis of gender, ethnicity, or age. However, there were seven significant differences among groups categorized on the basis of grade level assignment. Four of these were related to the question of how often student teachers heard homophobic remarks at school, in general, and more specifically in classrooms, hallways, and grounds. An interesting finding was that those placed at middle schools were far more likely than their high school counterparts to indicate that these remarks were made. Seventy-six percent of student teachers assigned to middle schools reported that they heard homophobic remarks frequently or sometimes, whereas 48.6 percent of high school students made the same report. Not surprisingly those assigned to elementary schools were least likely to hear homophobic remarks. Only 11.5 percent reported hearing the remarks frequently or sometimes.

Although student teachers assigned to middle schools were more likely to hear homophobic remarks, they were similar to student teachers assigned to high schools in their perception of whether homophobia was a problem in the schools. Fifty-two percent of those assigned to middle schools agreed or strongly agreed that homophobia was a problem; 56 percent of those assigned to high schools had similar perceptions. Only 23 percent of student teachers assigned to elementary schools perceived homophobia as a problem in the schools.

Similarly, those assigned to middle and high schools were more likely to agree that lgbt students have good reason to feel unsafe at school, with 68.4 percent of those assigned to middle schools agreeing or strongly agreeing and 65.8 percent of those assigned to high schools agreeing or strongly agreeing. Less than half (48.3 percent) of those assigned to elementary schools agreed or strongly agreed with this point.

Students at all levels reported very little preparation to deal with homophobia. However, those assigned to middle schools were more likely to report having received preparation. Even so, only 21.1 percent indicated that they had received any preparation. This compares with only 10 percent of elementary student teachers and 9.1 percent of high school student teachers.

CONCLUSION

The noted psychologist Erik Erikson (1963) indicated that the central tasks of adolescence and young adulthood are to find identity and to develop intimacy with another individual. If the young person is successful at these tasks, he or she will develop a sense of uniqueness and integration. If the young person is unsuccessful, the result is identity confusion. As the heterosexual adolescent's sexual awareness and discovery of how one relates to others evolves, he or she is given social approval for experimentation. Until society (especially adolescent peer groups) can offer the same support to lgbt youth, we will continue to see problems, including depression, school dropout, and even suicide.

Every institution should be working toward ameliorating this situation. Teacher education programs can serve a primary role in addressing homophobia by providing activities and practice experiences that increase awareness, sensitivity, and understanding. We can make changes in the curriculum to broaden our interpretation of multiculturalism by including lgbt cultures and lifestyles. We can encourage preservice teachers to consider the implications of their lesson plans for gay and lesbian students and children of gay and lesbian parents. We can also work towards creating "safe spaces" for gay and lesbian students and teachers. As the recent research of Ronni Sanlo reminds us, most lgbt teachers "would like to be open and honest about their sexual orientation. . . . They desire to be available as role models, mentors and advocates for homosexual and heterosexual students alike. . . . They would like to do their work without fear of harassment, humiliation or pressure to resign" (1999, 121). As teacher educators, we have a responsibility to address lgbt concerns and needs and create a more accepting environment for all students and teachers.

Our study indicates a particular need to better prepare early childhood and elementary preservice teachers. The elementary curriculum readily lends itself to addressing lgbt issues; some relevant topics include families, respect for others, and good citizenship. Greater teacher awareness at the elementary level may also increase sensitivity to playground bullying and facilitate teacher intervention.

Overall, our findings show that much work needs to be done at the southern university in this study. Other recent studies indicate that this university is not unique in this regard (Koerner and Hulsebosch 1996; Butler 1999). However, encouraging evidence has recently emerged suggesting that efforts toward intervention have been successful at increasing knowledge about lgbt concerns and changing attitudes toward gay men and lesbians (Anderson 1981; Butler 1999; Chesler and Zuniga 1991; Lance 1987). If we use this information to make appropriate changes, our new teachers will not be among those who stand by silently when harassment occurs because they don't know what they should or could do.

REFERENCES

Anderson, C. 1981. The effects of a workshop on attitudes of female nursing students toward male homosexuality. *Journal of Homosexuality* 7: 57–69.

Baker, D. F. 1980. A survey of attitudes and knowledge about homosexuality among secondary school teachers in training. Master's thesis, Southern Methodist University, Dallas, Texas.

Besner, H. F., and C. I. Spungin. 1995. *Gay and lesbian students.* New York: Taylor & Francis.

——. 1998. *Training professionals who work with gays & lesbians in educational and workplace settings.* Washington, D.C.: Accelerated Development/Taylor & Francis Group.

Bourdieu, P. 1991. *Language and symbolic power.* Cambridge, Mass.: Harvard University Press.

Butler, K. L. 1999. Preservice teachers' knowledge and attitudes regarding gay men and lesbians. *Journal of Health Education* 30 (2): 125–29.

Butler, K. L., and T. J. Byrne. 1992. Homophobia among preservice elementary teachers. *Journal of Health Education* 23 (6): 355–59.

Campaign to End Homophobia. 1990. *A guide to leading introductory workshops on homophobia.* Cambridge, Mass.: Campaign to End Homophobia.

Casper, V., and S. B. Schultz. 1999. *Gay parents/Straight schools.* New York: Teachers College Press.

Casper, V., S. Schultz, and E. Wickens. 1992. Breaking the silences. *Teachers College Record* 94 (1): 109–38.

Chesler, M., and X. Zuniga. 1991. Dealing with prejudice and conflict in the classroom. *Teaching and Sociology* 19: 173–81.

Coleman, G. D. 1997. The teacher and the gay and lesbian student. *Momentum (Washington, National Catholic Educational Association)* 28: 46–48.

Edwards, A. T. 1997. Let's stop ignoring our gay and lesbian youth. *Educational Leadership* 54 (7): 68–70.

Epstein, D. 1994. *Challenging lesbian and gay inequalities in education.* Buckingham, UK: Open University Press.

Erikson, E. 1963. *Childhood and society.* 2d ed. New York: Norton.

Fisher, T. R. 1982. A study of educators' attitudes toward homosexuality. Ph.D. diss., University of Virginia, Charlottesville.

Fontaine, J. H. 1997. The sound of silence. *Journal of Gay and Lesbian Social Services* 7 (4): 101–9.

GLSEN. 1999. *GLSEN's national school climate survey: Lesbian, gay, bisexual and transgender students and their experiences in school.* New York: GLSEN. Available: <www.glsen.org>.

Harbeck, K. M. 1992. *Coming out of the classroom closet: Gay and lesbian students, teachers and curricula.* New York: Haworth Press.

Harris, M. B. 1997. *The invisible minority: School experiences of gay and lesbian youth.* Binghamton, N.Y.: Harrington Park Press.

Jennings, K. 1998. *Telling tales out of school.* Los Angeles: Alyson Publications.

Kissen, R. M. 1993.. Listening to gay and lesbian teenagers. *Teaching Education* 5 (2, Spring/Summer): 57–68.

Koerner, M. E., and P. Hulsebosch. 1996. Preparing teachers to work with children of gay and lesbian parents. *Journal of Teacher Education* 47 (5): 347–54.

Lance, L. 1987. The effects of interaction with gay persons on attitudes toward homosexuality. *Human Relations* 40: 329–36.

Letts, W. J., and J. T. Sears, eds. 1999. *Queering elementary education: Advancing the dialogue about sexualities and schooling.* Lanham, Md.: Rowman & Littlefield.

Loutzenheiser, L. W. 1996. How schools play "smear the queer." *Feminist Teacher* 10 (2): 59–64.

MacGillivray, I. 2000. Educational equity for gay, lesbian, bisexual, transgendered, and queer/questioning students. *Education and Urban Society* 23 (3): 303–23.

Maddux, J. A. 1988. The homophobic attitudes of preservice teachers. Ph.D. diss., University of Cincinnati, Ohio.

Maney, D. W., and R. E. Cain. 1997. Preservice elementary teachers' attitudes toward gay and lesbian parenting. *Journal of School Health* 67 (6): 236–41.

Mathison, C. 1998. Invisible minority. *Journal of Teacher Education* 49 (2): 151–55.

Miller, H. M. 1999. Swimming with the sharks. *Reading Teacher* 52 (6): 632–35.

Pohan, C. A., and N. J. Bailey. 1998. Including gays in multiculturalism. *Education Digest* 63 (5): 52–57.

Sanlo, R. L. 1999. *Unheard voices.* Westport, Conn.: Bergin & Garvey.

Sears, J. T. 1989. Personal feelings and professional attitudes of prospective teachers toward homosexuality and homosexual students. Paper presented at the meeting of the American Educational Research Association, April, San Francisco, California.

———. 1992. Educators, homosexuality, and homosexual students. In *Coming out of the classroom closet: Gay and lesbian students, teachers and curricula,* edited by K. M. Harbeck, 29–79. New York: Haworth Press.

Seifert, K. L. 1988. The culture of early education and the preparation of male teachers. *Early Child Development and Care* 38: 69–80.

Unks, G. 1995. *The gay teen: Educational practice and theory for lesbian, gay and bisexual adolescents.* New York: Routledge.

Wickens, E. 1993. Penny's question. *Young Children* 48 (3): 25–28.

Young, A. J., and M. J. Middleton. 1999. "It never occurred to me that I might have a gay student in my K–12 classroom": An investigation of the treatment of sexual orientation issues in teacher education programming. Paper presented at the meeting of the American Educational Research Association, April, Montreal, Canada.

6

Education by Association: The Shortcomings of Discourses of Privacy and Civility in Anti-Homophobia Education

Cris Mayo

As John Dewey argued in *Democracy and Education* (1916), democracy is educative and strong to the extent that it enables a wide variety of strong associations among people. In this chapter I examine the language of liberalism and Southern civility circulating in North Carolina classrooms that impedes these associations as students begin to address homophobia and heterosexism. I use information from surveys given to preservice and in service teachers, administrators, and sexual minority youth, as well as information from personal communications and class discussions. The long-term purpose of my research is to work in collaboration with school leaders and practitioners to improve the school climate for sexual minority youth.

Surveys for the study came from students in a variety of classes in the Department of Educational Leadership and Cultural Foundations during the academic year 1999–2000, and were administered by the professor or teaching assistant during regular class time. Students were given fifteen minutes to fill them out. Classes had not yet specifically addressed the issue of anti-lesbian, gay, bisexual, and transgendered (lgbt) discrimination, although in some classes it was clear from the syllabus that the issue would be raised. Professors and teaching assistants explained that the survey sought information on the public school climate for lgbt youth. They briefly explained that survey information would help advocates for sexual minority youth, teachers, and administrators to critically examine school practices. The survey asked for information on anti-lgbt harassment and violence; antidiscrimination policies; and student perceptions of teacher, administrator, and school board support. In addition, the survey also asked students to assess the degree to which curricula and school resources adequately met the needs of sexual minority youth. Finally, respondents were asked if schools provided support services, adequate counselors, peer support groups, and information about community resources. The four groups of respondents included members of a sexual minority youth support group; former students from area schools (who were also preservice teachers); teachers, administrators, staff, student teachers; and respondents who did not specify their relationship to the public school (who were also preservice teachers).[1]

Various responses culled from 104 questionnaires are included in this chapter. In addition, members of Parents, Families and Friends of Lesbians and Gays (PFLAG), as well as the coordinator of the gay and lesbian hotline, contributed short telephone and e-mail interviews. Finally, the North Carolina State Board of Education website provided information on school antidiscrimination policies, providing student handbooks and employee protection information (none of the area schools protects against discrimination against sexual minority youth or employees). Since preliminary surveys and discussions suggested that changing laws was not enough, I have now turned to critical examination of the social context of particular schools, in conversation with people in those schools, to help generate ideas for locally sensitive approaches to anti-homophobia work.[2] But we continually come up against the perception that communities will not respond because they perceive sexual minority youth to violate codes of civility.

In other words, the very attempt to be locally sensitive is difficult if local sensibilities are, in some ways, part of the problem. In the discussion that follows, I use responses from surveys and class discussion to argue that Southern civility and its cousin, liberal civility, do as much to hinder progress on the rights of sexual minority youth as does overt discrimination.[3] Indeed, civility is a form of social discrimination, for it is predicated on making distinctions that support accepted practices and values, and entails enacting those distinctions to the detriment of the purportedly uncivil. In other words, civility can be seen as a central activity of discrimination rather than a force opposing it.

This interpretation of "civility" may help to explain the shortcomings of broad school conduct policies, civil tolerance, and blank respect as antidotes to discrimination. The discourse of civility and school codes of conduct assert that teachers, students, and administrators ought to be kind, respectful, and tolerant of everyone without specifying to whom they are being kind, respectful, and tolerant. This practice only serves to neglect issues that appear in and of themselves uncivil or distasteful. If civility requires leaving unspoken that which would disturb placid social interactions, the practice of civility will necessarily leave out sexual minority youth (among others). Further, advocacy of blank respect leads civil people to presume that all is well if they do not perceive overt acts committed against sexual minority youth. This blank tolerance papers over the specificity of homophobia and the particular experiences of sexual minority youth. Sexual minority youth themselves recognize that civility and tolerance act to privatize and remove their experiences of homophobia, placing them in a double bind. If they complain about homophobia, they are uncivil, violating the social practice of civility that only works by deracinating everyone. But by not complaining, they seem to give tacit approval to the social distinctions that frame homophobia. In short, they too are forced to structure public interactions and associations to maintain an empty, blank tolerance that removes the uncivil from recognized presence. These moments of enforced privacy and silence are precisely the problems that anti-bias education ought to attempt to overcome. One might easily argue, given the enforced silence sexual minority students face at school, that they already have far too much privacy, are already shunted away from public engagement, and need access to associations in public, not silenced, private lives.

PUBLIC CIVILITY: IGNORING THE
PROBLEMS AND AVOIDING THE SOLUTIONS

The first problem with civility may be its almost necessary presumption that everything is fine. This is doubtless a familiar refrain to anyone doing any kind of anti-bias education and is indicative usually of a dominant group's reluctance to acknowledge its dominance and, further, to acknowledge that its dominance negatively affects subordinate groups. In short, in an effort to minimize conflict, the discourse of civility ignores even the most blatant conflict. Survey results showed that sexual minority students consistently reported witnessing or experiencing more harassment in general and more harassment from faculty/staff in particular than did the other groups, although all groups did acknowledge in large numbers that such harassment and violence occurred. Whereas 100 percent of sexual minority students reported harassment and violence in and around school, only 67 percent of teachers, administrators, and school staff reported knowing about anti-lgbt harassment and violence in and around their schools. The responses of sexual minority youth and school professionals diverged most strongly in their assessment of what was being done about harassment and violence; 26 percent of faculty/staff respondents indicated that their school policy already protected sexual minority youth; half of those respondents indicated that more ought to be done. The other half indicated a dislike of sexual minority students and a desire not to see them specified as a protected class.

Sexual minority students themselves, in contrast, knew that school regulations did not protect them from homophobia; all of them stated that school policy offered no specific protection from anti-gay harassment. In addition, not surprisingly, all sexual minority students surveyed deeply desired more active, stated advocacy on the part of teachers, staff, and administration. As one sexual minority respondent put it, schools should provide "knowledge— i.e., pamphlets just to KNOW that there is help and access to some type of support network." Three other sexual minority respondents expressed a desire to see an informal school-based club that would encourage social connections among sexual minority students. In other words, they didn't want a group that just emphasized "at risk" aspects of sexual identity or specific issues like AIDS. One suggested, "If not a pride group, at least a hotline conducted by some teachers and brave students who have come out for the students who are scared or maybe just curious." This same student reported:

A few of our teachers know about some of us and are more than [willing] to give out their phone numbers so we can call and just talk to them if we want and others become distant when they find out. But other than just specific devoted teachers there are not groups or even conversations pertaining to the word "gay."

While respondents emphasized interactions between students and teachers, another sexual minority student suggested that "school counselors should also be better trained to handle the diversity of their students. School personnel are trained in cultural diversity regarding race and nationality, but they are not trained to help us." Still another suggested "explicit policies that forbid and punish discrimination and harassment of any kind (specifically including sexual orientation)." A survey of school policy indicates that these students were correct in the belief that they were not explicitly protected by school regulations or student conduct policies.

The fact that non-sexual minority students, teachers, and administration were more likely to presume that rules were already in place and that enough was being done, coupled with more than a few very hostile responses, indicates the working of an odd "hostility masquerading as civility" discourse that is not limited to the South. One administrator explained in a private conversation that he felt his school already addressed the needs of sexual minority youth because it taught students to respect everyone. When asked if his school could specify sexual minority students as a protected class, he responded that since homosexuality was a sin, that would not be possible, but they would be respected at school—although their sin would be pointed out to them. Although one can clearly see the crossover from civility to biblical proscription, I want to add another example that takes the same position in what the speaker took to be fully liberal terms. This teacher explained that although he personally supported the rights of sexual minority students, he also felt responsible for explaining to them the kind of harassment they would face from peers. He explained that when he had a "heinously non-conformist kid" in class, he would take that kid out of the classroom and explain that his or her nonconformity was going to lead to violence, so he or she should stop behaving in a provocative way. This avowed liberal was doing the work of conservatives in advance, seeking to smooth the social fabric before conflict could rend it and, of course, in the process insulting and degrading the student he was intent on protecting.

This discourse of civility enacts a new version of intolerance through unquestioning acceptance of the social practices in which one is embedded, questioning any challenge to those practices. I realize this observation is not earth shattering or new, but I am interested in the degree to which challenges to the discourse of civility raise hackles in my classes. When I discuss civility as a distancing strategy, whereby the codified social practices impede, rather than facilitate, social interaction and association, many students become angry. Indeed, it is, oddly, a moment wherein civility recedes as students defend a civility they cannot practice while engaged in its scrutiny. Although it is common in many regions for dominant groups to feel discomfort at the interrogation of invisible actions that structure their dominance, something else is at play in the South. Some students feel they are defending their Southern distinctiveness as they protect what they see as a particularly Southern attribute: the practice of good manners. When I intervene, I am doing so as a latter-day carpetbagger, ignorant and dismissive of Southern tradition. So my attempt to bring to the surface practices I find troubling is an enactment of power, not against discrimination per se, but as a potentially powerful outsider disrupting things I don't understand. (Lest I paint a monolithic picture of Southern civility, suffice it to say that there are dissenters and there are often differences of interpretation across race, class, age, and gender.) Because of my outsider status, explanations for the issues I raise are articulated through a North/South lens. When I question students' dominance, they question my regional dominance.

GETTING ALONG IN PUBLIC BY MOVING IDENTITY TO THE PRIVATE

Another regional difference arises as students point out that there is too much discussion of distasteful things in the North and a lack of recognition there that some things ought to be kept private. Their advocacy of public civil behavior moves to the private sphere anything that impedes smooth social action. In this version of how school life should proceed, students as non-acting, non-feeling bodies are allowed to be present, but the actions and feelings that define their identities are not. This is most familiar as "love the sinner, hate the sin," a position that does little to convince people that they are respected. Setting aside for the moment the response that all people are sinners (which never explains why the handy phrase only comes up when discussing sexual minorities), this discourse binds sexual minority students into inappropriateness in two ways. First, it does name them through their sin, despite the fact that the sin itself is not exactly what they are "doing" at school (my own experience in music practice rooms aside). Second, it implies that sinners do exist separately from their sin. The extent to which they are separate is the extent to which they are loved. But if we go back to the first point, this seems an empty promise, an impossibility couched as an imperative. The imperative is that to be loved one must not be oneself. Hence the distancing action of civility: We will only interact with you on the terms that you are not actually present. Interactions are structured by the open secret.

When I moved South, many well-meaning and kind Southerners explained that tolerance of oddity is common in the South in the form of the open secret. I realize this is a cliché, equally Northern as Southern (although my Northern students still insist that Northerners are more prone to face-to-face conflict and my Southern students occasionally want to know why anyone would want to live that way). It is, of course, paradigmatically liberal. The liberal argument that the private sphere is the space of diversity and distinctiveness and the public sphere the place of equality has been well criticized as hypocritical, inaccurate, and solipsistic. And the problem for public schools' role in maintaining liberal civility while continuing to acknowledge its tacit as well as overt support of particular identities is a difficult and vexed task. Still, the open secret is an interesting way to have one's diversity without having to have it. At the same time, as Eve Sedgwick (1990) reminds us, the open secret structures all of our interactions based on that secret. Its secrecy, in other words, is not a secret in that it is perpetually present, haunting the scene of its absence. I do not extol this paradox as a virtue: How does it feel to be an open secret? Not fabulous. Although it may sometimes feel perversely enthralling, one doesn't always want to be the thing structuring interactions and association. Sometimes one would like to interact and associate.

To put this more specifically, many respondents to the needs assessment survey and many students in class discussion claimed that homosexuality was not an issue in their schools. As one sexual minority student put it, "It's like they felt if they ignored it, it would go away. Nothing was said at all." Another respondent, a teacher, suggested that the issue of sexuality was not appropriate to schools: "A policy that include [sic] sexual orientation resources? [There ought to be] none. I feel that should be a home issue." But after viewing *It's Elementary: Teaching about Lesbian and Gay Issues in Schools* (Chasnoff and Cohen 1997), some students in a class of in-service teachers and administrators began to realize the very central way that homophobia structures student identity and interactions. They were faced with a challenge to their own belief that sexuality ought to be kept private. In addition, when asked if they were uncomfortable with the topic of homosexuality, after a few moments of silence, one student responded, "We wouldn't tell you if we were uncomfortable, we've been raised to sit quietly and smile through everything."

At the same time, many students steadfastly stuck to a discourse of professional responsibility and nonspecific tolerance. They recognized that this meant they would not be proactive about heterosexism in their schools, but at least they felt they could support sexual minority students as persons, when such persons became known and visible to them. Still, they couched this tolerance in terms of a desire to see sexual minority students maintain silence about their identity. As one student teacher put it, "I feel that if everyone followed the dress code there would be no need to know how anyone is sexually. Therefore, no need to be concerned." As class members articulated this support for privacy, they revealed their discomfort with sexual minority students *as* sexual minority students, preferring to refer to them as students who needed generalized tolerance. One student, a preservice administrator and in-service teacher, commented:

> I do not see sexual preference as a means of establishing a separate minority group, entitled to priviledges [sic] granted to minority groups. Sexual preference is an emotional/spiritual issue, not one inherited from one's parents. If this "minority" is given special focus, why not other "minorities" such as obese persons and/or pedophiles?

In the short answer section of the survey, comments about gay-inclusive nondiscrimination policies were equally divided between teachers and administrators who called for such policies and teachers and administrators contending that homosexuality was a sin and therefore ought not to be protected. As a middle school principal put it, "without a policy to support me, I can only advocate for those students I know are gay and I can't be open about supporting them as gay, but only as students. So I can't be proactive about addressing homophobia." A class discussion among principals and assistant principals indicated a strong fear of generating controversy in the community and of bad relations with school boards if overt discussions or workshops about homophobia were introduced into their schools. They were willing to give these students access to supportive resources, but they would not themselves (for religious or cultural reasons) support the students' sexuality. Tolerance, civility, and the right to privacy again became a rationale for avoiding the specific character of sexuality.

Nor are these ideas limited to students. A kind of blank tolerance was encouraged by a gay guest speaker whose presentation, generated through a national advocacy group, included a half hour discussion of "traits" in the context of left-handedness and then paralleled handedness with sexuality. The presentation encouraged students to dwell on the more comfortable topic of handedness without grappling deeply with the issue of sexuality. Useful in keeping students engaged, this approach nonetheless made "traits" appear ahistorical and unimplicated in power relations. In addition, the presentation actively avoided moral, religious, and value-related questions regarding sexuality, and so managed to leave personal bias intact while overlaying it with professional responsibility. This version of civic tolerance points to the shortcoming of civic morality, wherein privately held biases are not articulated, nor are their subtle (and not so subtle) public manifestations addressed.

INCIVILITY AS THE OPENING MOVE IN ASSOCIATION

By maintaining comfort with a bias-laden status quo, civility may present a greater barrier to change than incivility. Attempts to challenge bias against sexual minority students often appear on the surface to be making headway, while in reality one is just, as my student suggested, being smiled at and ignored. What may be needed instead is a distinctly uncivil approach to educating for diversity. One commonplace I have heard from diversity educators is that they need to approach prejudiced people as if those people were right. This seems precisely to miss the point of educating for diversity because, of course, prejudice is not "right." I think this particular turn of phrase embodies the way civility prevents education. If I approach you as if you are right, when I know or believe you to be wrong, I will be disinclined to challenge you. Education thus becomes a relation in which all who enter leave unchanged and unscathed. In the specific instance of educating about homophobia and heterosexism, and indeed any educational exchange, the point should be for all involved to be open to change and challenge.

Not too long ago, during a minor confrontation over fundamentalism and homophobia, a young woman chastised a friend and me for not knowing enough about the Bible. She reasoned that if we expected to talk to religious people we would have to do so on their terms. As it happens, her presumption that I wasn't conversant in relevant chapter and verse was incorrect. Indeed,

I have known many occasions when battling Bible verses was the order of the day. But the clear problem in attempting to explain something that is not strictly scriptural to such people is that meeting them on their own ground—faith supported by faith—means ceding the argument; for them there is no argument about their ground. That is pretty much the definition of faith, no matter how much one asserts that Jesus doubted, faith ought to be tempered by doubt, and so forth. So an attempt to engage civilly about sexual orientation means that one cannot engage.

Another approach to conservatives with whom one might have an argument, advocated by some activist groups, is not to engage at all. Rules for running demonstrations include, "No talking to counter-demonstrators." This too is an attempt to preserve some civility in public and to avoid getting bogged down in useless and escalating verbal disagreement. But there is another problem with this civility: It may maintain the peace, but then what is the point of demonstrating, particularly when demonstrations increasingly appear to happen in vacant downtowns on Sundays? As apathy keeps allies away and many see public protest as nearly barbaric, the only interlocutors we have are our purported enemies. These seem to be the very people with whom we ought to engage. I do not object to approaching people with the understanding that they believe themselves to be right and likely have very good reasons for so believing, reasons that can help me to understand them and revise my own views. This provisional willingness to revise beliefs and opinions is crucial to any educational undertaking. But it cannot be a one-way street, as we soon realized the young woman above was asking of us. For social interactions to lead to strong associations, we need to be more willing to be contentious, to risk incivility, and to expect that a disruption of placid, problematic interactions will be necessary. For sexual minority students, whose very presence may be seen by intolerant people as unsettling, advocating un-civility in anti-bias education may be the only way to start the conversation that needs to take place.

NOTES

1. No one in groups 2, 3, or 4 identified themselves on the survey as lesbian, gay, bisexual, or transgender.

2. Carolyn Riehl and I are working on this project. I am grateful to Carolyn for her suggestions on this project as well.

3. Michael Warner discusses a similar dynamic in sexual minority movements in *The trouble with normal: Sex, politics, and the ethics of queer life* (New York: Free Press, 1999). For a discussion of similar tension in school desegregation, see William Chafe, *Civility and civil rights* (Oxford: Oxford University Press, 1980).

REFERENCES

Chasnoff, D., director/producer, and H. S. Cohen, producer. 1997. *It's elementary: Talking about gay issues in school*. [Video.] (Available from Women's Educational Media, 2180 Bryant St., Suite 203, San Francisco, CA 94110, and distributed by New Day Films, Hohokus, NJ.)

Dewey, J. 1916. *Democracy and education*. New York: Macmillan.

Sedgwick, E. K. 1990. *The epistemology of the closet*. Berkeley: University of California Press.

7

The Gay Ghetto in the Geography of Education Textbooks

Allison J. Young and Michael J. Middleton

THE CONTEXT FOR THIS STUDY

Teacher preparation programs play a substantial role in shaping preservice teachers' beliefs about teaching, learning, and students. Since many preservice teachers have limited awareness about lesbian, gay, bisexual, and transgendered (lgbt) issues, it is incumbent upon these programs to discuss diversity in general, and sexual diversity in particular. Early childhood and elementary educators will encounter lgbt families in their classrooms (Casper and Schultz 1999). Secondary educators will also have students who identify as gay, lesbian, bisexual, or transgendered. At both levels, teachers will have colleagues who identify as lgbt. To create a truly inclusive community, it is important that preservice teacher preparation programs address lgbt issues directly (Mathison 1998).

Generally, we know that teachers' beliefs about diversity are likely to affect both the classroom climate and instructional practices (Grant and Secada 1990; Richardson 1996). Sears (1992) suggests that although preservice teachers' personal beliefs do not always correlate with beliefs about professional conduct, personal beliefs may in fact lead a teacher to treat a student unfairly. And a teacher who has not been exposed to a certain group may be unprepared to handle the social or learning challenges for members of that group. For instance, a 1994 study of prospective teachers in Ohio found a high incidence of negative stereotypes, as well as an unwillingness to address gay/lesbian issues adequately in the context of schools or to exhibit supportive behaviors toward lesbians and gays (Butler 1994). Given our understanding of the role of teacher beliefs, these findings are not encouraging, since they suggest that even if teachers were to present a "professional" demeanor as Sears (1991) suggests, their underlying beliefs would remain largely negative.

To address these personal beliefs about difference, many teacher preparation programs have begun to require multicultural education courses to help preservice teachers grapple with issues of diversity. Although race, gender, and social class are the usual signifiers of diversity, the treatment of lgbt issues in these courses remains unclear, as it does in preservice teacher education curricula in general. Furthermore, the methods and materials used to address lgbt issues remain unexamined.

Because there has been little investigation of how teacher preparation programs negotiate lgbt issues in the curriculum, we framed this study to investigate how textbooks present these issues, using a content analysis of a variety of popular textbooks (lifespan development, adolescent development, and multicultural/social foundations) used in teacher education programs. We focused primarily on texts for developmental psychology courses because we felt that these texts would be more likely to address issues of sexual diversity than would texts for instructional methods or educational psychology.

EXAMINING THE TEXTS

The twenty-three textbooks we studied, published between 1991 and 1998, are frequently used in teacher preparation courses including human development, adolescent development, educational psychology, and multicultural education or social foundations of education (see the appendix). We looked for content related to gays, lesbians, and/or homosexuality in eleven developmental psychology texts, five adolescence texts, and seven multicultural/social foundations texts. We did not examine any of the supplemental instructional materials, nor did we investigate interactive CD-ROM or textbook related websites, since not all teachers use these resources.

We assessed the textbooks' structural dimensions (such as index listings, placement among topics in chapters, and pictures and captions) by counting and categorizing references to lgbt issues. Further, we examined theoretical dimensions such as perspectives of psychological theories and topics such as etiology, human development, and social issues. We used an iterative process, looking for emerging themes in the content prior to and immediately following the sections on lgbt issues, as well as content specifically addressing these issues.

Where possible, we examined subsequent editions and compared these texts with the texts used in the initial analysis. Although this updated analysis was not possible for all texts, the sample of updated texts provides additional evidence of the authors' intentions toward sexual diversity.

VISIBILITY AND PLACEMENT

On a positive note, all the lifespan development and adolescence books dealt with lgbt issues, at least on some level. This was not the case in the seven multicultural texts, of which only two discussed lgbt issues: the Sadker and Sadker (1991) text and the Tiedt and Tiedt (1995) text. In all of the lifespan texts, lgbt issues appeared under the index heading "Homosexuality," while in one of the multicultural texts they were listed under "Homophobia." Of the eleven lifespan texts, three used the terms "Gay" and "Lesbian" in their indices. Of the five adolescence texts we investigated, only the Dusek (1996) text had an index heading for "Gay and Lesbian Parents," while still another, the Cobb (1998) text, used a cross-reference between homosexuality and heterosexuality.

Our examination of the texts' structural aspects led to several interesting observations. First, in the lifespan texts, lgbt issues were usually found in sections on social and personality development in early adulthood. Eight of the eleven texts (73 percent) followed this pattern. Lgbt issues also appeared in sections or chapters on adolescent social and personality development in five of eleven texts (45 percent), and on adolescent physical and cognitive development in four of the eleven texts (36 percent). Three texts discussed lgbt issues in sections on middle to late adulthood. One text discussed lgbt issues under genetics, another discussed them under the prenatal heading as part of a commentary on teratogens, and still another placed them within the context of preschool androgyny. The adolescence texts discussed lgbt issues in chapters on adolescent sexuality, whereas the two multicultural texts discussed them in sections on families and on homophobia's effect on education and schooling. Three of the texts (two lifespan and one adolescence) discussed the issue of gay and lesbian parenting.

Our other observations were specifically related to the content placement within the texts. In several cases in both lifespan and adolescence texts, the discussion of lgbt issues was directly preceded or followed by a discussion of STDs, teen pregnancy, or sexual abuse. We also analyzed the text within these discussions to examine how authors were portraying lgbt people. And finally, we examined pictures, figures, and tables, as well as special sections, often entitled "Highlights."

THE PROBLEMATIZATION OF LGBT ISSUES

Lgbt issues were often included as an example of problems associated with adolescent development along with teen pregnancy and drug abuse, and were often mentioned in conjunction with AIDS. In the three-page section entitled "Homosexual Attitudes and Behavior" in the Santrock (1997) text, a discussion of AIDS makes up half of the section, including a picture of an end-stage AIDS patient. Similarly, Bee's (1998) initial discussion of lgbt issues comes in a section entitled "Risky Behavior in Context" (281).

Such problematization was particularly evident in the structure of three of the adolescent development books, the Atwater (1996), Dusek (1996), and Steinberg (1996) texts, in which we found lgbt issues in the midst of sections on teen pregnancy, STDs, or sexual abuse. The same was true for seven of the lifespan texts. Positioning discussions of lgbt issues so near such topics connects them to problems, even if the text states otherwise.

Interestingly, four lifespan texts and one adolescence text listed AIDS in the index under "Homosexuality." In at least two cases, AIDS appeared only in the section on lgbt issues rather than under health concerns. The most recent edition of the Berk (2001) text offers a discussion of "bereavement overload over AIDS victims," explaining the effects of the AIDS epidemic on the gay community rather than focusing on infected individuals. While the connection between homosexuality and AIDS cannot be denied, addressing AIDS solely in this context colors student attitudes toward homosexuality.

MARGINALIZING LGBT IDENTITY

Most texts contrasted lgbt issues with heterosexuality, thereby marginalizing gay themes in much the same way that racial and ethnic differences are often marginalized. One text presented a discussion focused on etiology, ending with the comparative statement, "Like ethnic minority youth . . ." (Bee 1998, 314). Another text stated that "gays and lesbians adapt best when they don't define themselves in polarities, such as trying to live in an encapsulated gay or lesbian world completely divorced from the majority culture or completely accepting the dictates and bias of the majority culture" (Santrock 1997, 429). This same text then proceeded to compare lgbt identity to heterosexual norms, even though it had just cautioned the reader against such "polarity." Treatments like these serve to call attention to the primacy of the heterosexual perspective.

Within the section entitled "Divorce and Remarriage," Berk (1998), citing Bigner and Jacobsen (1989), discussed both never-married parents and gay and lesbian parents, and her depiction of gay and lesbian parents was generally positive:

> Families headed by a homosexual parent or a gay or lesbian couple are very similar to those of heterosexuals. Gay and lesbian parents are as committed to and effective at the parent role, and sometimes more so. Indeed, some research indicates that gay fathers are more consistent in setting limits and more responsive to their children's needs than are heterosexual fathers, perhaps because gay men's nontraditional gender-role identity fosters involvement with children. (475–76)

Similarly, Bee's (1998) discussion on debunking myths ended as follows: "All this means that gay partnerships are far more like heterosexual relationships than they are different" (368). Although these statements are literally positive in themselves, they continue to hold gayness up against a heterosexual norm. This pattern of presenting homosexuality only in contrast to heterosexuality is consistent with similar problems in the representation of other underrepresented groups (e.g., African Americans, women), resulting in the apparent "racelessness" or "womanlessness" of the research in psychology (Crawford and Maracek 1989; Graham 1992). The literature in psychology has often used white, middle-class, heterosexual, able-bodied males as the referent, leading to a marginalization of individuals or groups outside of those demographics. Marginalization was especially evident in the multicultural or social foundations texts, where only two of the seven books we examined mentioned homosexuality in passing. However, more recent texts show a growing sensitivity, addressing lgbt issues with greater variety (Berger 2001; Berk 2001).

It is interesting to note that there was little mention of transgendered people in any of the texts. The most recent edition of Feldman (2000) mentions gender identity in a section entitled "Sexual Orientation: Heterosexuality and Homosexuality." And the newest edition of the Cushner, McClelland, and Safford (2000) text includes a chapter entitled "Creating Collaborative Communities: Gender and Sexual Orientation." We hope that this awareness is the first step in addressing transgender issues in lifespan and adolescence texts.

COMMON THEORETICAL PERSPECTIVES

Three major common theoretical positions appeared in our initial analysis. First, most of the developmental/lifespan psychology and adolescence texts showed some concern with etiology or explanation. This was especially true of the five adolescence texts we examined. These texts attempted to answer the natural question, "How and why are people gay?" Typically, the answer included a combination of nature and nurture. One adolescence text, by Rice (1996), used "Biological Theories," "Psychoanalytic Theories," and "Social Learning Theories" in its discussion of etiology. Some texts recognized the prevalence of lgbt behavior but qualified this recognition by suggesting that it might be a phase many people outgrow. A review of more recent editions of some of these texts found little change in these discussions.

Second, some texts attempted to portray lgbt issues as part of the variability of development, focusing on individual differences. This was particularly true in the developmental or lifespan texts, which included lgbt issues throughout the text. Lgbt relationships were discussed during adolescence and early adulthood and, in a few of the texts, even into late adulthood. Some texts included a discussion of same-sex relationships under "non-marital lifestyles." Even the discussion of lesbian and gay parents was framed in relation to nonmarried parents, using heterosexual norms such as "married" or "non-married" rather than the range of relationships or of parenthood. Few if any of the texts in our initial analysis pointed out the sociopolitical circumstances that prevent gays and lesbians from participating in legal marriage, although more recent editions have begun to address this issue. For instance, Berk (2001) incorporates information on lgb parenting groups in an information box with other parenting and family issues, and includes a discussion of the importance of durable power of attorney for lgb couples.

Finally, some texts were careful to raise the issue of social context, pointing out that there is significant discrimination against lgbt people. These discussions focused on how societal beliefs and behaviors influence the development of individual gay men or lesbians. Many linked this discrimination to lgbt mental health. Often, discussion of lgbt issues used the individual as the "unit of analysis," a dominant paradigm in psychological theory and research. However, more recent texts indicate a shift, locating lgbt issues within the contemporary social context (Berger 2001; Berk 2001). It is important for readers of education texts to understand the interaction of the person and the environment (cf. Lewin 1935) as a major feature of both educational and developmental psychology, as well as education in general. Consideration of the social context is particularly important for preservice teachers. Although teachers cannot change characteristics of the individual student, such as sexual orientation, they *can* create classroom environments that are safe for all students.

A PICTURE IS WORTH A THOUSAND WORDS

We found a range of pictures, figures, and tables in the textbooks. At least nine of the eleven lifespan texts and four of the five adolescence texts presented photos representing men and women, youth and adults, single people and couples. Three of the lifespan texts showed photos highlighting political activism, and in one case, an AIDS patient. None of the multicultural education texts showed any such photos. Three texts, one lifespan and two adolescence books, used some representation of the Kinsey scale to supplement the text. One text offered a table depicting the likelihood of the incidence of gay/lesbianism in twins, while another illustrated differences among gays and lesbians on the basis of other demographic variables such as rurality versus urbanity and race/ethnicity. Of the twelve photos or figures we found, only one was immediately negative, a photo of a man on a respirator dying of AIDS. Non-group photos were equally likely to depict lesbians and gay men, but the people in the photos were predominantly white/Caucasian, marginalizing lgbt people of color. However, more recent texts such as Berk (2001) and Rice (1999) include gay men of color.

IMPLICATIONS FOR TEACHER EDUCATORS

Although these texts do raise lgbt issues in a straightforward way, it is clear that some need to consider the placement of lgbt issues as well as the choice of illustrative photos. Integration of lgbt issues throughout the text, as in the Berger text, is a crucial step in combating subtle homophobia (Whatley 1992) and would prevent the ghettoization we found in many of the texts we reviewed. In addition, texts should continue to present photos of gays and lesbians with positive connotations. The majority of photos we found were positive, showing lgbt people smiling and, we presume, happy, with partners and in groups, showing affection and doing mundane tasks. This range of images helps break down stereotypes about gay and lesbian people.

Authors and editors should consider carefully the language they use to discuss lgbt issues, as well as the way theoretical perspectives are presented. As Friend (1993) points out, it is important to emphasize contextual factors that create stress for lgbt people rather than locating distress within individuals, as is often the case in traditional psychological frameworks. Several of the texts we examined (Berger 1998; Feldman 1997; and Santrock 1997), did just this, but others such as Berk (1998), Papalia and Olds (1993), Sigelman and Shaffer (1995), and LeFrancois (1995), continued to focus on group or individual differences. While the discussion of the etiology of homosexuality in the life span texts may be important, it should be treated with some caution. For example, Feldman (1997, 2000) raises some questions regarding Freudian perspectives, which will help students to be appropriately critical of psychological theories. This perspective is important for teacher education students who may only take one or two psychology courses as a part of their coursework.

Textbook materials may be especially important in larger teacher preparation programs, where textbooks often serve to unify multiple sections of a course, and where a cadre of part-time or adjunct faculty may teach those sections. In such courses, textbook materials often form the basis for lectures and discussions. Since the individual instructor may not always be particularly sensitive to the nuances of lgbt issues, it is imperative that the text deal with them responsibly.

BROADENING THE DISCUSSION

It is also important for teacher educators to know about supplementary materials and how to find them. Many of our faculty colleagues indicated that they use supplementary resource material in their courses, which range from general education to educational psychology and from literacy to multicultural education and adolescent development. Teacher education colleagues report arranging panel discussions with representatives from Parents, Families and Friends of Lesbians and Gays (PFLAG) and the Gay, Lesbian and Straight Education Network (GLSEN). They also use handouts and other GLSEN sponsored materials, such as videos like *I Just Want to Say* (1998), featuring Martina Navratilova, and *It's Elementary* (Chasnoff and Cohen 1997). Careful use of Internet features like WebQuest can allow teacher education students to explore lgbt issues in more depth. Finally, gay-straight alliance student groups (GSAs) in the local high school can offer the secondary student's perspective.

Other ideas include appropriate children's literature with lgbt themes and personal narratives of experiences with gay and lesbian people. Examples of lgbt issues in other disciplinary areas may also be useful in the teacher education classroom; for example, Chesler and Zuniga (1991) describe a simulation they developed in a course on intergroup conflict and social change. A faculty colleague provides his students with a teaching case that deals directly with lgbt issues in area schools. Each of these methods has advantages and disadvantages, which need to be examined in future research. Educators should also explore materials designed to develop heterosexual allies of lgbt people, including the process of becoming a lgbt ally who can promote the incorporation of these ideas into textbooks. Finally, if lgbt issues are to be addressed in a systematic way, it is incumbent upon us to provide textbook authors and publishers with feedback on their respective approaches to lgbt issues.

Our study provides one framework for analyzing textbook materials. Further research should continue to examine the portrait of lgbt issues painted in mainstream textbooks. Most of the textbooks in our initial analysis were initially published in the mid-1990s, and an analysis of some newer editions indicates that authors and editors are becoming more sensitive to these issues. As teacher educators raise awareness and sensitivity to lgbt issues, the echo of these discussions promises to break the current conspiracy of silence in pre-K–12 schooling.

NOTES

An earlier version of this paper was presented as part of the symposium "Over the Rainbow and under the Multicultural Umbrella: Preparing Preservice Teachers for Sexual Diversity" at the Annual Meeting of the American Educational Research Association, Montreal, Quebec, Canada, 1999.

The authors would like to thank Rita Kissen and the Lesbian and Gay Studies SIG of the American Educational Research Association and the Gay, Lesbian and Straight Education Network for their support.

REFERENCES

Anderson, J. D. 1994. School climate for gay and lesbian students and staff members. *Phi Delta Kappan* 76 (2): 151–54.

———. 1997. Supporting the invisible minority. *Educational Leadership* 54: 65–68.

Bigner, J. J., and R. B. Jacobsen. 1989. Homosexual and hererosexual fathers: A comparison study. *Journal of Homosexuality* 18: 173–86.

Butler, K. L. 1994. *Prospective teachers' knowledge, attitudes, and behavior regarding gay men and lesbians.* (Tech. Rep. No. 143.) Kent, Ohio: Kent State University.

Casper, V., and S. B. Schultz. 1999. *Gay parents, straight schools: Building communication and trust.* New York: Teachers College Press.

Chasnoff, D., director/producer, and H. S. Cohen, producer. 1997. *It's elementary: Talking about gay issues in school.* [Video.] (Available from Women's Educational Media, 2180 Bryant St., Suite 203, San Francisco, CA 94110, and distributed by New Day Films, Hohokus, NJ.)

Chesler, M. A., and X. Zuniga. 1991. Dealing with prejudice and conflict in the classroom: The pink triangle exercise. *Teaching Sociology* 19: 177–81.

Crawford, M., and J. Maracek. 1989. Psychology reconstructs the female. *Psychology of Women Quarterly* 13: 147–65.

Crocco, M. S. 2001. Homophobic hallways: Is anyone listening? Paper presented at the meeting of the American Educational Research Association, April, Seattle, Washington.

Edwards, A. T. 1997. Let's stop ignoring our gay and lesbian youth. *Educational Leadership* 54: 68–70.

Friend, R. A. 1993. Choices, not closets: Heterosexism and homophobia in schools. In *Beyond silenced voices: Class, race, and gender in United States schools,* edited by L. Weis and M. Fine, 209–35. Albany: State University of New York Press.

Gay, Lesbian, Straight Education Network (GSLEN), producer. 1998. *I just want to say . . . students, parents, and teachers talk about anti-gay bias in our schools.* [Video.] (Available from GLSEN, 121 West 27th St., Suite 804, New York, NY 10001-6207.)

Graham, S. 1992. "Most of the subjects were white and middle class": Trends in published research on African Americans in selected APA journals. *American Psychologist* 47 (5): 629–39.

Grant, C. A., and W. G. Secada. 1990. Preparing teachers for diversity. In *Handbook of research on teacher education,* edited by W. R. Houston, 403–22. New York: Macmillan.

Lewin, K. 1935. *A dynamic theory of personality: Selected papers.* New York: McGraw-Hill.

Massachusetts Governor's Commission on Gay and Lesbian Youth. 1993. *Making schools safe for gay and lesbian youth: Breaking the silence in schools and families.* Publication No. 17296-60-500-2/93-C.R.

Mathison, C. 1998. The invisible minority: Preparing teachers to meet the needs of gay and lesbian youth. *Journal of Teacher Education* 49: 151–55.

Richardson, V. 1996. The role of attitudes and beliefs in learning to teach. In *Handbook of research on teacher education,* 2d ed., edited by J. Sikula, 102–19. New York: Macmillan.

Sears, J. T. 1991. Helping students understand and accept sexual diversity. *Educational Leadership* 49 (1): 54–56.

———. 1992. Educators, homosexuality, and homosexual students: Are personal feelings related to professional beliefs? In *Coming out of the classroom closet: Gay and lesbian students, teachers and curricula,* edited by K. Harbeck, 29–79. Binghamton, N.Y.: Harrington Park Press.

Simoni, J. M. 1996. Confronting heterosexism in the teaching of psychology. *Teaching of Psychology* 23: 220–26.

Whatley, M. H. 1992. Images of gays and lesbians in sexuality and health textbooks. In *Coming out of the classroom closet: Gay and lesbian students, teachers and curricula,* edited by K. Harbeck, 197–211. Binghamton, N.Y.: Harrington Park Press.

APPENDIX: TEXTBOOK LIST

* Indicates a revised edition or an addition to the previous analysis.

Lifespan Development/Human Development

Bee, H. 1998. *Lifespan development.* 2d ed. New York: Addison Wesley Longman.

Berger, K. S. 1998. *The developing person through the lifespan.* 4th ed. New York: Worth Publishers.

——. 2001. *The developing person through the lifespan.* 5th ed. New York: Worth Publishers.*

Berk, L. E. 1998. *Development through the lifespan.* 1st ed. Needham Heights, Mass.: Allyn & Bacon.

——. 2001. *Development through the lifespan.* 2d ed. Needham Heights, Mass.: Allyn & Bacon.*

Craig, G. J. 1999. *Human development.* 8th ed. Upper Saddle River, N.J.: Prentice-Hall.

Feldman, R. S. 1997. *Development across the lifespan.* 1st ed. Upper Saddle River, N.J.: Prentice Hall.

——. 2000. *Development across the lifespan.* 2d ed. Upper Saddle River, N.J.: Prentice Hall.*

Gormly, A. V. 1997. *Lifespan human development.* 6th ed. New York: Harcourt Brace College Publishers.

LeFrancois, G. R. 1995. *Of children: An introduction to child development.* 8th ed. New York: Wadsworth.

Paludi, M. A. 2002. *Human development in multicultural contexts: A book of readings.* Upper Saddle River, N.J.: Prentice Hall.*

Papalia, D. E., and S. W. Olds. 1993. *A child's world: Infancy through adolescence.* 6th ed. New York: McGraw-Hill.

Santrock, J. W. 1997. *Lifespan development.* 6th ed. Madison, Wis.: Brown & Benchmark Publishers.

Seifert, R. L., R. J. Hoffnung, and M. Hoffnung. 1997. *Lifespan development.* Boston: Houghton Mifflin.

Sigelman, C. K., and D. R. Shaffer. 1995. *Lifespan human development.* 2d ed. Pacific Grove, Calif.: Brooks/Cole Publishing Company.

Adolescence

Atwater, E. 1996. *Adolescence.* 4th ed. Upper Saddle River, N.J.: Prentice-Hall.

Cobb, N. J. 1998. *Adolescence: Continuity, change, and diversity.* 3d ed. Toronto, Ont.: Mayfield.

Dusek, J. B. 1996. *Adolescent development and behavior.* Upper Saddle River, N.J.: Prentice-Hall.

Rice, F. P. 1996. *The adolescent: Development, relationships & culture.* 8th ed. Needham Heights, Mass.: Allyn & Bacon.

——. 1999. *The adolescent: Development, relationships & culture.* 9th ed. Needham Heights, Mass.: Allyn & Bacon.*

Steinberg, L. 1996. *Adolescence.* 4th ed. Boston: McGraw-Hill.

——. 1999. *Adolescence.* 5th ed. Boston: McGraw-Hill.*

Multicultural Education/Social Foundations Texts

Cushner, K., A. McClelland, and P. Safford. 1992. *Human diversity in education: An integrative approach.* New York: McGraw-Hill.*

———. 2000. *Human diversity in education: An integrative approach.* 3d ed. New York: McGraw-Hill.*

Garcia, E. 1994. *Understanding and meeting the challenge of student cultural diversity.* Boston: Houghton Mifflin.

Grant, C. A., and M. L. Gomez. 1996. *Making schooling multicultural: Campus and classroom.* Columbus, Ohio: Merrill.

Sadker, M. P., and D. M. Sadker. 1991. *Teachers, schools, and society.* 2d ed. New York: McGraw-Hill.

Strouse, J. H. 1997. *Exploring themes of social justice in education: Readings in social foundations.* Columbus, Ohio: Merrill.

Tiedt, P. L., and I. M. Tiedt. 1995. *Multicultural teaching: A handbook of activities, information, and resources.* 4th ed. Needham Heights, Mass.: Allyn and Bacon.

Tozer, S. E., P. C. Violas, and G. Senese. 1998. *School and society: Historical and contemporary perspectives.* New York: McGraw-Hill.

II

"ADD LGBT AND STIR": MULTICULTURALISM AND SEXUAL DIVERSITY

In part II, five teacher educators explore the place of lesbian and gay issues in the multicultural enterprise. Paula Kluth and Kevin Colleary begin by suggesting how the tenets of inclusive special education can help us prepare teachers to welcome lesbian and gay students into their classrooms. Emphasizing the building of multicultural bridges, Kluth and Colleary propose a model in which tolerance and inclusion are more important than the different kinds of "difference." In contrast, Will Letts imagines a "queer multiculturalism" whose practitioners would "advocate dialogue and exchange across difference, rather than trying to craft or impose some mythical set of shared values." Letts's approach is not wholly theoretical, however; he presents us with activities in which autobiographical writing, encounters with literature, and a "cultural plunge" into an unfamiliar environment can help students "interrogate constructions of and assumptions about subjectivities, identity categories, and what is 'normal.'"

Tim Bedford's description of the GLEE project, founded by the European Union (EU), and of the Theory of Knowledge course he has taught in Finland and Japan, presents yet another model of lesbian and gay awareness within a multicultural perspective. Bedford bases his vision of multiculturalism on the four core values of diversity, human rights, human dignity, and equity/equality, and addresses the challenge of breaking the silence about all forms of oppression, including heteronormativity and homophobia. Using a stage model of intercultural sensitivity, he outlines a participant-centered pedagogy in which teachers create gay-sensitive curricula and develop electronic networks connecting schools from a variety of EU countries.

Genét Simone's chapter, like Bedford's, describes pedagogic practices that encourage students to construct and reconstruct their own understandings of heterosexism and homophobia. Mere knowledge, as Simone points out, does not necessarily change hearts and minds, and so her Personal Transformation Exercise engages students in self-analysis and personal risk-taking. Like the students in Will Letts's Cultural Plunge, Simone's students design an exercise to address their own self-acknowledged fears and assumptions. Simone grounds this process in multiculturalism but focuses on two students who chose to address their own homophobia. She draws from the mind/body movement, meditation, and other contemplative practices, while insisting that "[a]nything less than . . . passion and rigor will keep our preservice teachers from relating to their own students as whole human beings."

Despite their differences, all these writers draw on the rich history and insights of multicultural education as they write and teach about sexual diversity, and all insist that theory be grounded in the lived experience of students and teachers.

8

"Talking about Inclusion Like It's for Everyone": Sexual Diversity and the Inclusive Schooling Movement

Paula Kluth and Kevin P. Colleary

During a preservice teacher education class titled "Inclusive Schooling," a student handed in a course evaluation that read: "When I first signed up for this class I thought inclusive schooling was about disability issues. Thanks for talking about inclusion like it's for everyone. I like how you said 'partner' instead of boyfriend or girlfriend. I like how you talk about lesbians as a diversity. I like how you encouraged relationships in here."

Inclusive schooling as a catalyst for thinking about sexual diversity? Some might see the two issues as distinct and separate, but we have come to see them as similar and overlapping. It was the evaluation quoted above, however, that prompted us to consider formally what the two issues have in common and how associating them can benefit learners in schools and teachers in higher, secondary, and elementary education.

We have come to believe that this important political, social, and educational movement can help us to better understand issues of sexual diversity; teach to and about sexual diversity; and better support learners who identify as lesbian, gay, bisexual, transgendered, and/or queer (lgbtq) as well as those who do not. Our interest in the intersection of these issues has prompted us to examine the question, "What can we learn from the inclusive schooling movement about incorporating and celebrating sexual diversity in teaching and learning?" This chapter is a result of our thinking about that question. It is also a summary of our hopes for education in this new century.

INCLUSIVE SCHOOLING:
A REFORM TO BENEFIT ALL LEARNERS

The inclusive schooling movement, which has influenced teacher education programs throughout the United States for over twenty years (Meyer et al. 1997; Villa, Thousand, and Chapple 2000) helps in-service and preservice teachers develop pragmatic strategies for teaching students with diverse needs, abilities, and strengths. More important, the philosophy of the movement helps teachers expand their thinking, expectations, and understandings of how students can learn and how teachers can teach.

Although many have understood inclusive schooling as a reform implemented to benefit learners with disabilities, most of its proponents understand it as a movement that concerns all students. It is a way of thinking about and engaging in teaching and learning to benefit and support all students in higher education and in K–12 schools, and it is inspiring promising new practices, behaviors, supports, and ideals in American education.

In this chapter we share our vision of how this educational movement can help preservice teachers broaden their definitions of student diversity and better understand their role in helping all students learn, feel comfortable, and have a healthy educational experience. We also hope to use what has been learned from this movement to show how it can be extended to help teacher education programs as they work to incorporate issues of sexual diversity into their philosophy and practice.

SEXUAL DIVERSITY AND INCLUSIVE SCHOOLING

Without ignoring or minimizing the many unique characteristics of sexual diversity and dis/ability, we have noticed multiple intersections between teaching about inclusive education and teaching about sexual diversity. We believe teacher educators wrestling with incorporating sexual diversity into their curricula or programs can benefit from looking to an educational reform that has inspired both classroom teachers and university educators to make positive shifts in their philosophies and practices. Inclusive schooling has motivated countless elementary, secondary, and postsecondary educators to consider and appreciate the individuality that each student brings to the classroom. Perhaps most important, the inclusive schooling movement is prompting teachers and administrators to attend to differences broadly and positively. The inclusive schooling movement has much to share as we work to construct new models for preservice programs that challenge emerging teachers to embrace, support, and understand *all* diversities.

There are many ways the inclusive schooling movement can move teachers to better understand issues of sexual diversity and welcome lgbtq students, families, and issues into their classrooms. Specifically, inclusive schooling offers both a progressive ideology and a useful set of practices. Supporters of inclusion promote a *new* type of education. Inclusive schooling stresses interdependence and independence, views all students as gifted, and values a sense of community (Falvey, Givner, and Kimm 1995). In addition, it is an educational movement that supports civil and human rights:

> [Inclusive schooling] propels a critique of contemporary school culture and thus, encourages practitioners to reinvent what can be and should be to realize more humane, just and democratic learning communities. Inequities in treatment and educational opportunity are brought to the forefront, thereby fostering attention to human rights, respect for difference and value of diversity. (Udvari-Solner 1997, 142)

Like Udvari-Solner, we define inclusive education as something that supports, has an impact on, and benefits all learners. We see inclusion as an educational orientation that embraces differences and values diversity. Further, we view inclusion as a revolution, a social action, and a critical political movement. Inclusive education is not conditional; we believe it must be creatively pursued and realized for all learners, including students who are lgbtq and those who share their schools.

LEARNING FROM THE INCLUSIVE TENETS

There are five important tenets related to the philosophy and practices of the inclusive schooling movement that may be used to guide teachers as they work to better support all students in their classrooms. We examine the ways in which each of these tenets relates to inclusive education and, further, how they can be used to educate preservice teachers about incorporating sexual diversity issues in their teaching. These tenets are

- Recognizing differences,
- Interrogating labels,
- Preserving student dignity,
- Designing sensitive and relevant curricula, and
- Encouraging advocacy.

Recognizing Differences

We all know that every child is unique and special and that when we walk into our classrooms each new school year, we are faced with twenty-five to thirty-five "different" people entrusted to our care. Yet seeing those differences and understanding them are sometimes complicated matters for a teacher. For example, teachers often say, "I don't see color, I see a child," or "I don't see disabilities; all of my students are special." These statements may spring from a well of goodness and concern, but they are often misguided. It is impossible to "not see" color, race, or the other differences that make up all of our lives. These elements are distinct and real. They are an integral part of who we are as individuals and as members of our communities. "Not seeing" is not a positive response to difference. Recognizing and doing our best to really understand how differences affect students' lives and educational experiences helps us to better know and serve each individual student.

As citizens of such a diverse nation as the United States, we must always be ready to meet and engage with others who are very different from ourselves. This is especially true in the workplace, in civic life, and in an increasingly diverse set of virtual communities in which we choose to exist. This is a lesson that we as adults must understand, and it is a lesson that we as teachers can share with and model for our students during their earliest years in school.

In inclusive schools, students are encouraged to express their individuality and to acknowledge "not only what is good and enjoyable in their lives but also what is painful and hard" (Sapon-Shevin 1999, 35). As Sapon-Shevin stresses, we need to encourage students to feel comfortable with their differences; to do so, teachers must first create a context in which differences can be exposed and accepted:

> We want to create chances for students to share all aspects of themselves: the good, the laudable, the troublesome, and the confusing. Because community and cultural values and standards concerning what's appropriate to share are apt to vary considerably, it is important for teachers to be extremely sensitive in respecting children's differences. (1999, 36)

The inclusive schooling movement has inspired a paradigm shift in education. This critical educational reform has helped teachers conceptualize differences as an essential and valued aspect of classrooms. Inclusive teachers, in fact, welcome differences in the classroom and view them as critical to student learning. In good inclusive schools, "the view that differences among individuals in education pose difficulties and need to be fixed, improved, or made ready to fit (i.e., homogenized) is replaced by the recognition that differences are valuable assets to capitalize on" (Stainbeck 2000, 508).

Of course, students must also be given opportunities to share similarities and to see beyond differences. Seeing *beyond* differences, in fact, is a critical part of *recognizing* differences, as former Vice-President Al Gore has indicated:

> It's a two-step process. You have to first establish absolute and genuine mutual respect for difference. And that respect for difference has to include both an appreciation for the unique suffering that has come about because of the difference, and the unique gifts and contributions that have come about because of the difference. And a basic appreciation for the unique perspective that is based on that difference. Then the second step is a transcendence of that difference to embrace all the elements that we have in common in the human spirit. (quoted in Lemann 2000, 62)

Gore's charge reminds us that seeing differences and looking beyond them to find similarities, connections, and relationships allows us to fully serve and honor each child in a more honest and relevant way.

Interrogating Labels

Teachers in diverse classrooms must recognize the benefits of celebrating student differences, while at the same time working to know students as individual learners. During busy classroom days, teachers may rely on stereotypes, assumptions, and perceptions in their daily social interactions with students and in the planning of curriculum and instruction. Educators may also fall into the trap of using labels or one-dimensional descriptions of students in conversations with colleagues, in formal reports or other types of communication, and even in interactions with students themselves.

The labeling of differences presents a difficult challenge. Although labeling and identity politics can certainly promote self-affirmation, positive self-image, and connectivity with others, the limitations presented by labels are many. Labels can be constricting and limiting. Further, the inclusive schooling movement teaches us that the labels used to define students of various abilities have a checkered and often disturbing past. Some sources suggest, for example, that the etymology of handicap is "cap in hand" (Snow 1998), evoking the image of a person with a disability begging on the street with "cap in hand."

In inclusive schooling classrooms, teachers are encouraged to avoid using labels to define students and to consider using People First Language (Snow 1998) when communicating about learners with disabilities. People First

Language is a way of speaking and writing that "puts the person before the disability"(14). Instead of saying, "Jane is an LD student," for example, a teacher should say, "Jane is a student with learning disabilities." Snow, a disability activist who advocates the use of Person First Language, stresses the need to see the important differences in individuals, while recognizing the complexity of differences at the same time:

> The disability community is the largest minority group in our country. It includes people of both genders and from all religions, ethnic backgrounds, and socioeconomic levels. About the only things people with disabilities have in common with one another are: 1—having a body function that operates differently; 2—facing prejudice and discrimination; and 3—having a desire to be treated with the same dignity and respect afforded people without disabilities. (1998, 14)

Labeling has also been problematic for those identifying as lgbtq. Often when a student comes out to classmates or is identified by peers as lgbtq, that individual becomes *the* "gay kid" in the school, identified for that characteristic alone. This framing of an individual strips him or her of personality, interests, beliefs, values, skills, talents, gifts, and other elements that make that person whole. In other words, no student is simply "gay"; a person who is lgbtq is also defined within the constructs of race/ethnicity and gender. He or she may also be a member of a religious tradition, a political organization, or a number of other communities. Although much is shared by people who self-define as lgbtq in the United States today, the complexity of differences among them mirrors that found within the disability community and within all other such communities.

Proponents of inclusive education believe that seeing labels and groupings as socially constructed and getting to know and appreciate the individuality of students can encourage all of us to value the contributions, gifts, and unique traits of groups, but also to recognize and understand the uniqueness of each learner.

Preserving Student Dignity

Preserving student dignity is one of the most important and least talked about goals in education programs. Although no teacher would admit to intentionally treating students without respect, and every teacher would claim to value the preservation of student dignity, teachers can easily reduce a student, especially a student questioning his or her own sexuality, to emotional rubble with a word, a glance, or the silence provoked by fear or uncertainty.

Inclusive schooling teaches us much about preserving student dignity; self-determination and self-respect are central themes of the movement. A teacher who embraces inclusive schooling might work to make sure that students have authority in their own lives, protect their privacy when possible, and demonstrate respect for their individuality. Preserving student dignity in inclusive classrooms can also involve protecting and positively supporting students who manifest challenging behaviors, encouraging and empowering a student with low self-esteem, helping students to resist and challenge an oppressive school culture, or facilitating relationships for students without a single friend.

Teachers can also preserve and promote dignity by caring in small and consistent ways. Expressing care can be especially important to those students who are depressed, or ridiculed or teased because they are different. Gallagher (1997) describes one teacher who took the charge of showing concern so seriously that she initiated a systematic program of expressing caring in her classroom. This teacher became conscientious about greeting students as they entered the classroom. She also "made a list of words that conveyed caring and found that the following affected the students the most: responsible, worthy, valuable, brave, courageous, treat, special, thoughtful, and on the edge of greatness" (7).

Helping students learn how to live in community with one another, learning from their differences, and learning how to react to new or unknown situations are all important life lessons offered by the inclusive classroom. This openness and flexibility can be an excellent model for learning how to deal with students who are grappling with sexual diversity, for example, helping teachers preserve the dignity of students who do not fit stereotypical gender roles or who come from families that do not fit such roles. Knowing the power of society's rigid restrictions on what "boys can do" and what "girls can do" and how that may manifest itself in the classroom is critical in helping students who may challenge these restrictions in their own lives thrive in school.

Teachers who create supportive, fluid spaces where children can be themselves freely allow for the preservation and promotion of all students' dignity. In these truly inclusive classrooms, intimidation, taunting, name calling, or bullying of students who appear, behave, sound, or dress somewhat differently from the accepted codes are challenged by teachers and students alike. As Sonia Nieto (2000) points out, in the best classrooms such behaviors can even be turned into a lesson on dignity and integrity:

> The name-calling that goes on in many schools provides a tremendous opportunity for teachers and students to engage in dialogue. Rather than addressing these as isolated incidents or as the work of a few troublemakers, as is too often done, making them an explicit part of the curriculum helps students understand these incidents as symptoms of systemic problems in society and schools.

Making explicit the biases that are implicit in name-calling can become part of a "circle" or "sharing time," or can form the basis for lessons on racism, sexism, ableism, or other biases. (356)

Dignity can also be preserved by cultivating and maintaining personal relationships with students. In an inclusive classroom, students have time to share and be listened to, and they feel comfortable bringing their personal lives to the teacher and the classroom. As Jim Cummins (1996) suggests, and as truly effective teachers know, "good teaching does not require us to internalize an endless list of instructional techniques. Much more fundamental is the recognition that human relationships are central to effective instruction" (73). Inclusive principles can be a guide to help all teachers remember what is most important in the schooling experience.

Designing Sensitive and Relevant Curricula

Inclusive schooling advocates find fault with traditional approaches to schooling and call for more inspiring, collaborative, and tolerant classrooms. Specifically, supporters call for changes in teaching strategies (Graves, Graves, and Braaten 1996; Udvari-Solner 1996; Vaughn and Arguelles 2000); a broader and more meaningful curriculum (Fisher and Roach 1999; Jorgensen 1998; Kluth 2000; Peterson 1996; Sapon-Shevin 1999; Thousand, Nevin and McNeil 2000); new ways to identify and teach to the gifts all learners possess (Renzuli 1995); and the promotion of friendships, community, and cooperation (Sapon-Shevin 1999; Staub 1998; Strully and Strully 1996) within the school setting.

The inclusive schooling movement can also offer inspiration about the teacher's role in creating and implementing sensitive and relevant curricula. Teachers in inclusive classrooms are concerned about reaching and motivating all learners. In the best cases, they are versed in adapting materials, lesson formats, instructional arrangements, curricular goals, and teaching strategies (Udvari-Solner 1996) and can meet students' academic and social needs. A teacher in an inclusive classroom might create graphic organizers for visual learners, give some classroom directions in Spanish for bilingual students, engineer a peer tutoring relationship for a student who may need extra assistance, or connect a student who is questioning his or her sexual orientation with appropriate family and community resources.

In addition, a teacher might ask students to deconstruct materials from a political perspective or to consider the social justice implications of the school curriculum. They might also ask students to name "Who is missing?" from their standard curriculum materials or help them learn how to examine issues from a wider variety of perspectives. This is especially critical when teaching lgbtq students and their classmates, as most published materials or approved curricula documents do not even note the existence of lesbian, gay, bisexual, transgendered, and/or queer issues, history, or individuals.

Good inclusive teachers also design a curriculum and engage in pedagogy that reflects the diversity found in classrooms and communities. The classroom library must include books written by and about people with individual and group differences. Further, classroom lessons should include information about the diversity students represent. A teacher might achieve this by providing information about Thomas Edison's learning difficulties during a lesson on invention or by explaining the impact of sexuality and sexual orientation when discussing the writings of Langston Hughes. Kumashiro (2000, 33) stresses that such lessons about "the Other" should not be limited to "once or twice a year," but instead should be integrated across subject areas, in natural contexts, throughout the year. This movement away from isolated lessons on diverse groups and toward a curriculum that creatively includes the experiences and perspectives of the Other "can work against the tendency to treat different groups as mutually exclusive" (Kumashiro 2000, 33) and can teach a "hidden curriculum" lesson: that the recognition of diversity is important and educationally relevant.

We realize that teachers face pressures and responsibilities, including teaching and learning curriculum guidelines, standardized testing, and parent and community expectations. As difficult as it can be in practice, however, we suggest that conscientious teachers put student learning, health, and safety above politics and look for links between what the system demands and what the students need. Clearly, all students will benefit from a classroom that appreciates diversity. Despite outside pressures, teachers in inclusive classrooms must design curriculum and instruction and engineer classroom activities that are personally and culturally appropriate, engaging for a range of learning styles, and suitable for learners with various talents and interests. This practice is critical not only for students with unique learning or social needs but for all learners in the classroom as they grow and learn, not just from the daily curriculum but from the ways in which schools respond to difference.

Encouraging Advocacy

Ideally, children would grow up with a wealth of excellent models in their families, neighborhoods, and religious and civic institutions from which they would learn the most important elements of advocacy and agency for the oppressed and others who suffer discrimination. In reality, however, some students may have no other model except their teacher for these values. The role of the teacher as a model for advocacy and agency is a historic one. Teachers have long taken important stands on economic, cultural, political, and social issues of the day (Kliebard 1987). The need for this role continues, and the inclusive schooling movement has much to teach us.

Teachers in inclusive classrooms are often asked to serve as student and family advocates. They are challenged to work as social agents and to interrogate the codes, systems, and structures of schools and communities. The positions teachers take and the example they set are important lessons to students about the role of an active citizen in a pluralistic democracy. Most important, teachers who choose advocacy and political action as a way of life will be models for all students, but especially for those with learning differences, students of color, poor students, language minority students, and lgbtq students, who desperately need to learn self-advocacy skills as they negotiate an often difficult and discriminatory world.

In addition to advocating for all students, teachers must encourage students to share their ideas and hopes for change. A classroom cannot truly be considered inclusive if students have no power or if their voices are not central to classroom practice. All students, especially those who have experienced oppression, need opportunities to express ideas, thoughts, challenges, and criticisms. Unfortunately, however, students' voices are not always valued in classrooms. Students with learning differences may have an even harder time being heard and valued because they employ different methods of communicating or nonstandard language. Other students who have been disenfranchised may also struggle to be heard. Sensitive teachers will attempt to identify silenced students, encourage them to use their voices, seek opportunities to listen to them, and create supportive spaces for sharing.

Listening to students is not simply a matter of providing attention and opportunity, however. In fact, listening can be the hardest work teachers do. Writing about the mounting power of texts authored by people with disabilities, Danforth and Rhodes (1997) point out that "seeking, hearing, and taking seriously the words and ideas of the persons served by special programs, although seemingly innocent enough, is often disruptive" (363). Students may present teachers with information or ideas that challenge authority or criticize institutional practices and structures. As representatives of schools, teachers may find this a challenging but important reality to face.

Teachers who value inclusion as a political movement will welcome the unsettling process of shifting power to students. Students' voices must be a primary focus of the classroom. They must take part in shaping school structures and policies, providing leadership, constructing curriculum, and designing instruction. In addition, students must be provided with opportunities to serve as advocates in their own lives. Teachers must facilitate this advocacy and give students tools to communicate their ideas and opinions. For example, students can be taught a language of "critique and possibility" (Brady and Dentith 2000) whereby they can be encouraged to discuss issues of concern and learn to "read the world" (Brady 1995; Freire 1970). For students who have struggled in a traditional schooling experience, learning critical language and thinking skills can empower them to see their potential and question their assumptions. For example, students who are learning to be self-advocates can be taught about the political implications of being labeled "at-risk," learning to deconstruct the ambiguity and use of the term and the assumptions surrounding the label. Similarly, lgbtq students can critique the silences that surround sexual diversity in our schools and challenge the many discriminatory and homophobic legal restrictions that still exist in our communities and religious, social, and cultural organizations.

USING THE TENETS IN THE TEACHER EDUCATION CLASSROOM

There are two primary ways in which we can use the tenets of inclusive schooling to make teacher education classrooms safe and comfortable for lgbtq students and to integrate issues of sexual diversity into our curricula. The first is to model the tenets ourselves. That is, in our classrooms we can recognize differences, interrogate labels, preserve student dignity, design sensitive and relevant curricula, and encourage advocacy. Any teacher educator can engage in these practices whether he or she teaches special or general education, educational theory, educational psychology, or curriculum studies. Teacher educators can use materials that recognize and celebrate diversity, recognize the differences their students experience, and challenge classroom dynamics that exclude learners. Specifically, educators in preservice programs might use gender neutral language such as "partner" rather than "girlfriend" or "boyfriend"; encourage classroom community; use student-centered learning; discuss personal concerns with students; and use materials, examples, and content that reflect differences in their classrooms.

A second way teacher educators can use the inclusive schooling tenets is to teach them to students. No matter what type of teacher a preservice educator wants to be, he or she must learn to be politically and socially savvy about issues of difference. All teachers, including physics teachers, music teachers, elementary education teachers, and school counselors, should leave their preservice educational program with an understanding of what inclusive education means for all students. They should also understand that tenets of inclusive schooling can help us better support learners who have been marginalized, hurt, and forgotten.

As we teach preservice teachers these tenets, we must remind them specifically that sexual diversity should receive as much attention as any other kind of diversity. This idea can be challenging when the religious or moral tradition of the teacher educator or the students in preservice classes is at odds with the concept of equality and sexual diversity. Nonetheless, our responsibility to all students mandates that we challenge exclusionary philosophies or beliefs to ensure a safe, challenging, and equitable educational experience for all students in our pluralistic society.

CONCLUSION

In this chapter we have explored how the inclusive schooling movement can help us learn about preparing and presenting educational experiences that will be relevant and appropriate for preservice educators and the students they will teach. Examining sexual diversity and inclusive education together also pushes us to consider what characteristics we want to see in teachers beyond competence and professionalism. In considering the needs and gifts of diverse learners we must ask ourselves: What values do we want teachers to hold? What practices should we promote for use in a diverse classroom? In what ways should we encourage and model understanding and caring in our own teacher education classrooms?

Comparing the experiences and educational needs of two oppressed groups has challenged us to think about the wide range of learners in the classroom and the "myth" of the average student. While our preservice teacher population continues to grow in diversity, we know that most preservice teachers are not now and will never be persons with disabilities or lesbian, gay, bisexual, transgendered, and/or queer. We recognize and appreciate the challenge of teaching preservice teachers about what they are not. In teaching to and about the inclusive movement, however, we hope to shatter the impressions of preservice and in-service educators that "diversity" is something about *other* people, when difference is for and about every student and every teacher.

REFERENCES

Brady, J. 1995. *Schooling young children: A feminist pedagogy for liberatory learning.* Albany: State University of New York Press.

Brady, J., and A. M. Dentith. 2000. A critical feminist postmodern pedagogy: Linking theory with practice. Paper presented at the meeting of the American Education Research Association, April, New Orleans, Louisiana.

Cummins, J. 1996. *Negotiating identities: Education for empowerment in a diverse society.* Ontario, Calif.: California Association for Bilingual Education.

Danforth, S., and W. C. Rhodes. 1997. Deconstructing disability: A philosophy for inclusion. *Remedial and Special Education* 18: 357–66.

Falvey, M., C. Givner, and C. Kimm. 1995. What is an inclusive school? In *Creating an inclusive school,* edited by R. Villa and J. Thousand, 1–12. Alexandria, Va.: Association for Supervision and Curriculum Development.

Fisher, D., and V. Roach. 1999. *Opening doors: Connecting students to curriculum, classmates, and learning.* Colorado Springs, Colo.: PEAK Parent Center.

Freire, P. 1970. *Pedagogy of the oppressed.* New York: Continuum.

Gallagher, P. A. 1997. Promoting dignity: Taking the destructive D's out of behavior disorders. *Focus on Exceptional Children* 29: 1–19.

Graves, M., B. Graves, and S. Braaten. 1996. Scaffolding reading experiences for inclusive classes. *Educational Leadership* 53: 14–16.

Jorgensen, C. 1998. *Restructuring high schools for all students: Taking inclusion to the next level.* Baltimore, Md.: Paul H. Brookes.

Kliebard, H. 1987. *The struggle for the American curriculum.* New York: Routledge.

Kluth, P. 2000. Community referenced instruction and the inclusive school. *Remedial and Special Education* 21: 19–26.

Kumashiro, K. 2000. Toward a theory of anti-oppressive education. *Review of Educational Research* 70: 25–53.

Lemann, N. 2000. Gore without a script. *The New Yorker*, July 31, 44–63.

Meyer, L., G. Mager, G. Yarger-Kane, M. Sarno, and G. Hext-Contreras. 1997. Syracuse University's inclusive elementary and special education program. In *Teacher education in transition,* edited by L. Blanton, C. Griffin, J. Winn, and M. Pugach, 18–38. Denver: Love Publishing Company.

Nieto, S. 2000. *Affirming diversity: The sociopolitical context of multicultural education.* New York: Longman.

Peterson, M. 1996. Community learning in inclusive schools. In *Inclusion: A guide for educators,* edited by S. Stainback and W. Stainback, 271–93. Baltimore, Md.: Paul H. Brookes.

Renzuli, J. 1995. Teachers as talent scouts. *Educational Leadership* 52: 75–81.

Sapon-Shevin, M. 1999. *Because we can change the world: A practical guide to building cooperative, inclusive classroom communities.* Boston: Allyn & Bacon.

Snow, K. 1998. To achieve inclusion, community, and freedom for people with disabilities, we must use person first language. *TASH (The Association for People with Severe Handicaps) Newsletter* (October): 14–16.

Stainbeck, S. 2000. If I could dream: Reflections on the future of education. In *Restructuring for caring and effective education: Piecing the puzzle together,* edited by R. A. Villa and J. S. Thousand, 503–12. Baltimore, Md.: Paul H. Brookes.

Staub, D. 1998. *Delicate threads: Friendships between children with and without special needs in inclusive schools.* Bethesda, Md.: Woodbine House.

Strully, J., and C. Strully. 1996. Friendships as an educational goal: What have we learned and where are we headed? In *Inclusion: A guide for educators,* edited by S. Stainback and W. Stainback, 141–54. Baltimore, Md.: Paul H. Brookes.

Thousand, J., A. Nevin, and M. McNeil. 2000. Achieving social justice through education for responsibility. In *Restructuring for caring and effective education: Piecing the puzzle together,* edited by R. A. Villa and J. S. Thousand, 137–65. Baltimore, Md.: Paul H. Brookes.

Udvari-Solner, A. 1996. Examining teacher thinking: Constructing a process to design curricular adaptations. *Remedial and Special Education* 17: 245–54.

———. 1997. Inclusive education. In *Dictionary of multicultural education,* edited by C. A. Grant and G. Ladson-Billings, 141–44. Phoenix, Ariz.: Oryx Press.

Vaughn, S., and M. Arguelles. 2000. Adaptations in general education classrooms. In *Restructuring for caring and effective education: Piecing the puzzle together,* edited by R. A. Villa and J. S. Thousand, 166–85. Baltimore, Md.: Paul H. Brookes.

Villa, R., and J. Thousand. 1996. Student collaboration: An essential for curriculum delivery in the 21st century. In *Inclusion: A guide for educators,* edited by S. Stainback and W. Stainback, 193–99. Baltimore, Md.: Paul H. Brookes.

Villa R. A., J. S. Thousand, and J. W. Chapple. 2000. Preparing educators to implement inclusive practices. In *Restructuring for caring and effective education: Piecing the puzzle together,* edited by R. A. Villa and J. S. Thousand, 531–57. Baltimore, Md.: Paul H. Brookes.

9

Revisioning Multiculturalism in Teacher Education: Isn't It Queer?

Will Letts

> Like any social institution that has a long history, education is intolerant of any form of diversity that it has never recognized.
>
> —*Corson, Changing Education for Diversity,* 7

Although perspectives focused on inequities related to sex, gender, socio-economic status, "race," ethnicity, and disability have drawn the increasing attention of educators and researchers, there is almost complete silence about queer, or non-normative, sexual identities. Recognition of "queer" aspects of multiculturalism, when it does exist, rarely extends beyond adding a place-holder (i.e., lesbian, gay, bisexual, and transgendered [lgbt] students, gays and lesbians, queers) to a list of diversity categories. This "add lgbt and stir" approach leaves untheorized the multiplicity of ways that sexuality is a crucial dimension of teacher practice, student learning, and the production of knowledge. We might ask ourselves, But why does this matter? Couldn't this be easily remedied by simply acknowledging gays and lesbians in aspects of our curriculum and teaching?

As an alternative to this approach I describe and advocate a queering of multiculturalism in teacher education programs. Eschewing "laundry list" multiculturalism for a more critical examination of the assumptions that infuse current conceptualizations of equity in education, queering multiculturalism extends beyond a concern for the identities of the students who sit before us in our classrooms. Instead, this stance explicitly uncovers and works against heteronormativity, deconstructs the powerful allure of dichotomies (such as male/female, nature/culture, knowledgeable/ignorant, reason/emotion, neutral/biased, homosexual/heterosexual), and originates from a unique epistemological standpoint. In this chapter I use a critique of the dominant models of multicultural teacher education that render issues related to minoritized sexualities invisible as a starting point to advocate bringing queer theories to bear on conceptions of multicultural education. I delineate some aspects of a queered multiculturalism in teacher education and offer a few examples of what this stance might look like in our practice as teacher educators.

MULTICULTURALISM IN TEACHER EDUCATION

Multicultural education courses in the United States have long been a part of teacher education programs (Edgerton 1996; King, Hollins, and Hayman 1997; Ladson-Billings 1995), although as Nancy Lesko and Leslie Bloom (1998) note, the forms the courses take and the topics that they discuss are still open to vigorous debate. And despite the range of approaches taken to engage with this topic in tertiary classrooms, Lesko and Bloom describe "an absence of discussion and debate about teaching multiculturalism from the perspective of theories of knowing and learning, that is, in relation to epistemology" (378). Instead, "far too often what gets called *multicultural education* is weakened and watered-down through appropriation by those who would use it as a new way to silence rage rather than honestly and faithfully address it" (Edgerton 1996, 6). Still, much if not most of the work in multiculturalism in teacher education seeks to improve the experiences and outcomes of schooling for students and teachers. Despite the compelling critiques of the use of "multicultural" as a qualifier of such words as education and research (Ellsworth 1999), I use that terminology here because of its continuing prevalence in teacher education.

It would not be an overstatement to characterize texts that deal with multicultural education as "thin," if not emaciated, in their treatment of sexual diversity and minoritized sexualities. Often these issues are not raised at all in these texts that argue convincingly for changing the way we teach to both take account of diversity and educate for diversity. Part of this is surely a function of the multiple definitions of "cultural diversity" and "multiculturalism" that currently circulate. For many, issues of sexual diversity and minoritized sexualities do not fall under the definition of "culture" that their work addresses. Nick Couldry (2000) has captured the fraught nature of these debates: "A separate difficulty involves questioning whether the types of culture or cultural formation to which we assume individuals to 'belong' are themselves stable, coherent entities" (44–45).

When these issues are raised, it is usually in a long list with other identity categories. The focus is on individual identities and on collectivities based on "common" sexualities, rather than on the more far-reaching issues that I discuss later in this chapter. Such texts may focus on several forms of difference—language, social class, gender, ethnicity, disability, and sexual orientation,—in articulating approaches to multicultural education. Although issues of sexual orientation and even sexuality more generally are explicitly named in these texts, they receive cursory treatment for the most part. "Gay and lesbian" are added unproblematically to the roster of identity categories that it is important for prospective and practicing teachers to acknowledge. But rarely are the issues mentioned and discussed in enough detail to give the reader a sense of the scope of these issues and their relevance to both multiculturalism and teacher education.

So why is sexuality important to attend to? And what still gets obscured when the focus is primarily turned to students' sexualities? Rendered invisible by the heteronormative nature of much multicultural education, these questions remain uninterrogated and unremarked as viable and relevant areas of study. Moving both in concert with and beyond what critical pedagogy or cultural studies have provided, I examine what a queered multiculturalism can contribute to teacher education.

CONSIDERING CULTURE

One place to start in a critique of the approaches to multicultural education in teacher education is to investigate the meanings of "culture" referenced and reinscribed in this work. Culture is a highly contested notion, with debates raging across the humanities and social sciences; to comprehend its meaning in multiculturalism it is necessary to think beyond the immediate understandings that might arise from these courses and to excavate the deeper structures to which such concepts refer. The traditional model sees cultures as discrete but interacting, coherent "natural" units marked by a particular time and place. But as Nick Couldry notes, this "holistic" model of culture is fraught with problems: It's impossible to sustain the notion of cultures as discretely contained entities, the ties of the notion of culture to place and time have been loosened, and there is a dangerous link between essentializing notions of "culture" and essentializing notions of "race" and ethnicity" (2000, 96). But this does not mean that we make a simple retreat to what appears to be the opposite of homogenization: that all cultures are de-localized. Again, following Couldry, "Instead of searching for . . . unified cultures or proclaiming their abolition, we must investigate the nature of cultural flows, and the space within which they work" (97). Thinking in terms of cultural flows, rather than autonomous bounded cultures, might be a more useful way to consider the aims and means of teaching about multiculturalism in teacher education. Instead of worrying about a set cultural order, we as educators are freed to envision and teach about culture as something that far exceeds tidy boundaries, something that flows. Suddenly, spaces for discussion and analysis are opened up, rather than foreclosed. This is often quite at odds with the intent (whether tacit or enacted) of multiculturalism to bound and essentialize cultures or identity categories.

Our intent in multiculturalism must be to better understand the complexities of these cultures and identity categories with an eye to recognizing but not essentializing difference, and without assuming that some "natural" order exists to explain them. We must advocate dialogue and exchange across difference, rather than trying to craft or impose some mythical set of shared values. This is not to wholly deny the utility of examining structural dynamics and power differentials in terms of categories (such as women, the rich, or lesbians), but only to signal quite strongly that an overreliance on these categories or an overattribution of what these categories "tell" us about people or what they "mean" to individuals would be a gross distortion of the limited use they have in these discussions. Further, as Jay Lemke notes, "we are permeable to cultures; we are not consistent, not all of one sort or all of another. We are all hybrids, mixtures, and not nearly as well integrated as we are supposed to pretend we are" (1995, 151). In this way we might work more effectively with the realities of cultural complexity while still framing these issues and debates in ways that are useful to us in our teacher education classrooms. So clarifying what is meant by "culture" is an important facet of understanding and teaching multiculturalism. But is it enough?

BRINGING QUEER THEORIES
TO BEAR ON MULTICULTURALISM

From the outset I want to make clear that I do not envision the project of bringing queer theories to bear on multicultural education as about replacing one hegemonic master narrative with another. I am not envisioning a "new" multiculturalism that "work[s] toward reproduction, toward identity and duplication, and thus away from difference" (Lesko and Bloom 2000, 244). On the contrary, what I believe queer theory contributes to these discussions is a movement away from identity politics toward recognizing multiple, contested, even seemingly contradictory subject positions, and the epistemological imperatives that accompany this new constellation of subject positions. I should also note that I am engaged here in what many will see as a bankrupt project: trying to pin down something as necessarily elusive as queer theory. Although I acknowledge the tensions in trying to make clear the tenets of a body of theory known for its definitional indeterminacy, I insist that my project here is not to fix the meaning(s) of queer theory but to hold it still long enough to get a good look at it so that we may then think about how we can best make use of it in our classroom practice. I am interested, then, in catching queer theory to examine it, not in keeping it in a jar with a perforated lid and taking it home.

As a body of theory, "queer theory" is the product of specific theoretical and historical contexts, marked by a move away from what were seen to be the constraints and limitations of gay and lesbian studies. Examining "queer," Annamarie Jagose writes:

> Broadly speaking, queer describes those gestures or analytical models which dramatise incoherencies in the allegedly stable relations between chromosomal sex, gender, and sexual desire. Resisting that model of stability—which claims heterosexuality as its origin, when it is more properly its effect—queer focuses on mismatches between sex, gender and desire. . . . .[Q]ueer locates and exploits the incoherencies in those three terms which stabilise heterosexuality. Demonstrating the impossibility of any "natural" sexuality, it calls into question even such apparently unproblematic terms as "man" and "woman." (1996, 3)

Queer theories debunk as illusions the notion of stable sexes, genders, and sexualities. These theories deconstruct normative insistence on stable binaries for sex, gender, and sexual object choice. Queer is relational in reference to the normative rather than a fixed positivity, and in this way works to resist rampant essentializing discourses. Identity, like culture, is a relational process of identification rather than fixed and immutable. Importantly, these queer theories also shift concerns from an assimilationist politics of identity to a politics of difference.

"To queer" is to denaturalize coherent selves, to resist the narrow logic of binaries, and to dislodge the sense of safety that comes with "really knowing." Queer insists "that non-straight sexualities are simultaneously marginal and central, and that heterosexuality exists in an epistemic symbiosis with homosexuality" (Luhmann 1998, 144). In relation to multicultural education, queer theory does not ask that curricula and pedagogies "*become* sexualized, but that [they] excavate and interpret the way that [they] already [are] sexualized" (Sumara and Davis 1999, 192). This is a very different project, one that requires very different resources and frameworks. Thus, multicultural pedagogy and knowledge "might be posed as a question (as opposed to the answer) of knowledge: what does being taught, what does knowledge do to students?" (Luhmann 1998, 148).

What are the effects of bringing queer theories to bear on multiculturalism? It is shortsighted to think of the value of these discussions only in terms of potentially teaching lgbt students or students having lgbt parents or guardians. This is much more a project of digging up and examining one's beliefs about sex, gender, and sexuality and coming to terms with one's comfort and knowledge (or lack thereof) about these topics and the epistemological implications that all of this has for each of us. This project explicitly marks the desire to move beyond an inclusion of lgbt as identity categories that run the risk of essentializing groups of people (Pohan and Bailey 1997). A queered notion of identity "upends jaundiced conceptions of equity work that suggest by knowing the categories a person belongs to, you then know the 'formula' for how to teach them" (Letts and Fifield 2000, 9).

Instead, identities as positionings are malleable and encourage thinking from the margins, decentering categories marked as "the other." We must contest "the automatic slippage that superimposes dichotomous notions of gender—femininity and masculinity—[or sexuality] onto 'biological' sex in such a way that makes gender [and sexuality] also seem dichotomous, discrete, polarized and 'natural'" (Letts 1999, 103). Further, the refusal of *any* normalization, based on sex, ethnicity, social class, and so forth, necessarily also must be part of the queer agenda. It is important to be aware that the term "queer" "is in danger of stabilizing into an identity rather than remaining a radical critique of identity and a challenge to extend the study of sexuality and gender beyond the signifiers 'gay' and 'lesbian' and 'man' and 'woman' and into the domain of sexual and gender minorities" (Halberstam 1997, 260). We must actively resist this danger and make evident the fluidity of queer as we work with it.

WHAT THIS DOES FOR QUEER ISSUES

Critics may see the moves I am proposing as "attempts to politicize previously apolitical domains and to contaminate universal knowledge claims through partisan self-interests" (Chun, Christopher, and Gumport 2000, 233). It is no wonder, for it is the hegemony that these critics are overinvested in and explicitly benefiting from that is really made more visible and challenged by multicultural education. And a queering of multicultural education even more directly locates the source of contamination in the conservative and essentializing discourses and actions of these critics. Suddenly *they* become subject to the gaze, and not surprisingly, they don't find it very comfortable.

Although a queered multiculturalism doesn't guarantee that lgbt students, teachers, and parents will necessarily be attended to, it does bring with it a critical orientation that ensures that issues previously rendered invisible or simply actively ignored will be tackled. And as I have stressed throughout this chapter, it also brings with it some important theoretical commitments. First, a queered multiculturalism aims to expose and deconstruct binaries by "destabilizing the certainties of such oppositional categories" (Lesko and Bloom 2000, 249) and the resultant denial of diversity that is harbored in such restrictive discourses. Alternatively, "*queer* aims to spoil and transgress coherent (and essential) gender configurations and the desire for a neat arrangement of dichotomous sexual and gendered difference, central to both heterosexual and homosexual identities" (Luhmann 1998, 145). We don't want our students (or the children that they will teach) to uncritically take up their teachers' understandings of race, class, gender, sexuality, and so forth via a pedagogically barren model that envisages teachers' roles as primarily coercive rather than co-constructive. Susan Edgerton notes that institutions, such as schooling, that are "based on the logic of binary opposition are ill-equipped to deal with the nuances of these (non)categories and their implications for the production of subjectivity" (1996, 39). We need to foster student engagement with these issues that goes well beyond facile understandings, and we should support our students as they negotiate their way through these issues to make decisions about what kinds of teachers they want to be. One possible way to envisage this is for teachers to "help students destabilize these dualities and think about them critically, so that even when they rely on them, they are consciously aware of what they are doing, rather than blindly and uncritically falling back on them" (Letts 1999, 106).

Another resource gained by this turn to a queered multiculturalism is a different epistemological standpoint. Feminist epistemologies have enabled me to think about "how to move from including others' lives and thoughts in research and scholarly projects to *starting* from their lives to ask research questions, develop theoretical concepts, design research, collect data, and interpret findings" (Harding 1991, 268). Further, just as was the case for postcolonial standpoints, the "queer" standpoint I am articulating here is "an epistemological stance . . . positioned against the 'positivist', internalist epistemological ones that, explicitly or implicitly, largely continue to frame knowledge-seeking projects about nature and society" (Harding 1998, 17). In this framework queer is viewed as a subject position rather than as a positivity that is essentialized or socially fixed. Identity categories, then, are fluid and shifting and allow people to construct, deconstruct, reconstruct, and move more or less freely among them. This is not to deny structural impediments, for example, that might make this movement difficult. But it is to assert that despite such barriers, the fluidity of a queer positioning cannot be denied. Deborah Britzman (1995) challenges, "Those who seem uncomfortable think the term queer is a noun or an identity. But the queer and the theory in Queer Theory signify *actions*, not actors. It can be thought of as a verb, or as a citational relation that signifies more than the signifier" (153). Thus, this act of positioning is malleable and encourages thinking from the margins, often from people whose consciousness is bifurcated as they alternate between queer thinking and hegemonic thinking (yet another problematic binary).

What can be seen from the borders? What access to knowledge do people on the margins have, and how can it enhance and alter what gets seen from the center? Now that queer is not the topic of investigation, as "lesbian" and "gay" tended to be, what questions will be asked from queer standpoints? The purpose of adopting this epistemological view here is to acknowledge the importance and validity of these new and fruitful ways of knowing. Different things can be seen, the same things can be seen differently, and thus different questions will be valued and asked. We need to interrogate the discursive vehicles used in multicultural education—the methods, models, narratives, metaphors, and production of knowledge—from queer standpoints. Again, it is important not to view this epistemology as essentializing but rather as a lucrative and powerful means for the generation of new knowledge.

What might we gain by thinking, teaching, and acting through a lens of queered multiculturalism? Although I have continually asserted the need to think and move beyond a simplistic notion that this lens will merely afford inclusion to lgbt people heretofore excluded in the majority of multicultural education discourse, the importance of this move as one of many shouldn't be overlooked. It is, in fact, essential that multicultural education come to terms with lgbt people and take seriously the ways that education has and continues to both include and exclude them. That said, this shift in the lens through which we view and enact multicultural education also marks a shift away from identity politics to a view of bodies and identities as continually negotiated and always under construction. Our "selves" are not stable; we just work very hard to make them seem that way! A more critical view of identity construction and maintenance must start with the notion that "sexuality is a necessary companion to all knowing" (Sumara and Davis 1999, 203) and that identity and epistemology are mutually embedded—who we understand ourselves to be intersects with what counts as knowledge (see chapter 14). This view offers us as teachers and allows us to envision for our students more viable narratives about acceptable and accepted constellations of sex, sexuality, and gender. It also engenders a more reflective stance on the power of language to label and name by uncovering assumptions about what is natural and bringing to the forefront issues of power in its discussions about the "normal."

A third resource gained by a queering of multicultural teacher education is a move beyond containing and understanding identities to a critical textual engagement that works to destabilize rather than fix these constructs. A queered multiculturalism brings to the fore issues relating to how texts, understood widely to include visual and spoken images, behaviors, utterances, and identities as well as printed words, are taken up or refused. As Jay Lemke states, "In politics, as in education, as in literacy, the issue of central concern is how our discourses, our texts, mediate meanings that actions and events have for us, and so how we act" (1995, 153). This marks a move away from a concern with how "accurately" people are represented within curriculum and toward a concern with reading practices and how knowledge is taken up and understood: "How do we insert ourselves in the text? What positions do we refuse? Which ones are desirable?" (Luhmann 1998, 149). This could serve to move us from the perceived safety of certainty, of needing to fix our knowledge, to a tolerance of ambiguity and an appreciation of hybridity (Anzaldúa 1987). In turn, these critical textual engagements identify, resist, and deconstruct the heteronormativity that is reified through social relations and grammar and offer us a far more varied repertoire for "making sense."

WHAT MIGHT THIS LOOK LIKE?

A question before us then is, what spaces of intervention has this turn to queer theories opened up? How might we engage in "teaching to support unassimilated difference" (Ellsworth 1992)? Rather than aiming to be prescriptive, I offer several examples of attempts to enact this vision of multiculturalism in teacher education classrooms. Although all three examples could be understood and enacted in ways that maintain a problematic, essentialized, and unexamined focus on "others," my intention in describing them here is to advocate their use in teacher education classrooms to interrogate constructions of and assumptions about subjectivities, identity categories, and what is "normal."

The first, *autobiographical writing as a queer curriculum practice*, can be used to defamiliarize or queer the identity categories we inhabit and the versions of the self we enact (Edgerton 1996; Miller 1998). Students are asked to write a short autobiographical piece about some period from their schooling that was "troubling" to them. As they explore the many facets of what was troubling to them, students can write in ways that shift "autobiography in education from its modernist emphasis on producing predictable, stable, and normative identities and curricula to a consideration of 'selves' and curricula as sites of 'permanent openness and resignifiability'" (Miller 1998, 367). Using autobiography in this way can enable us to strategically evoke difference, something not possible through modernist autobiographical tales that reinscribe normative silences and reiterate stable, coherent selves.

By denaturalizing taken-for-granted identity categories we write against the grain about our lives and our relations with others. Autobiography as queer curriculum practice can allow us to "explore how we are situated simultaneously in multiple and often conflicting identity constructions—some of which may be hidden in order to remain normal [in] school" (Miller 1998, 370). Autobiography has a place in a queered multicultural education because it enables a focus not only on a range of sexualities but also on the classed, racialized, and gendered aspects of identities that exceed monolithic, fixed constructions. This explicit, though undervalued, stance can allow students and us to engage in more generative modes of thinking about the ways that difference matters.

A second approach entails production of a *critical incidents paper* in which the students attempt to deconstruct notions of difference and how they play out in educational settings. The intention of this piece of writing is to help students move beyond an uncritical reporting of their experiences to an examination of those experiences with an eye toward deconstructing them to uncover the assumptions and biases that are at the heart of how we make sense of things. To that end, students are asked to identify two scenarios in which they recall being aware of their own or someone else's "difference" in an educational setting. (I have tried to leave the term "difference" as open-ended as possible, resisting the desire to define it specifically for students.) Students are to think about what that term means to them and then to translate that into a recollection of memories. My aim is not to have students commit to some fixed and definite sense of difference; rather it is to give them access to instances of difference in order for them to speak and write "into existence denaturalized ways of being that are obscured or simply unthinkable when one centered, self-knowing story is substituted for another" (Miller 1998, 368).

A variation on this assignment is to identify incidents of difference in fiction or nonfiction and analyze them in a similar way. Writings from the margins are in a unique position to reveal that lives are marked as much by the gaps that they disclose as by the coherence that seems to belie them. Susan Edgerton comments that:

> Literary works of marginalized groups can provide a passage to a shifting of the discourse away from conceptions of multiculturalism as something we "add on" to the curriculum, "do for" marginalized groups, or as a means to simply change attitudes. Such a shift away is a shift toward a more fluid and thoughtful "discourse of encounters" in its abrogation of the problem of representation— representation as it concerns such entities and notions as identity, culture, and civilization [and I would add sexualities]. (1996, 6)

Focusing specifically on novels that depict transgenderism, Judith Halberstam observes, "Teaching novels of gender variance, indeed teaching the topic of gender variance, is a pedagogical challenge because it requires that the instructor hold apart definitions of transgenderism and definitions of gay and lesbian identity. For many students, unconventional gender is already the sign of homosexuality; gender and sexuality become, for them, inextricably combined under the heading of deviance" (1997, 270). In both cases, what is gained by using others' writings as the basis for an examination of critical incidents is being able to raise issues of difference that teacher education students themselves might not raise, in order to interrogate and analyze the various manifestations of difference and its effects on teaching and learning.

A final suggestion, called the *cultural plunge*, is a field-based experience intended to have the students make the strange familiar, and the familiar strange. In this out-of-class exercise the students are asked to put themselves in a situation that is not the "norm" for them, to make themselves feel like an "other." This immediately evokes and opens up for contestation definitions of "normal" and "other." Students are challenged to think about how they define themselves, noting that identity, like culture, "is not a demonstrably empirical category but the product of a process of identification" (Jagose 1996, 9). Once they identify some of the assumptions and attitudes that shape their identities, they choose a site to "take the plunge." The students are then asked to write up a description of their plunge: where they went, why they chose it, what happened while they were there. The most important part of the written account is a critical analysis of their personal responses to the plunge. Students are asked to consider such questions as: Why did you feel the way(s) that you did? What prompted your dis/comfort? How did your own identity become apparent to you as you plunged? How does "normal" become assigned a subject position? What did this experience teach you about yourself? Were any of your taken-for-granted norms and assumptions exposed or challenged during the plunge?

The cultural plunge is not intended as an exercise in cultural tourism, a safari to gaze upon "others," although I acknowledge that this may be to some extent unavoidable if indeed students submerge themselves in totally new environments. But while the students may find themselves as "voyeurs-for-a-day" (Lesko and Bloom 1998), the focus of the experience is meant to be a more substantive and critical examination of one's own assumptions about "the normal" and how these oft-unexamined assumptions shape what we think and how we act. I have found the cultural plunge quite effective because I maintain from the start that the focus is on the students themselves rather than on the people they are plunging with. The salient question is What did you learn about yourself and your own epistemological investments, rather than What did you learn about "them?" And a salient response to that question is not a fixed or certain answer that indicates that students have "become fully knowledgeable and enlightened about themselves, their students and their teaching practices" (Miller 1998, 369), but rather a reflexive reworking and continuous revisiting of the question to see what can be seen and learned each time it is asked.

Multicultural education as queer curriculum practice exceeds a focus on identities, individuals, or collectivities. It must move beyond the very important issues of lgbt people to also consider knowledge construction and validation, the allure of heteronormativity, the power of dichotomies, and critical textual practices. A queered multiculturalism, one that includes interrogations of the multiplicity of sexual and gender configurations and their bearings on identities *and* epistemologies, is a provocation. Viewing the process of queering as subversion, we might be able to re-vision multicultural teacher education, and wouldn't that be queer?

REFERENCES

Anzaldúa, G. 1987. *Borderlands/La frontera*. San Francisco: Aunt Lute Press.

Britzman, D. 1995. Is there a queer pedagogy? Or, stop reading straight. *Educational Theory* 45 (2): 151–65.

Chun, M., S. Christopher, and P. J. Gumport. 2000. Multiculturalism and the academic organization of knowledge. In *Multicultural curriculum: New directions for social theory, practice, and policy,* edited by R. Mahalingam and C. McCarthy, 223–41. New York: Routledge.

Corson, D. 1998. *Changing education for diversity*. Buckingham, UK: Open University Press.

Couldry, N. 2000. *Inside culture: Re-imagining the method of cultural studies*. London: Sage.

Edgerton, S. H. 1996. *Translating the curriculum: Multiculturalism into cultural studies*. New York: Routledge.

Ellsworth, E. 1992. Teaching to support unassimilated difference. *Radical Teacher* 42 (Fall): 4–9.

———. 1999. Multiculture in the making. In *Multicultural research: A reflective engagement with race, class, gender and sexual orientation,* edited by C. A. Grant, 24–36. London: Falmer Press.

Halberstam, J. 1997. Who's afraid of queer theory? In *Class issues: Pedagogy, cultural studies, and the public sphere,* edited by A. Kumar, 256–75. New York: New York University Press.

Harding, S. 1991. *Whose science? Whose knowledge? Thinking from women's lives*. Ithaca, N.Y.: Cornell University Press.

———. 1998. *Is science multicultural? Postcolonialisms, feminisms, and epistemologies*. Bloomington: Indiana University Press.

Jagose, A. 1996. *Queer theory: An introduction.* New York: New York University Press.

King, J. E., E. R. Hollins, and W. C. Hayman, eds. 1997. *Preparing teachers for cultural diversity.* New York: Teachers College Press.

Ladson-Billings, G. 1995. Multicultural teacher education: Research, practice, and policy. In *Handbook of research on multicultural education,* edited by J. Banks and C. Banks, 747–59. New York: Macmillan.

Lemke, J. L. 1995. *Textual politics: Discourse and social dynamics.* London: Taylor & Francis.

Lesko, N., and L. R. Bloom. 1998. Close encounters: Truth, experience and interpretation in multicultural teacher education. *Journal of Curriculum Studies* 30 (4): 375–95.

———. 2000. The haunting of multicultural epistemology and pedagogy. In *Multicultural curriculum: New directions for social theory, practice, and policy,* edited by R. Mahalingam and C. McCarthy, 242–60. New York: Routledge.

Letts, W. J. 1999. How to make "boys" and "girls" in the classroom: The heteronormative nature of elementary-school science. In *Queering elementary education: Advancing the dialogue about sexualities and schooling,* edited by W. J. Letts and J. T. Sears, 97–110. Lanham, Md.: Rowman & Littlefield.

Letts, W. J., and S. Fifield. 2000. Sexualities, silence, and science teacher education. Paper presented at the meeting of the American Educational Research Association, April, New Orleans, Louisiana.

Luhmann, S. 1998. Queering/querying pedagogy? Or pedagogy is a pretty queer thing. In *Queer theory in education,* edited by W. F. Pinar, 141–55. Mahwah, N.J.: Lawrence Erlbaum.

Miller, J. L. 1998. Autobiography as queer curriculum practice. In *Queer theory in education,* edited by W. F. Pinar, 365–73. Mahwah, N.J.: Lawrence Erlbaum.

Pohan, C. A., and N. J. Bailey. 1997. Opening the closet: Multiculturalism that is fully inclusive. *Multicultural Education* (Fall): 12–15.

Sumara, D., and B. Davis. 1999. Interrupting heteronormativity: Toward a queer curriculum theory. *Curriculum Inquiry* 29 (2): 191–208.

10

Queer Developments in Teacher Education: Addressing Sexual Diversity, Homophobia, and Heterosexism

Tim Bedford

INTRODUCTION

Educational institutions mirror the dominant views, perspectives, and values of the broader society. Teachers are products of an educational system reflecting the pervasive heterosexism and homophobia prevalent in almost all societies, and in turn, act as agents for the social reproduction of heteronormativity. Both pre-university and teacher education institutions maintain a culture of silence about nonheterosexuality which, according to Epstein and Johnson (1994),

> discriminates by failing to recognize differences. It posits a totally and unambiguously heterosexual world in much the same way as certain forms of racism posit the universality of whiteness. In this way the dominant form is made to appear "normal" and "natural" and the subordinate form perverse, remarkable and dangerous. (198)

Uncovering heterosexual privilege and raising awareness of its destructive personal and societal effects is central to breaking the culture of silence. Rich (1986) describes invisibility as a "dangerous and painful condition" and adds that

> when those who have the power to name and socially construct reality and choose not to see you or hear you, whether you are dark skinned, old, disabled, female, or speak with a different accent or dialect than theirs, when someone with the authority of a teacher, say, describes the world and you are not in it, there is a moment of psychic disequilibrium, as if you looked in a mirror and saw nothing. Yet you know you exist and others like you, that it is a game with

mirrors. It takes some strength of soul—and not just individual strength, but collective understanding—to resist this void, this non-being, into which you are thrust, and to stand up, demanding to be seen and heard, and to make yourself visible, to claim that your experience is just as real and normative as any other. (199)

Since prejudice against lesbians, bisexuals, and gays, along with the belief in the superiority of heterosexuality, are learned attitudes and cultural constructions, teacher education lies at the heart of combating homophobia and heterosexism and faces the challenge of breaking the culture of silence. This challenge is twofold: uncovering the system of compulsory heterosexuality and heterosexual privilege and transforming heterosexist perspectives into ones that are accepting of the diversity of sexual identities in the same way one may work to transform ethnocentrism within the tradition of multicultural education. I consider this twofold challenge as a teacher in both teacher education and high school. The first part of the chapter considers how multicultural education can be an instrument for the social deconstruction of heterosexism. The remaining parts present two examples of my current work to affirm the diversity of sexual identities in educational settings.

MULTICULTURAL EDUCATION, SOCIAL CHANGE, AND SEXUALITY

Multicultural education has often been described as an instrument to transform schools and society that sees schools as sites for social change, equity, and justice. Multiculturalism enables individuals and institutions to function within a pluralistic society where diversity is cherished. It is part of a process of redressing inequities arising from a system in which difference is ranked, giving privilege to certain groups based on sex, ethnicity, class, religion, sexual orientation, and so forth.

Confronting issues of power and power relations (compulsory heterosexuality being one of these) is central to multicultural education and plays an important role in creating just and equitable schools and societies. Furthermore, multiculturalism is an ideology and an orientation, a way of viewing the world. As David Abalos (1989) states:

[M]ulticulturalism is an attitude; it's a spirit of openness and celebration; of inclusion that honors the history and cultures of all peoples. It's not just tolerance; it's not begrudging acceptance; it's not stony silence or expedient allowances. It's not the lie of behavior modification. (67)

In the context of this chapter, this means being open to persons who do not identify themselves as heterosexual—whether lesbian, gay, bisexual, or transgendered. It means inclusion of these sexual minorities in the curricula, policies, and practices of schools, and redressing the invisibility of their experience. It is about uncovering a system of compulsory heterosexuality that reinforces the notion that everyone either is or should be heterosexual, that is, pervasive heterosexism. It is about ending a system of heterosexual privilege. It is about valuing difference as a source of learning and not a source of division and inequity. It is about redressing injustices, and above all it is the affirmation of the diversity of sexual identities.

Although I recognize the many views of multiculturalism, I believe there arc four core values: affirmation of diversity, human rights, human dignity, and equity/equality. It may seem surprising that many who seem to embrace the multicultural philosophy find sexuality, especially nonheterosexuality, problematic; I believe this can be said of gender, too. Programs within multicultural education have often been heterosexist or sexist, especially when the focus is ethnicity and everyone is implicitly assumed to be male and straight. This bias can be likened to the discrimination that lesbian women of color have faced in both the civil rights and women's movements in the United States. If multicultural education is serious about being a counteroppression tool, then it has to recognize that in the words of Martin Luther King Jr., there can be "no end to oppression without an end to all forms of oppression."

During April 1999, three bombs were planted in London, England. The bomber was said to be targeting minorities, and the first bomb went off in a predominantly West Indian neighborhood. The second bomb went off in a Bangladeshi neighborhood, and the third was planted in a gay bar. How could one argue that any minority is more or less deserving of prejudice, discrimination, or hate attacks? Paraphrasing the words of Audre Lorde, "Silence will not save us."

THE CHALLENGE OF BREAKING THE SILENCE

Teacher education and schools face the challenge of either perpetuating homophobia and heterosexism or striving to build a society free of prejudice, discrimination, injustice, and hate. As Pharr (1988) states:

> We must take a very hard look at our complicity with oppressions, all of them. We must see that to give no voice, to take no action to end them is to support their existence. Our options are two: to be racist, or anti-Semitic, or homophobic (or

whatever the oppression may be), or to work actively against these attitudes. There is no middle ground. With an oppression such as homophobia where there is so much permission to sustain overt hatred and injustice, one must have the courage to take the risks that may end in loss of privilege. We must keep clearly in mind that privilege earned from oppression is conditional and is gained at the cost of freedom. (52)

Breaking the silence is therefore a challenge of breaking with the orthodox faith of heteronormativity. It is the challenge of becoming and being a heretic. However, breaking the silence can produce an increase in homophobic discourse, as a target previously out of view comes into sight. This increase is part of a developmental process. Although silence may seem a state of harmony, the exposure of homophobia-prompted visibility is a step toward sexual diversity. Bennett's work on a developmental model of intercultural sensitivity (1993) supports this view. He describes an interactive continuum of stages to describe different ways of experiencing cultural difference, with each stage representing a greater degree of intercultural sensitivity. The first stage is the denial of difference, where one's own worldview is unchallenged as central to all reality; this is often the case when physical or social isolation precludes any contact with significant cultural differences. This stage is the position of heterosexism in which one assumes everyone is heterosexual, oblivious to the existence of other sexual identities. Stage two represents the defense against difference and involves attempts to counter perceived threats to the centrality of one's (heterosexist) worldview. The usual response is the denigration of difference and the belief in the superiority of one's own culture. This stage produces homophobia, where there is now recognition of nonheterosexuals who are then disliked, feared, or hated. Further stages include "acceptance," in which individuals acknowledge and respect difference as fundamental, necessary, and preferable in human affairs. The final stage of "integration" represents the ability to adapt to difference and function in various cultural ways. It is embodied in the multicultural human who experiences diversity as an essential and positive aspect of all life. From the perspective of this chapter, this individual is someone with a positive view of his or her own sexual identity and "other" sexual identities.

Breaking the silence is the first step in combating homophobia and heterosexism. I consider further steps to move toward the affirmation of sexual diversity, beginning with a consideration of pedagogy and moving on to a description of the GLEE project,[1] which I coordinate at the Oulu University department of teacher education, and Theory of Knowledge, a course I teach at high schools in Finland and Japan.

PEDAGOGY AND
EDUCATIONAL TRANSFORMATION

Sears (1992) found in a two-year survey in the United States that teachers generally avoided the subject of homosexuality and that two out of three teachers felt uncomfortable discussing homosexuality; 75 percent had negative attitudes toward homosexuals; 52 percent of prospective teachers would feel uncomfortable working with an openly lesbian or gay colleague; and more than eight out of ten opposed the integration of lesbigay themes into existing curricula. Two out of three guidance counselors harbored negative feelings toward lesbians, and only one in five had received any training in serving gay and lesbian students.

Although some counter-homophobia materials and lesbigay-inclusive curricula have been developed, they will only be used if teachers have the confidence and support to address sexuality. Studies such as Sears's (1992) highlight the need not only for materials but also for teacher training to redress the detrimental effects of homophobia and heterosexism. The training needs to focus on engaging teachers in reflecting on how they were schooled to deal with diversity, gaining an understanding of the social construction of prejudice, and becoming familiar with ways to transform curricula to counter prejudice and affirm sexual diversity. The provision of safe space and ongoing support are also essential components in such a training program.

CHALLENGING HOMOPHOBIA AND
HETEROSEXISM: THE GLEE PROJECT

The GLEE Project, funded by the European Union, is an educational response that seeks to combat homophobia and heterosexism. In line with the Amsterdam Treaty,[2] which outlines the European Union's commitment to combating all forms of discrimination, the project is developing an interactive network of teacher training, curriculum development, and research initiatives to combat discrimination on the grounds of sexual orientation.

Educational transformation requires three mutually supporting elements: research, training, and curriculum development. In the GLEE Project's creation of a network of educational initiatives to combat homophobia and heterosexism, these three elements interact as an effective model for change. Unlike programs that produce growing shelves of unused research, training and curriculum development by "experts" devoid of classroom experience, and "top down" and prescriptive change, the GLEE model is bottom-up, focusing on locally contextualized teacher-facilitated initiatives. The project aims to provide a stimulus for more research to inform training and curriculum development.

Raising awareness and uncovering invisible systems of privilege are basic to the pedagogical approach for the project. This approach is based partly on theories of transformative pedagogy such as Freire's (1975), which aim to build a learning community supporting the individual growth of each member of the community while at the same time fostering solidarity and dialogue among members of the community, and also with the wider society. It aims to create critical consciousness and to promote an analysis of the processes of mindset construction. Its methodology addresses inequity and discrimination by deconstructing stereotypes and prejudices.

The GLEE Project course is also based on participant-centered pedagogy as well as experiential learning. These approaches emphasize sharing personal experiences and opinions and creating a safe learning community in which all voices are valued. This kind of community creates a climate for raising awareness, developing understanding of diverse viewpoints, giving theory personal meaning (connected knowing), and supporting the critical exchange between the participants of the project and the surrounding community. Together these approaches aim to increase awareness and develop critical consciousness, providing the foundation for action to end discrimination.

The first phase of the project began in September 1999 and focused on in-service teacher training. With funding from the EU Commission, a team of educators from four European Union countries (Finland, the United Kingdom, Portugal, and Italy) and the United States set about designing a leadership training course for teachers from primary and secondary schools. The main objective of the course was for participants to develop an action plan for establishing education initiatives within their own school communities or university teacher education programs to (1) raise awareness of the extent and destructive effects of homophobia and heterosexism on all members of the school or university community; (2) develop strategies to combat heterosexism and homophobia in school or university policies, practices, and curricula; and (3) work toward combating all forms of discrimination. These initiatives were tailored by course participants to local needs and priorities, reflecting the diverse cultural contexts in which participants worked. Initiatives might include teacher and/or student groups meeting regularly; workshops for teachers in schools or universities and at conferences; curriculum development; student counseling and support services; and action research on a particular issue or theme.

During the course, participants learned to use GLEENET, an Internet-based support network. This network provides a resource center for use after the course as well as a means of ongoing communication among participating schools and universities to share ideas and collectively develop materials for their own local initiatives. GLEENET has chat and mailing facilities, along with an environment for distance learning and collaborative work. Thus it will be possible to create further initiatives on a national and international level, as participants from three to five schools from different EU countries will form partnerships to develop their own transnational projects. They will then submit an application for three years of funding from the EU Commission under its Socrates Education Program.

In August 2000 the Leadership Training Course was piloted with a group of twenty-five educators from Europe and North America. The participants then became part of a one-year pilot of the GLEENET. Participants developed their own action plans and in May 2001 presented an evaluation of their activities along with an assessment of GLEENET. Activities ranged from development of materials and classroom activities to research related to lesbian, gay, bisexual, and transgendered (lgbt) issues, to teacher training and workshops at conferences. In addition, a school partnership (the Pilot School Project) based in Finland, Ireland, Portugal, and the United Kingdom submitted an application for its own in-service teacher training project, which aims to combat prejudice and create a more tolerant and inclusive society. Participant teachers create a staff training pack to deliver this to their own school staff and students, and participating schools link up with one another to discuss diversity and respect within their own communities. This Pilot School Project began in August 2001, and provided a model for teachers participating in the first Leadership Training Course in Oulu, Finland in July 2002, to develop their own projects. Further courses will increase the impact of the GLEE Project.

THE CHALLENGE OF PERSPECTIVE
TRANSFORMATION: THE TOK COURSE

The pedagogical approach of the GLEE Project also forms the basis of the Theory of Knowledge (TOK) course I teach. Although I have only taught this course in high schools in Finland and Japan, it has much relevance for teacher education. Theory of Knowledge is a course for high school students who are candidates for the international baccalaureate diploma; it gives them the opportunity to explore and analyze perceptions, attitudes, values, and knowledge, and in particular, to gain an understanding of the social processes constructing their own and others' mindsets and worldviews. The course can be a valuable tool for lessening ethnocentrism and transforming perspectives by unmasking the existing dominant beliefs, ideas, and assumptions that shape the world.

Like the GLEE Project, the TOK course is, in the words of Gray (1982), a "struggle for liberation from a set of malignant mindsets"—including heterosexism and homophobia. Both TOK and the GLEE Project emphasize radical critical analysis of the underlying values and systems of beliefs that guide actions, as well as a consideration of how to bring about social transformation. Both view the student not as a passive onlooker but as a shaper of a new order. Both recognize that education has often been an instrument for perpetuating heterosexism, playing a role in the social construction of homophobia, and denying the intrinsic value of all humans. And both seek a more inclusive curriculum, welcoming diverse views and perspectives, as an important part of building partnership, unity, and respect for all.

The TOK course encourages students to put their own and others' belief systems to the test. Are these systems, such as compulsory heterosexuality, compatible with a belief in the intrinsic value of all? As we consider questions like these, I have noticed that a student's dualistic world of black/white, right/wrong, gay/straight, soon blends to grey, with emerging uncertainty. This is part of a process in which students become more open-minded, better able to live with ambiguity, and more aware, as engaged knowers, that they are an intimate part of what is and what is not known. Challenging homophobia, heterosexism, and the invisibility of lesbigay voices in the curriculum helps to illuminate connections among all forms of discrimination and to see the broader picture of the "Theory of (Whose?) Knowledge."

At the beginning of the course I ask students to name a scientist, a mathematician, an economist, a religious leader, a politician, and so forth. We analyze this sample of responses by sex, race, and social class. The racial and gender imbalance in the answers, previously invisible to most students, comes as a shock. As one student from India commented in a journal entry:

> The education system even in an international school setting seems to value the West more than any other part of the world and Whites more than Blacks. . . . I recall being told, at the age of six, that I was stupid and ugly because I am dark. For three years I believed it. I wished every day for light skin, blond hair and blue eyes. I kept at a distance from people who resembled me. I aspired to be like the norm and tried hard to be accepted. I was conscious of the White, Christian boys and girls and unconscious of the dark, non-Christian boys and girls.

This journal entry shows the student's internalized negative views of her ethnic identity—what Banks (1988) calls ethnic psychological captivity. This phenomenon parallels the internalization of homophobia by lesbian and gay youth. Both have the same negative effect on self-worth and self-esteem.

Invisibility is a complex phenomenon when it comes to sexuality. There are many gay and lesbian voices in school curricula, but they are unacknowledged. This raises another interesting question: To what extent does an individual's sexuality influence knowledge? Is there such a thing as queer literature, science, or economics? At this stage we move into a discussion of curricular revision and discuss questions such as: "What would each of the subject areas look like if they had a more inclusive base?" and "In what ways would the questions and answers vary?"

The history section of the course provides many opportunities for identifying heterosexual and other biases in the curriculum. Invisibility is again addressed: "Herstory," Black history, Third World history, gay and lesbian history. Where are they? What is the reason for and effect of their exclusion? Following are excerpts from another student's work addressing the question, "To what extent does history education reflect the power structures dominant in the world, and what consequences might this have?":

> History education should be liberating and should teach the students to question and find alternatives for the existing system and ideas, as opposed to domesticating students and preserving the "status quo" by passing on past values and existing social conventions of the dominating class/elite. People need to learn more about a world in which people like themselves play a role, in which they may find role models that represent their own race, gender, sexual orientation . . . and group.

When high school students begin to engage in such a critique of their educational experience, reconstruction of the dominant body of knowledge has begun. Edward de Bono, in *Handbook for the Positive Revolution* (1991), states:

> The weapons of the positive revolution are not bullets and bombs but simple human perceptions. Bullets and bombs may offer physical power but eventually will only work if they change perceptions and values. Why not go the direct route and work with perceptions and values? (59)

The TOK course goes some way toward planting the seeds to begin a journey down the direct route.

CONCLUSION

The development of broader perspectives, and the appreciation of otherness, depend on recognizing one's own blind spots and seeing the world through someone else's eyes. Confronting and understanding one's own cultural lens is an essential part of the process, whether for students in a TOK class or teachers participating in the GLEE Project. The challenge for teacher education is to create opportunities to begin the long journey to affirm diversity and redress inequity and injustice. What is needed is the creation of a social awareness that impels action—a framework reflected in research, teacher training, and curriculum development initiatives.

NOTES

1. See <http://glee.oulu.fi> for further details about the project and courses.
2. The Treaty of Amsterdam came into force on May 1, 1999. It includes a new clause, Article 13, which bans discrimination on the grounds of sexual orientation.

REFERENCES

Abalos, D. 1989. Multicultural education in the service of transformation. Paper presented at Multicultural Education Conference, Montclair State College, Montclair, New Jersey.

Banks, J. 1988. *Multiethnic education: Theory and practice*. Newton, Mass.: Allyn & Bacon.

Bennett, M. J. 1993. Towards ethnorelativism: A developmental model of intercultural sensitivity. In *Education for the intercultural experience,* 2d ed., edited by R. M. Paige. Yarmouth, Maine: Intercultural Press.

de Bono, E. 1991. *Handbook for the positive revolution.* Harmonsworth, UK: Penguin.

Epstein, D., and R. Johnson. 1994. On the straight and narrow: The heterosexual presumption, homophobias and schools. In *Challenging lesbian and gay inequalities in education,* edited by D. Epstein, 197–230. Buckingham, UK: Open University Press.

Freire, P. 1975. *Pedagogy of the oppressed*. Harmonsworth, UK: Penguin.

GLEE Project. <http://glee.oulu.fi>.

Gray, E. D. 1982. *Patriarchy as a conceptual trap*. Boston: Nimrod.

Pharr, S. 1988. *Homophobia: A weapon of sexism*. Little Rock, Ark.: Chardon.

Rich, A. 1986. *Blood, bread and poetry: Selected prose*. New York: Norton.

Sears, J. T. 1992. Educators, homosexuality, and homosexual students: Are personal feelings related to professional beliefs? In *Coming out of the classroom closet,* edited by K. Harbeck, 29–79. Binghamton, N.Y.: Harrington Park.

11

Getting to the Heart of Teaching for Diversity

Genét Simone

> The significant problems we face cannot be solved at the same level of
> thinking we were at when we created them.
>
> —Albert Einstein

As teacher educators work toward helping preservice teachers satisfy requirements for certification, they often encounter the standard of "diversity."
The goals within that standard are oriented toward better understanding who
teachers are in relation to others and how social events and interpersonal dynamics shape groups of people by ethnicity, class, gender, sexual orientation,
and ability. There is an emphasis on building respect for oneself and others
and valuing all human contributions to society.

The methods typically employed to help attain a degree of fluency with the
diversity standard include case studies and autobiographies, field experiences, documentaries, and journal writing. These can strongly affect personal
beliefs about diversity (González et al. 1993; Liston and Zeichner 1996; Merseth 1996; Noordhoff and Kleinfeld 1993; Sykes and Bird 1992; Zeichner and
Hoeft 1996; Zeichner and Melnick 1995). Exposed to different cultures, students learn that their particular perceptions of others are exclusive to their
own history, language, and socially-constructed classifications, such as ethnicity or socioeconomic status. They also learn that, in spite of differences,
people across our nation and around the world struggle with the same issues
of anger and sadness, grief and depression, hope and joy.

Given the relative newness of gay issues in mainstream society, it is safe to
say that most diversity training for preservice teachers neglects the concerns
and needs of lesbian, gay, bisexual, and transgendered (lgbt) people as a vital

143

part of the social fabric. Although their needs could easily be highlighted within the language of the diversity standard (e.g., valuing people regardless of perceived or true differences), they are often given only lip-service in teacher education curricula. Vaid (1995) calls this "virtual equality," where equality in the basic human right to live a life free of persecution is offered with one hand (such as by law) but then taken away with the other (not enforced).

Many groups of people in the United States—African Americans, American Indians, Latinos, Jews, handicapped people, and so forth—continue to experience virtual equality on a daily basis. It is critically important for teacher education programs to address the challenges these groups face. However, focusing on those groups must be tempered with an equally respectful approach to the concerns and needs of lgbt people. Fortunately, an increasing amount of suitable material has been published for use in higher education (Casper and Schultz 1999; Friend 1991; Jennings 1994; Kozik-Rosabal and Macgillivray 2000; Lesbian and Gay Parents Association 1994; Rofes 1989; Woog 1995). These materials can be beneficial, and many more should be sought for use in courses where working with the diversity standard is an expectation and goal.

Unfortunately, a pervasive attitude among teacher educators is that, if simply exposed to a variety of information about other people's lives through case studies, panels, and other personal venues, preservice teachers will automatically understand the concept and reality of injustice and discrimination and will therefore work toward creating more equitable and compassionate schools. The assumption is that preservice teachers will face their own biases and strive to overcome prejudicial beliefs. Exposed to stories and factual information about certain groups of people in our society, they will naturally replace damaging opinions and attitudes and gravitate toward supporting their own students in the future, regardless of the differences those students bring to the classroom setting.

Those of us who work as teacher educators, however, need to be cautious about making such assumptions. Although they are hopeful and vested in the belief of the inherent goodness of people who pursue teaching as a career, these assumptions are dangerous to make and rely upon. There is no guarantee that preservice teachers will use common sense and switch biased habits and ideas for neutral or supportive ones. Such change requires a more intentional strategy, as the following story illustrates.

On the first day of one of my teacher education courses called "School and Society," I prompted my twenty-seven students to think about what they had learned from the foundations course that served as a prerequisite to the one in which they were now sitting. I wanted to find out what issues remained fresh for them so I could get a feel for where they were "at" with regard to some of the topics typically covered in the first class, ones to which we would return again in the coming weeks. After several rounds about how much they liked the field experience and other special projects, one student named Elaine[1] remarked, "In my class, we talked a lot about racism, sexism, being gay, and things like that, but you guys never told us what to do with it."

I was struck by this young woman's honesty, and I asked her to elaborate. Within a few minutes, the entire class had poured out their frustration with the treatment of diversity in previous education courses. Some did not believe that education was the place for examining systems of oppression in our society, while others stressed that, in our zeal to help students understand the dynamics inherent within and between socially-constructed groups, those of us who taught the foundations courses had forgotten to address the emotional impact the information would have on students. We had inadvertently adopted a mechanical stance on the "isms," or what one instructor in a personal conversation with me referred to as "the flavor of the week": one week on racism, one week on sexism, one week on heterosexism, and so forth.

In spite of the stunted format of our courses, I knew that the instructors worked hard to bring the preservice teacher population—largely Caucasian, heterosexual, suburbanites—to new places of understanding about how some groups of people enjoyed "unearned privilege" (McIntosh 1988) and how many did not. We pursued that goal through case studies, videos, journal writing, field experiences, and other methods supported by research on diversity and teacher education. Yet there continued to be a rift between what we presented to the students and what they were willing to grapple with.

As a result of that discussion, I changed the orientation of the course. I needed a common thread with which to weave the topic of diversity into my students' lives so they *would* know what to do with the information. But how could I redirect our approach to the topics being addressed? There was no model to follow, nor any ready-made exercises at my disposal.

I remembered the earnestness on Elaine's face and her desire to truly understand how to live with what she was learning about these issues and how to work with that new information so that it would make sense to her as a teacher. I realized that the thread I was searching for needed to begin with the students themselves. Somehow, I had to find a way to help them individually break out of the self/other dynamic that my colleagues and I had inadvertently perpetuated through the curriculum, even as we strove to help students personally identify with groups of people whose lives might be different from their own. I had to help Elaine and all of the other students find their own grounding in diversity and provide support to each of them as they ventured forth on a more personal exploration than they were accustomed to or comfortable with in a class. I had to prepare the playing field so they could run about freely and explore what *they* felt was worthy of attention on these issues. Since each student had a different orientation to and experience with diversity, it was critical that the support, encouragement, and information I provided follow some kind of structure.

Finding such a structure, or strategy, was going to be especially tricky when we came to the part of the class where we talked about heterosexism and homophobia. Throughout my years as a teacher educator, these issues had continually elicited feelings of confusion, resistance, guilt, and anger that were clearly more potent than when we discussed what I thought were equally difficult issues, such as racism or sexism. I frequently heard from other faculty and graduate student instructors how the topic of gay sexual orientation was enough to move an entire class from relative openness to outright rebellion. One graduate student instructor told me one day how a student of his went to the dean to complain that "the curriculum on gay issues was top-heavy." This young male student was offended that so much of class time was aimed at "recruiting preservice teachers to a complete acceptance of the gay lifestyle." In reality, the course met for sixteen weeks, with only one week exclusively devoted to the topic.[2]

This anecdote is just one example of a student who followed through on a sentiment that I had heard and knew from first-hand experience was a common feeling among students in education classes. Comments were frequently aired during class time and in student writings, such as, "I am really sick and tired of dealing with diversity, and the whole gay agenda," or, "As far as I'm concerned, school is not the place for these issues. What does being gay have to do with teaching? I treat everyone equally, and I always will."

With good reason, I anticipated that the highest resistance from students was going to occur when we talked about these issues. I was beginning to realize that all of my good intentions to have them read stories and meet nice gay people were not going to work. My approach to helping them through their resistance needed to be more personal, and to take place at a level where each student had the belief and courage to enter into a new realm of learning—not so much about gay people per se, but about themselves and what was happening to them mentally and emotionally when we dealt with this topic. In essence, the diversity standard was asking preservice teachers to develop the ability to respect themselves and others, regardless of perceived differences. I started to understand that perhaps the only way to meet the intent of the standard was to begin with the students' ideas and worldviews first, as opposed to parading a lot of "others" in front of them.

In the past, I had used a process in my education classes at a Midwest university that had become known as the Personal Process Transformation Exercise.[3] It was a tool to help identify a goal and then plot the path of students' personal development on any issue. For example, students would work on dispositions they wanted to nurture in themselves as teachers, like self-esteem, honesty, or dependability. They also worked on larger societal issues, like racism or homophobia. I decided to try this exercise again with my class, but this time I would require my students to deliberately choose to work on a disposition related to diversity, such as openness and understanding of issues of ability or race. Although I would have liked to focus exclusively on sexual orientation, I knew that I could not push that topic forward with the class, because doing so would likely backfire and was antithetical to my philosophy of inviting students into their own learning where *they* believed they needed it the most.

During the next class session, I announced that I was replacing one of the required papers with a different assignment, called the Personal Process Transformation Exercise. I also briefly explained that my reasoning for the switch had come from their concerns the week before. Then I asked students to get out a sheet of paper and complete in writing a series of sentences I was going to read out loud to them. I explained that they needed to write honestly and even bluntly, because they were going to use these thoughts as a foundation for the assignment that would stretch over the course of the entire semester. "No one is going to look at these," I added, and I began with the first sentence: "I would characterize my personal strengths as . . . ."

After giving the students a few minutes to finish that phrase, I continued with another statement: "I will take risks with others only when . . ." Again, I allowed time for students to finish their thoughts. The third and fourth sentences read, "I am less likely to be assertive when . . ." and "I tend to respond to conflict by . . ."

Then, I read, "I am likely to value and support differences in people with respect to race, class, sexual orientation, ability, or gender, when . . ." I asked them to consider each category, and then asked them to add their thoughts to this statement: "I think this happens because I . . ."

After giving the students time to respond to this set, I invited them to consider another angle of that question. "Okay, now I want you to write about this," I continued: "I am *less* likely to value and support differences in people with respect to race, class, sexual orientation, ability, or gender, when . . ." Again, I asked them to reflect on each grouping, and then finish with, "I think this happens because I . . ."

I directed the students to quietly review their writing and add to it, if necessary. Their homework assignment was to return the following week with a paragraph describing one goal they wanted to work on during the semester, which needed to be focused on diversity. This first stage was not going to be graded,[4] but I wanted them to take it seriously. When students returned the following week, I walked them through the rest of the exercise, which included clarifying their goals; listing a few reasonable strategies for measuring their progress toward those goals; naming a supportive person with whom to share their process; identifying a way to track their growth; and identifying a reward system, verbal or tangible.

The most important part of the process was that it established a structured way to intentionally reflect on their thoughts and feelings—even their physical reactions—when dealing with their goals. For example, when Margie handed in her paragraph about wanting to express her thoughts and feelings "even when they differ from those of the person or persons I am talking with," I encouraged her to pay attention to what happened when she did *not* express her thoughts and feelings. Was there a difference in her mental, emotional, and physical responses when she spoke honestly about some issues rather than others? Was it easier for her to express herself with some people and not with others? Why?

Other students wrote about wanting to work on their judgmental natures or overall discomfort with groups of people who were different from themselves. Much to my surprise, two students deliberately chose the topic of sexual orientation. Marc wanted "to see sexual orientation with open mindedness, and not jump to conclusions," while Sarah wanted "to question anti-gay slurs and jokes."

Regardless of the goal students chose to work on, I steered them toward putting it within the context of diversity. If they wanted to work on taking more risks, for example, they had to do so on diversity. Likewise, if they wanted to learn how to speak openly and honestly about their feelings, they needed to speak up on issues of diversity. I wanted to give them some freedom, but I felt that framing the assignment this way would help them stay on track with what they had identified on that first day as a very important dilemma: learning to live with new information that had the potential to challenge and perhaps change drastically their worldviews.

First in small groups, and then as a whole, we brainstormed ways that students could start working toward their goals. They listed things like attending events hosted by groups on campus, like the Black Student Alliance or the Chicano Center. They listed visiting the campus offices of groups like the Gay, Lesbian, Bisexual, and Transgender Alliance, or the Women's Resource Center. Some students realized that their required thirty-two-hour school practicum would place them in an ethnically or economically diverse neighborhood, a perfect opportunity to learn about communities that were different from their own. They suggested reading books and attending lectures, and asked me for magazine and journal articles to supplement their findings. The list was long, and students left with a number of ideas.

It is important to note that not all of the students in this class were white and heterosexual, typically the bulk of the teacher education population. There were three Latina/o students and one who identified as Native American, as well. These students were not exempt from the demands of the assignment; they, too, sought opportunities to learn about people who were different from their own experience.

I was heartened by the students' willingness to try out this activity, and made a special effort to check in with them throughout the semester, in person, via e-mail, and as a class. It was very important to allow in-class time for processing, too, privately and collectively. I wanted them to know that spending time for personal reflection and contemplation on difficult aspects of human interaction was critical to their ability to witness personal progress toward their goals. I also wanted to assure them that their goals might change direction depending on their circumstances, and it was important to follow where that was taking them.

I had found in the past that some students' goals were merely symptomatic of deeper needs, so I made it clear early on that my role as their instructor was not to counsel them. If I felt they were headed into personal territory that required the assistance of a counseling professional, I was going to encourage them to pursue that. My job was to teach them to get closer to the core of their own thought processes and feelings so that when we covered information on diversity, they could move through their initial feelings of confusion, guilt, frustration, or anger (the typical responses) to a deeper understanding and resonance with the topics at hand. The overall goal was to help them get to the heart of diversity in their own lives so they could be more responsive (rather than reactive) to situations that made them uncomfortable and unproductive as students and teachers.

The results at the end of the semester were powerful. Many students chose to work on simply becoming more comfortable around groups of people who were different from themselves. The main avenue for accomplishing this goal was attending cultural events on campus or in the larger community. For some students, this was a very big step in transforming not only their knowledge about others but also their knowledge about themselves in situations that were unfamiliar, and where the acceptable behavior was undefined.

Margie, whose goal was to express her thoughts and feelings (even when they differed from others'), found the courage to speak up in situations that she would have previously ignored or avoided. She wrote in her final report, "I forced myself to speak up if I heard something I disagreed with or that made me feel uncomfortable, no matter how small an issue it was. By doing this, I became more comfortable speaking out when bigger issues came up."

For example, Margie described a situation in a teachers' lunchroom, a site of frequent "racial or derogatory comments": She challenged one teacher's comments that students of color (mostly Black and Hispanic) "had bad tempers" and "parents who don't care about education." Margie countered his statement by saying that that there was probably "a lot more to the picture than the children just having bad tempers." To her surprise (she wrote), "two other people chimed in that they agreed with me." At the same school, Margie also came to the defense of a young boy who she felt was not being assessed fairly as a "special needs" student. After she shared her feelings with her practicum teacher, the teacher initiated another test for the boy, which resulted in the school's meeting his academic needs. "If I hadn't spoken up," she said in her report, "this child may not have gotten the service he needed."

One important thing that happened for Margie happened for others as well. By paying close attention to what they were really thinking and feeling in certain situations, they realized that they tended to acquiesce to authority for fear of losing their privileged status. Margie realized that if she hadn't spoken up in the teachers' lounge, or said anything to her practicum teacher about the young student, she would only have perpetuated the problem and ended up complying with the discrimination at hand. Not challenging that discrimination certainly would have felt less dangerous to her, but not acting on her instincts and sense of fairness, which were based on new information she obtained in our class about discrimination, felt much worse. In essence, her awareness of those dynamics and her internal responses to them forced two outcomes: (1) It was harder for her to hide behind a perceived ignorance about what was really being said, and (2) her awareness became a launching point for empowerment. "This was a great exercise for me," she wrote, "because for a long time I needed to work on these issues, but this gave me a reason to have to face them. Now I feel [that] I will be all the more ready when I do start teaching."

The two students in my class who set goals to work specifically on sexual orientation had mixed results. Sarah had a difficult, but life-changing, experience with her project. She started out wanting to "question anti-gay slurs and jokes," but found that she also needed to do something much more personal and powerful: She needed to "come out" as a lesbian. She wrote in her final report, "The underlying core of my goals was making my entire self known to people and learning not to care how they reacted. . . . I found that throughout the semester my self-worth has dramatically improved, although I feel increasingly alienated from mainstream society. [But] I am no longer willing to hide who I truly am by pandering to others' wishes and pretending I have no weekend social life, just because it may have included going to gay-themed events."

Sarah chose to tell close friends that she was a lesbian, and she tried expressing a little more affection for her girlfriend when in public. She read books about lesbians like Eleanor Roosevelt, Marguerite Cammermeyer, and Georgia O'Keefe. She also came out to a co-worker and then to her mother. Coming out to her mother proved to be an extremely painful experience, however. Sarah wrote that she "had been trying to broach the subject with her for over a year and had been deathly afraid of her reaction." Sarah continued, "My mother became angry and stated that she did not want to hear about my 'lifestyle.' She thought it was just a phase." Sarah described how she wrote a letter to her mother after that heated discussion but received only anger in response. Still, through this ordeal Sarah remained steadfast in her commitment to herself that she was not going to hide any longer. "Although my mom's reaction to my coming out was even worse than I imagined, I'm glad that I no longer have to live in fear of her accidentally discovering my sexual orientation."

The power of honest introspection, along with support and a clearly defined goal, brought Sarah to this resolution by the end of the class: "This assignment helped me gain a greater understanding of myself and address an area of my life that had been kept a secret to many—a secret that gnawed at my insides. It has been one of the most personally rewarding assignments ever given to me in school." I was overjoyed with Sarah's growth over the course of the semester, and was duly impressed that she found the courage not only to choose a difficult issue at the outset, but then to redirect her focus into such a tender and vulnerable place in her heart.

A student named Marc also chose to work on the sexual orientation issue. Marc started out by wanting to "see other sexual orientations with open-mindedness," but he found that it was going to be a lot harder to change deeply held prejudicial beliefs than he thought. He wrote at the end of the semester, "[It] never really got going, because I wimped out and never went back more than twice to see if I could accept the alternate lifestyle." I knew that Marc's views on a number of issues tended to be conservative, so I encouraged him to speak to me, or to seek out information from the lgbt center on campus. I made the point that many students on campus—heterosexual as well as gay—utilized that office's resources. I found out later that his main approach to dealing with this particular diversity issue was to get "slightly drunk" in order to "get up the nerve" to go to an all-gay bar in a nearby city. He said at the end, "Going to a bar really didn't change my views or opinions of the lifestyle that homosexuals choose to lead, although now I think that some of the stereotypes of the flaming and real feminine guys that I had in the past are not true."

Marc had set a clear goal, but the main method he chose to obtain his goal did not promote the kind of introspection I had intended for the exercise.

Instead of examining what was happening inside of his own mind and body when faced with "the gay lifestyle," he kept it at arm's length. He did not deal with issues of the heart. Although he said that going to the bar helped him make "incredible strides," those strides took him only a short way down the road to his goal of acceptance and understanding. I am not discounting the value of Marc's experience but rather pointing out that his attempts managed only to gain a peripheral entrance to the real issues of what he honestly felt when he sat on a bar stool and watched gay men dance.

There is a critical difference between Marc's story and Sarah's. Although both of them were receiving the same information in class about lgbt people through case studies, panel discussions, and videos, their point of departure into that information was quite different. Marc, who identified as heterosexual, was an outsider with this topic. Sarah identified as lesbian, which placed her in an insider role with the group she was exploring. These different stances—in conjunction with information provided in class and the Personal Process Transformation Exercise—forced different results. Marc's results were peripheral and intellectual; he tried to change his beliefs about gay men simply by spending time in their space. By getting "slightly drunk," he ensured that he would not be in touch with his true feelings. Further, because he did not make any personal connection to any of the gay men, the new information he was gathering at the bar remained at a self/other level of analysis.

Sarah, on the other hand, took a very personal journey to her goal, and was radically transformed by the experience, accepting herself to the extent that she could be open about her sexual orientation regardless of others' negative attitudes or treatment of her.

These differences agree with research findings that simply adding new information about diversity to a preservice teacher's repertoire does not guarantee that it will change actions or beliefs, especially in situations that call for sensitivity to other cultures (Noordhoff and Kleinfeld 1993; Zeichner and Hoeft 1996; Zeichner and Melnick 1995). Further, research on the role of teacher education in changing beliefs—like the ones we were challenging in our foundations courses—suggests that personal beliefs do not change substantially, regardless of the intent and practice of teacher education courses (Zeichner and Tabachnick 1981).

These studies, and others, clearly indicate that a person's prior beliefs about a particular subject will affect his or her subsequent curriculum development, teaching strategies, and tenor of relationships with students and colleagues. Although most research on teachers' prior beliefs has been conducted in subject areas, such as reading, math, science, and writing, it is fair to say that prior beliefs about *any* issue will influence current behavior and thought. This is painfully clear when we address sexual orientation. Students hold deeply embedded beliefs that "normal" intimate unions occur between members of the opposite sex. When faced with information to the contrary, preservice teachers don't know what to do with the information. They struggle with their discomfort—an understandable response, given the heterosexist hegemony of our society.

Case studies, video and film documentaries, and panel presentations can help preservice teachers work through their confusion, misconceptions, and general lack of ease. However, the changes in their beliefs typically remain at a level of intellectual analysis, not the deeper level of understanding that is essential for personal transformation (Mezirow 1991). The whole point of analysis is to examine something outside of oneself. Hence, it establishes a self /other dynamic (Murray 1989), which can be useful in many situations, but not necessarily when aimed at studying and understanding the complex lives of human beings. Without intending to do so, teacher educators create an us/them polarization when they ask students to analyze other groups to find out what "they" are like. This analytic process defeats the intent of valuing and celebrating diversity, because the nature of that method allows only a glimpse of what they are "*not* like." In other words, when students analyze someone else, they are not walking in that other person's shoes; they are walking *around* them, as if examining a specimen at the zoo.

This is what happened to Marc with his experience at the gay bar. He was only one of dozens of students I have taught over the years who tried to "accept the gay lifestyle" but who was not yet ready to examine his own feelings about why he felt he could not. Marc, like many others, chose to work at a cerebral level when his heart needed to be summoned instead.

Teaching this course, and using the Personal Process Transformation Exercise, helped me understand that, just as the technical changes to school policies will not necessarily make people change their minds on a particular issue (Evans 1996; Fullan 1991), so simply reading and talking about "other people" will fall short of preparing teachers to work with diverse populations. Preparing for diversity requires more than an intellectual jaunt through a different neighborhood; it requires intentional soul-searching and reflection, which can lead to meaningful personal growth and transformation. Activities that can compassionately expose who we are as human beings with biases, beliefs, needs, and desires are desperately needed in adult education, which often takes for granted the good intentions of people who plan to teach and mentor youth.

There is evidence that contemplative practice, such as meditation, can work well for this kind of venture (Miller 1994b). Practices that invite people to pay attention to the present moment, free of personal judgment and analysis, have the capability to bypass the self/other approach typically used in traditional teacher education for issues of diversity. Rather than upholding an us/them tension, the contemplative practitioner simply grows more acutely aware of what is happening in the present moment, and then lets it go. There is no endless grasping after analysis and right answers; rather, there is an opening of the heart toward authentic and nonjudgmental living.

I did not introduce contemplative practices in my class; however, the use of reflection and ongoing discussion between peers and with me helped us avoid (more often than not) the self/other dynamic. We talked about being more compassionate with ourselves, because we were all inheritors of the heterosexist, racist, classist assumptions in our society. The point of dealing with diversity and the intent of the Personal Process Transformation Exercise was not to sift the pros and cons on certain issues. Rather, the emphasis was to try to peel back all of the misinformation and misunderstanding about different groups of people to discover more personally, clearly, and honestly the complexity of what was hidden there. Awareness is the first step toward healing the heart (Goleman 1998; Krishnamurti 1999) and developing into a professional teacher in the truest sense of that word. Simple awareness of our mental, emotional, and physical processes—which we flushed out through discussions and reflection papers—helped unearth the fears and misunderstandings associated with issues that were masked by a host of damaging and misleading information absorbed over a lifetime.

I firmly believe that, if treated with respect, people who dare to open their hearts to what they see, as well as what they cannot readily see, will be in a much better position to "deal with diversity" (as we often describe it) than people who merely analyze differences between their lives and the lives of others. "[B]ecoming a teacher is not a matter of learning how to teach but of personal discovery—of learning how to use one's self well" (Heck and Williams 1984, 2).

The population of youth and adults who are coming to terms with, and expressing openly, their gay, lesbian, and bisexual identity is growing at a steady rate. It is critical, therefore, that people who pursue teaching as their life's work learn about the particular challenges that gay people face. More important, however, they need to be invited into a process of personal inquiry that can help them negotiate their own internal dispositions and beliefs about diversity, as well. Anything less will remain at a self/other analytical level, which pays no attention to the emotional aspects of learning and living and thus falls short of the true meaning of education.

To educate means to "draw out." A real education, therefore, is not only focused on transferring information from one generation to the next; it is concerned with human relationships and the telling of stories that give meaning to our lives. It is about liberation (Freire 1970) and teaching that reaches "the intellectual and spiritual growth of our students . . . that respects and cares for [their] souls" (hooks 1994, 13).

In the same way, teacher education needs to be empowering and filled with opportunities that invite preservice teachers to grapple with the complexity of diversity and sexuality in ways that challenge but also encourage them to engage in meaningful and heart-felt self-inquiry. In the eloquent words of the late Paulo Freire,

> Educating involves a heart-felt passion to know that should engage us in a loving search for knowledge that is—to say the least—not an easy task. . . . [T]hose wanting to teach must be able to dare to have the disposition to fight for justice and to be lucid in the defense of the need to create conditions conducive to pedagogy in schools; though this may be a joyful task, it must also be intellectually rigorous. The two should never be viewed as mutually exclusive. (1998, 4).

Anything less than this kind of passion and rigor will keep our preservice teachers from relating to their own students as whole human beings in their own right—as far more complex and beautiful than a conglomeration of socially constructed categories of existence. To practice authentic teaching, therefore, teacher educators must have the tools to intentionally guide preservice teachers toward the kind of powerful and life-changing self-awareness that can help them realize their own diversity, potential, and promise. As the students in my class showed themselves (and me), the Personal Process Transformation Exercise is one way to do just that.

NOTES

1. All names of students are pseudonyms.

2. It's quite possible that the student was also taking offense with the instructor being an openly gay man.

3. In another article (Kozik-Rosabal 2001) I describe in more detail the steps of this exercise, and how it helped students deal with a range of personal and interpersonal issues. I was introduced to the exercise in 1994 when working as an adjunct faculty member at another university.

4. The final grading at the end of the semester for this assignment was both a self-assessment of individual effort and my own assessment of how thoughtful and well-written the final reports were.

REFERENCES

Casper, V., and S. B. Schultz. 1999. *Gay parents, straight schools: Building communication and trust.* New York: Teachers College Press.

Evans, R. 1996. *The human side of school change: Reform, resistance, and the real-life problems of innovation.* San Francisco: Jossey-Bass.

Freire, P. 1970. *Pedagogy of the oppressed.* New York: Continuum.

———. 1998. *Teachers as cultural workers: Letters to those who dare to teach.* Boulder, Colo.: Westview.

Friend, R. A. 1991. Choices, not closets: Heterosexism and homophobia in schools. In *Beyond silenced voices: Class, race, and gender in United States schools,* edited by L. Weis and M. Fine, 209–35. Albany: State University of New York Press.

Fullan, M. G. 1991. *The new meaning of educational change.* New York: Teachers College Press.

Goleman, D. 1998. The mechanics of attention. In *Inner knowing: Consciousness, creativity, insight, intuition,* edited by H. Palmer, 139–43. New York: Jeremy P. Tarcher/Putnam.

González, N., L. C. Moll, M. Floyd-Tenery, A. Rivera, P. Rendon, R. Gonzales, and C. Amanti. 1993. *Teacher research on funds of knowledge: Learning from households.* Washington, D.C.: National Center for Research on Cultural Diversity and Second Language Learning, Center for Applied Linguistics (1118 22nd Street, N.W., Washington, DC 20037).

Heck, S. F., and C. R. Williams. 1984. *The complex roles of the teacher: An ecological perspective.* New York: Teachers College Press.

hooks, b. 1994. *Teaching to transgress: Education as the practice of freedom.* New York: Routledge.

Jennings, K., ed. 1994. *Becoming visible: A reader in gay and lesbian history for high school and college students.* Boston: Alyson Publications.

King, J. E., E. R. Hollins, and W. C. Hayman, eds. 1997. *Preparing teachers for cultural diversity.* New York: Teachers College Press.

Kozik-Rosabal, G. 2001. How do they learn to be whole? A strategy for helping preservice teachers develop dispositions. In *Unfolding Bodymind: Exploring possibility through education,* edited by R. B. Hocking, J. Haskell, and W. Linds, 100–114. Brandon, Vt.: Holistic Education Press.

Kozik-Rosabal, G., and I. Macgillivray, eds. 2000. Sexual orientation and gender identity in America's urban schools. *Education and Urban Society* 32 (3) (special issue).

Krishnamurti, J. 1999. Listening to the silence. In *Inner knowing: Consciousness, creativity, insight, intuition,* edited by H. Palmer, 136–38. New York: Jeremy P. Tarcher/Putnam.

Lesbian and Gay Parents Association. 1994. *Both of my mom's names are Judy: Children of lesbians and gays speak out.* [Video.] (Available from Lesbian and Gay Parents Association, 6705 California St., #1, San Francisco, CA 94121.)

Liston, D. P., and K. M. Zeichner. 1996. *Culture and teaching.* Mahwah, N.J.: Lawrence Erlbaum.

McIntosh, P. 1988. White privilege: Unpacking the invisible knapsack. In *Experiencing race, class, and gender in the United States,* edited by V. Cyrus, 194–97. Mountainview, Calif.: Mayfield.

Merseth, K. 1996. Cases and case methods in education. In *Handbook of research on teacher education.* 2d ed., edited by J. Sikula, 722–44. New York: Macmillan.

Mezirow, J. 1991. *Transformative dimensions of adult learning.* San Francisco: Jossey-Bass.

Miller, J. P. 1994a. Contemplative practice in higher education: An experiment in teacher development. *Journal of Humanistic Psychology* 34 (4): 53–69.

———. 1994b. *The contemplative practitioner: Meditation in education and the professions.* Westport, Conn.: Bergin & Garvey.

Miller, R. 1993. We need a holistic teacher training program. In *Holistic education: Principles, perspectives, and practice,* edited by C. L. Flake, 112–14. Brandon, Vt.: Holistic Education Press.

Murray, E. 1989. Krishnamurti, education, and wholeness. *Holistic Education Review* (Summer): 52–57.

Noordhoff, K., and J. Kleinfeld. 1993. Preparing teachers for multicultural classrooms. *Teaching and Teacher Education* 9 (1): 27–39.

Rofes, E. 1989. Opening up the classroom closet: Responding to the educational needs of gay and lesbian youth. *Harvard Educational Review* 59 (4): 444–53.

Sykes, G., and T. Bird. 1992. Teacher education and the case idea. In *Review of research in education*, vol. 18, edited by C. Grant, 457–521. Washington, D.C.: American Educational Research Association.

Vaid, U. 1995. *Virtual equality: The mainstreaming of gay and lesbian liberation.* New York: Anchor.

Woog, D. 1995. *School's out· The impact of gay and lesbian issues on America's schools.* Boston: Alyson Publications.

Zeichner, K. M., and K. Hoeft. 1996. Teacher socialization for cultural diversity. In *Handbook of research on teacher education,* 2d ed., edited by J. Sikula, 525–47. New York: Macmillan.

Zeichner, K. M., and S. L. Melnick. 1995. The role of community field experiences in preparing teachers for cultural diversity. Paper presented at the meeting of the American Association of Colleges for Teacher Education, February, Washington, D.C.

Zeichner, K. M., and B. R. Tabachnick. 1981. Are the effects of university teacher education washed out by school experience? *Journal of Teacher Education* 32: 7–11.

TELLING OUR STORIES

In this third and final section, teachers, teacher educators, and a school administrator describe their struggles to integrate lesbian, gay, bisexual, and transgendered (lgbt) awareness into teaching and teacher education. "How My Teacher Education Program Failed" is a poignant account by a recent teacher education graduate, reminding us, if we needed reminding, of how much work still needs to be done. Starr's essay also suggests our responsibility as teacher educators to really listen to the concerns of all our students, especially those who are lesbian or gay, and demonstrates the devastating effect of a first year teacher's having to go back into the closet after having been visible and proud at her university campus.

The two chapters that follow trace discoveries arising in the relationship between teacher educator and preservice teacher. My account of what I learned from Karen reveals how a diversity workshop, even one in which lgbt students were given the opportunity to come out, could still end up silencing one lesbian intern. Steve Fifield and Lee Swain engage in a dialogue on the limitations of heteronormativity within the science curriculum and explore the consequences of coming out to one another as gay student and teacher educator. As he discovers that his students could read homophobic meanings even into scientific terms, Lee moves from a positivist view of his role in the classroom, in which he "did not expect his sexuality to have much to do with teaching science," to a clearer understanding of the way heteronormativity underlies all classroom discourse, especially assumptions about what is "normal" in nature. For Steve, sharing Lee's classroom experiences became the catalyst for making lgbt identity more visible in his own work with future science teachers.

Writing as an activist with long experience in the gay communities of New England and San Francisco, Eric Rofes muses on the consequences of teaching as an openly gay instructor in a state university in Northern California. Preparing teachers in a rural environment forces him to rethink the best strategies an activist-educator might employ to challenge homophobia in educational settings. And while his own openness about his sexual orientation helps empower the lesbian and gay students in his cohort and brings new awareness to others in his program, Rofes still finds himself "disheartened by the huge work still ahead. . . . [E]ven as an openly gay professor who feels that his own identity struggle has reached a place of peace, there are continuing complications, confusions, and contradictions. . . . When will this struggle end?"

Teaching as an openly gay instructor is also the focus of the two following chapters. James King and Roger Brindley describe what happens when a gay professor introduces lgbt issues into a weekly undergraduate seminar. Students' questions about whether they "were going to do anything in the seminar 'besides the gay stuff,'" once again illustrate the paradox of "surplus visibility" described previously in this volume. At the same time, King discovers that he is unconsciously reenacting heterosexist prescriptions about normality and propriety, casting himself and his partner as "Ozzie and Ozzie (as contrasted with Ozzie and Harriet)."

Like King and Brindley, Karleen Pendelton Jiménez writes about teaching and being out. Despite the ethnic disconnect between Pendleton Jiménez and her mostly Anglo students, she is eventually able to connect with students, both straight and gay. For Pendleton Jiménez, teaching begins with her "queer body": holding her five year old child on her lap at a student potluck, hugging her students at graduation, and presenting herself as a butch lesbian whose "masculine" affect, she believes, paradoxically accords her more power than she might find if she looked more feminine.

Karen Glasgow writes as a biracial Jewish lesbian who brings her multiple identities to her role as school principal in Los Angeles. She draws parallels between the invisibility of her lesbian identity and the invisibility of the Black experience that she found as a child, and recounts the way a parent's homophobic remarks forced her to choose between tacit acquiescence and coming out. In choosing the latter, Glasgow recognizes the difficulties she will now face as a school principal, "working so hard to build relationships and show my abilities." But Glasgow comes out squarely on the side of breaking the silence, urging school administrators and teachers to do the same.

Part III concludes with Ronni Sanlo's account of her journey from lesbian mother to "campus dyke" to teacher educator. Losing custody of her two children in the homophobic environment of Anita Bryant's Florida, Sanlo vowed to "do everything in my power for the rest of my life to try to make this world a better place for other lesbian and gay people." Most recently, this vow has taken her to UCLA, where she teaches a social justice course in the Teacher Education Program. Her essay describes the readings, videos, and activities that situate lesbian and gay awareness within a reconstructionist, social justice framework with a strong local focus: Los Angeles history, the particularities of racism in California, and the Rodney King uprising. She also includes student quotations that reveal how such a curriculum can affect a diverse cohort of preservice teachers.

The many voices in this last section of *Getting Ready for Benjamin* share a vision of teaching as intellectually honest, authentic, and relational. Although most of the writers are searching for answers, the questions they raise are at the heart of this book, and of all teaching.

12

How My Teacher Education Program Failed

"Starr"

I discovered that I wanted to become a teacher when I was a senior in high school, and already an out lesbian. Not only did I know that I wanted to teach, I knew that I wanted to teach high school agriculture.

Agriculture is a diverse subject covering topics from business management and horticulture to biotechnology and public relations and is traditionally taught in public high schools in rural areas throughout the country. Agriculture courses are usually taught in a "hands-on," experiential format, and include students with a broad range of abilities, from honor students to students enrolled in special education. I was led down the route to becoming an agricultural educator by a wonderfully charismatic, dedicated, and passionate man who taught agriculture in my high school. He was like a father to me, and he still serves as my mentor and one of my greatest sources of encouragement. In fact, he is the only person who has not questioned my decision to teach because of my lesbianism.

I knew I was headed down a difficult path when my mother, who has always been one of my most ardent supporters, asked me how I would reconcile my need to be open about my lesbianism with my desire to teach in a male-dominated and heterosexual-dominated field in a public high school. I still do not know the answer to that question.

I began my postsecondary education as a biology major at an Ivy League university. Shortly afterward I joined the teacher education program to dual certify as a high school biology and agriculture instructor. At the time I knew my lesbianism could threaten my career plans—I had often heard the horror stories about teachers who lost their jobs because they were outed or refused to go back in the closet simply because they were working with students. Yet

I thought I had plenty of time to work out any potential problems and many excellent resources at my disposal. After all, my university is a very liberal institution, and I was out at the time, and serving as the lesbian, gay, bisexual, transgendered (lgbt) representative to the student government. I assumed that the faculty in my department would work with me to allay my fears. However, when I began to take graduate level education classes to work toward my MAT (master of arts in teaching) degree I started to realize that this was not the case.

The classes I was required to take to complete my MAT requirements included many discussions of topics such as multicultural education and diversity. I remember many class discussions about racism, classism, gender discrimination, and able-ism; yet sexuality, homophobia, and heterosexism were consistently ignored. In each of these classes I outed myself as a lesbian and tried to bring up questions about sexuality and sexual orientation, yet even these direct inquiries were met with resistance. My professors did not seem willing to admit that such issues existed, let alone facilitate class discussions concerning them. Feeling alienated, I spoke to some of my professors and teaching assistants. The few who seemed at all receptive to speaking about my sexual orientation still did not feel comfortable giving me advice or guidance or bringing the topic up with other students. Often I was told that class time should be used to focus on diversity issues that affected all of us, not just a small minority. My professors explained that since I was the only one in the class who would need to deal with these issues they could not justify spending valuable class time on them. These faculty members never considered that I might not have been the only lgbt student in their course (I wasn't, I was just the only one who was out), and they never thought about the hypocrisy of their message to me: that diversity affects us all, unless that diversity involves sexual orientation.

In fact, I found that some of the faculty in the Education Department of my university could not even comprehend that there might be students in the department who did not identify as heterosexual. I tried many times to come out to one of my favorite professors, a man who I thought might be able to provide me with some advice and support. However, when I told him that I was a lesbian he literally laughed and said, "You can't be serious!" Needless to say, his response did not encourage me to pursue this topic with him. When I confided in another faculty member about problems I was having with my girlfriend, she responded by saying, "I'm sorry you're having trouble getting along with your roommate." Other faculty members, although they might have accepted my identity as a lesbian, were not willing to discuss the problems I might face in education because of my identity. I have received more support from online networks such as GLSEN (the Gay, Lesbian and Straight

Education Network) than I have from the Education Department in my own, supposedly progressive, university. As a result I have not had any guidance or support to help me sort through what it means to want to be an out lesbian and teach in a public school. Furthermore, my peers have not been given the tools to deal with sexuality in their classrooms and in their schools.

I am currently beginning my student teaching experience in agricultural education in a rural area of the Northeast. I still feel I do not have enough knowledge of my rights to be out in the classroom. As a result, I have had to go back into the closet. Psychologically this has been very difficult for me. If I were not completely dedicated to teaching I would not go through being closeted again, even for a short period of time. I have been very out for the past five years of my life, and my lesbianism has become as much a part of my visible identity as my race and my gender. It is not something I feel I should have to hide; in fact, I feel that it is so inseparable from my identity that people do not really know me if they do not know I am a lesbian. A friend of mine came up with a wonderful analogy to what it is like for me to be closeted: He compared it to having to pretend your mother died when you were very young and always being afraid that you will make a reference to her, or that you will slip up and talk about her to other people. It is as hard for me to pretend that I do not date women as it would be for someone who is very close to his or her mother to pretend he or she grew up without a mother. My lover is a very important part of my life, a part of my life I feel I should be able to talk about and celebrate, not hide.

Some people have told me there is an easy way to resolve the issue of being a teacher and being a lesbian: Just don't talk about it. Your sexuality is your business, and no one but you should have to know whom you are sleeping with. Please! I cannot think of a single workplace where home life is not discussed. In the lunch room, the break room, the office, the teachers' room, and the classroom personal life is discussed constantly. Every job I have ever held has been in an office where people's personal lives are discussed freely at work; in fact personal issues are discussed *more often* than other topics. Why should the school building be any different? I have been student teaching for a week, and already I know a good deal about my cooperating teacher's husband and son. She knows virtually nothing about my personal life, except that I have pets. I almost slipped and mentioned my lover, but stopped myself just in time. She hasn't yet asked if I have a boyfriend, but I'm sure she will in time. What do I say in these situations? Just saying no doesn't seem like the truth. What do I say when students ask me if I have a boyfriend or if I am married? I feel deceitful if I do not tell the entire truth. And how can I expect honesty and respect from my students if I feel I am not being truthful with them? I *want* to be honest with my students, but I also want to keep my job as a teacher. How do I accomplish both? Where do I go for the answers to these questions? Who will talk to me about my concerns?

In approximately a year I will begin my job search. I have been told that the field of agricultural education is wide open. I have been told I will not have any trouble finding a good job. I am sure that this is true, but the question is, will I be able to find a job I can be happy with? Will I be able to find a job in an area where I can be out, where I can speak freely about my lover and not lose my job? I know there are some areas of the country where this is possible. Last year I met a science teacher who is out to his students. Overnight he became my personal hero. I did not agree with many of his teaching practices or with his theories about education, and I have a feeling we wouldn't get along very well on a personal level, yet he became someone I look up to. I find it extremely depressing that someone I hardly know, and would probably not agree with, became a role model for me in such a short period of time. But he was an *out teacher* in a public high school! After all, when you are a lesbian who is a prospective teacher, role models are in short supply. How many talented and dedicated potential teachers have we lost because they are not getting the support and the role models they need?

If I sound angry, it is probably because I am. I guess I thought teacher preparation programs were supposed to be exactly that, preparation programs. However, I am entering my first formal teaching experiences without necessary preparation. How open should I be with students? What laws (if any) protect me? Will I lose my job if I am outed? Do I have to go back into the closet to be a successful teacher? Either the faculty in my particular preparation program do not know the answers to these questions, or they are too intimidated by the topic to respond. If this is the case at a supposedly liberal Ivy League university, I hate to think how other programs are "preparing" teachers.

Sexual orientation—like race, religion, and gender—is an issue not only for the classroom teacher but for all students. Even if the teachers themselves are not gay or lesbian, chances are they will have gay or lesbian students at some point. Where are gay and lesbian students going to get the support they need if their teachers are not prepared to deal with homosexuality? I have been in many classrooms where the word "nigger" was definitely not allowed, yet I heard the words "faggot" and "homo" used on a regular basis without so much as a second glance from the teacher.

The lack of support for gay, lesbian, and bisexual students is not entirely the fault of classroom teachers. Every single school mission statement I have read includes a phrase about teaching children to be critical thinkers and accept diversity among all people. However, most school districts do not include sexual orientation in their nondiscrimination policies, and teachers are still not learning how to deal with lgbt youth, let alone with lgbt teachers. Maybe those mission statements should read, "We believe in educating youth to think critically and accept diversity among all people, *if* said people are heterosexual."

One of the main reasons I wish to teach is that I believe in the original premise of those school mission statements. I *want* to help the next generation of children learn to think critically and challenge the world around them. How can we expect our teachers to provide these opportunities to their students if we do not teach them the same skills? The key to educating youth is to educate future teachers about the issues facing their students and their colleagues. Unfortunately, sexual orientation is one issue that is still not addressed.

13

Visibility, Invisibility, and the "Thickness of Nondiversity": What I Learned from Karen

Rita M. Kissen and Karen Phillips

INTRODUCTION

Although teacher education programs have begun to teach teachers how to create classrooms free of racism, sexism, able-ism, and classism, little has been done to integrate preparation for sexual diversity into the teacher education curriculum. Few programs address the knowledge, attitudes, and beliefs of preservice administrators and teachers about these issues (Butler 1994; Geller 1990; Mainey and Cain 1997; Rofes 1995; Sears 1989), and even fewer recognize the dilemmas faced by preservice teachers who are lesbian and gay. How does their sexual identity affect their development as teachers, and how does societal and institutionalized homophobia affect them as they interact with peers and professors, student teach in school classrooms, and prepare to enter the world of professional education? Most important, how will they cope with the unique paradoxes of visibility, invisibility, and "hyper-visibility" (see chapter 2) that they will face in their professional lives?

This chapter is an attempt to begin a discussion about these questions. It did not come out of a quiet scholarly moment or a provocative phrase in a journal article. Like most important educational insights, its genesis was an encounter with a student, a young lesbian intern in my teacher education program, who took the risk of coming out to a cohort of eighty interns and faculty members at a diversity workshop several years ago. What follows is reflection on what both of us learned from that day and its aftermath, and what those insights offer to teacher educators.

MEETING KAREN

The graduate teacher education program at my university is a one-year program based at five sites, where interns fulfill their course work while working with host teachers in partner schools. Each site is administered by a
school-based educator with half-time university status and a university professor. The program is based on a developmental approach to eleven outcomes, ranging from knowledge of child and adolescent development, to instructional planning and strategies, to sensitivity to and respect for diversity.
Interns are selected in a rigorous admissions process that includes the usual
transcripts and recommendations, a personal essay about the candidate's
teaching and learning philosophy, and an interview conducted by university-
and school-based faculty and current interns.

When Karen applied to our program, I was the university-based coordinator for the only urban site, which at that time included two high schools
and a middle school. Karen was the first Asian American to interview at
our site, where many of the students are children of color. In addition, she
had been highly recommended to me by a women's studies colleague; at
the time of our interview I knew she was a lesbian, although she did not
know I knew. Karen did not choose to share her sexual identity with the interview team; why should she, when it was irrelevant to the merits of her
candidacy for the program? Yet my knowledge of her sexual orientation,
and the likelihood that everyone else on the interview team would assume
she was heterosexual if they thought about it at all (since heterosexuality
is assumed in our society until a lesbian or gay person comes out) meant
that her silence about her sexual orientation was not neutral. It was part of
the complicated web of safety and disclosure that all lesbian and gay people face, especially in educational environments. In any case, Karen was
an outstanding candidate and there was no doubt about her suitability for
the program.

As the semester progressed, Karen began to feel safer about disclosing her
sexual orientation to her peers. Our program is cohort-based, with a great deal
of trust-building activity at the beginning of the internship. Before many
months had passed, Karen had come out to the thirteen students at our site,
and had even brought her girlfriend to an intern party. As one of her mentors,
I was pleased to see how smoothly this disclosure process seemed to be happening, how comfortable the other interns seemed with the knowledge that
one of them was a lesbian.

Later in the semester, interns at all five sites came together for a diversity
workshop, a full-day event that took them out of their classrooms to introduce
them to pressing issues in multicultural education. That year, we hired two fa-

cilitators to run the workshop, which began with a "crossing the line" exercise in which various group identities were called out and people were invited to step forward and be applauded.

KAREN'S JOURNAL (1)

I watched as others moved and squirmed to get around each other, making their way to the front of the room. Once there, the participants turned to face the rest of the teacher interns and the crowd applauded. As the din died down, the people maneuvered their way to blend back in with the crowd until the next category was called out.

I was positioned at the back of the group, pushed up against the far wall, unable to see the facilitator. I stared at the back of the head in front of me and listened to the categories being called out. I waited. And waited. The classifications of identity were becoming more personal. Religions and ethnicities were being announced. The only category I was concerned with, however, was the one which would announce my sexuality. . . . The contrast between the other categories and the one which addresses who I sleep with amplified my anxiety and level of discomfort. Being gay is my most intimate form of identity and knowing this would eventually be exposed made me feel the secrecy of my own being in a way which the other categories could not. The privacy of my sex life was suddenly going to be made visible [with] a few words. With the anticipation creeping up . . . I realized there was always more than one person who stood at the front of the room at any given time throughout these exercises. Quickly the statistic ran through my head, one out of ten people are gay, right? At least. So, won't it be interesting to see who goes up there with me? I had expectations of meeting some fellow gay teacher intern(s) since I was the only one in my cohort group of thirteen. So much for statistics. But, surely, there were other gay people in this mass of sixty to seventy educators.

I recall hearing "Japanese/Asian American" and perked up. That's me! The pride with which I embraced my racial heritage fueled my path through the forest of bodies. I stumbled into the clearing after reaching the edge. I turned to find myself alone, facing the thickness of nondiversity, or so it seemed, and waited for the echoes of applause to cease. Since I grew up in Brunswick, Maine, it didn't surprise me to be the only Asian American person in the crowd. I was conditioned to accept my assimilation and to bury my awareness, having lived in a state which is virtually 90 percent white. Still, I felt unique and flattered to have others clap for me due to my physical appearance and cultural self.

I made my way back through the thicket and, no sooner had I reached the wall, when I immediately heard "gay/lesbian/bisexual/transgender" from the front of the room. I took a breath and paused for a moment, then excused myself as I again moved toward the clearing. I remember being very aware of the slight pause in my step. Thoughts of remaining stationary and thinking that I [had] a choice raced through my mind. I did not have the same feelings I had when I previously identified myself as a Japanese American. I suddenly felt my steps were riskier on both a personal and professional level and that the possibility of rejection was a reality. I tried to feel proud and unique in my insecurity. What motivated my steps, I realized, was the feeling of obligation to not lie to myself . . . [a]nd that I would hopefully find strength in numbers.

I looked far to my left and equally far to my right. I stood alone. The accolade of hand-clapping was not flattering. I felt like something on display and that my sexuality was something to be observed. I was proud of myself, yet felt slightly resentful that no one else came forward. In a way, I was offended by the other gay people who chose not to expose themselves, even though coming out remains a personal decision. I observed my aloneness from afar and fought off the feelings of being embarrassed and sorry for myself. I hoped that seeing my isolation would be enough to draw the others forward so that I wouldn't have to stand alone. But no one came forward.

I also struggled with the idea that I was now going to be identified as a gay person instead of as an educator. I could not bring the two together in my mind and was certain that others couldn't either.

RESPONDING TO KAREN (1)

Reading Karen's reflection, I am struck by the contrast between her feelings about being the only Asian American to come forward and being the only lesbian. Her racial heritage is an obvious form of difference, setting her apart from her fellow interns and from most other people in "the thickness of non-diversity," yet it brings her a sense of pride and pleasure at the applause she receives. Sexual difference, on the other hand, feels unsafe, uncomfortable, embarrassing; the applause there is "not flattering." Karen attributes her feelings to her sense of betrayal when other lesbian and gay interns in the room would not stand up with her, and to her belief that her sexuality is the most personal part of her identity. She is also worried about being perceived henceforth as "a gay person rather than an educator." Talking to her later, I pointed out how heterosexism sexualizes the process of coming out, since heterosexual references to spouses, children, or living arrangements are not assumed to be "about" sex. Nevertheless, knowing this did not prevent her from seeing her sexual orientation as the part of her identity that made her most vulnerable.

KAREN'S JOURNAL (2)

Afterwards . . . many people came up to me and expressed . . . appreciation and support for having come out to the crowd. A few individuals personally came out to me and said how much they wished they could have done the same thing. I was surprised and overwhelmed by the fear and lack of confidence which came through in their tone and manner. I realized how my exposure became a vehicle for others and that there is strength in numbers. No matter how lonely it appears for one to be standing alone, there will always be someone else who is present.

Acknowledgment is also a form of communication, and I encourage educators and interns alike to try and validate the experiences and existence of gay people in your programs. Coming out to my cohort group was a personal decision so that I could comfortably be myself, since I knew we would be spending every day in classes together for a whole year. What left me feeling detached from my peers and program [in the workshop] was that being gay didn't seem to matter, either personally or professionally. I was never asked any questions about my life as a lesbian intern or as a lesbian teacher. Even though I wanted my sexuality to remain hidden, I was not prepared for the consequences of feeling invisible as a social or professional being. I realized I did want to be acknowledged and felt that my coming out should have been a catalyst for interaction. . . . I felt as though people were curious but it seemed my peers were reluctant to be inquisitive since my lifestyle didn't necessarily involve them on a personal level.

RESPONDING TO KAREN (2)

Karen's ability to empathize with the other gay interns' failure to stand with her shows a transition from distress at her abandonment to sympathy for those who abandoned her. She can understand, and even sympathize with, the fear that the other gay interns felt, and she is also beginning to understand why her self-disclosure might threaten someone still in the closet. In coming out, she has become both an inspiration and a threat, something she will probably experience many times in her teaching career.

Yet the silence that followed her self-disclosure at the workshop—a silence in which I and the other teacher education faculty colluded—denied her the opportunity to integrate this discovery into her developing identity as a teacher.

Karen's comments on visibility (wanting "to be acknowledged" as a lesbian and wanting "to blend in" at the same time) describe the pull between safety and disclosure, visibility and invisibility, familiar to so many lesbian and gay teachers. Her words remind me of Dianne, a teacher I interviewed for a book about lesbian and gay educators (Kissen 1996). Dianne went back and forth about using her own name or a pseudonym in the book. She finally said that using her own name didn't feel safe, but she would use it anyway—and told me to be sure I spelled it correctly, "D-I-A-N-N-E."

KAREN'S JOURNAL (3)

In order to establish that yes, indeed, students are aware of same sex issues and feel the need for exposure in the classroom, I distributed a survey to both students and teachers at the high school where I did my student teaching. I should note that the students I asked to participate I knew were grappling with their own sexuality. I realized this put a slant on the outcomes but, as an intern, I could not afford to out myself. I pictured certain students not being able to understand the objective of the survey and then perhaps targeting me for broaching the subject.

The very first question of the survey asked [respondents] to describe the climate of the school in terms of its openness for discussing same sex issues. The responses are indicative of the misconceptions between teacher and student within the same school system. [One] teacher stated that the "climate neither encourages nor discourages discussions that arise from classwork" and that sexual issues should be left to sex education classes. [A] student, on the other hand, stated that "the majority of the school is really not open or even tolerant of any discussion of homosexuality."

The teacher's perception of the climate of the school seems unrealistic and intentionally neutral. The student's reply appears much more honest, active, and involved. These two points of view are worlds apart, which reflects the conflict of understanding not only between administration and student but also between adult and adolescent. . . . Teacher education programs which address and foster openness will create teachers who are accepting and tolerant of sexual diversity. What takes place in the classroom will eventually transmit into the halls and spaces between the walls.

RESPONDING TO KAREN (3)

Karen undertook this project as an independent study for her curriculum course. In an anonymous survey, she asked a small sample of students and teachers six questions about the climate around same sex issues in their school and the importance of teaching about gay and lesbian people. Karen's reflection shows that she understands the way "neutrality" can silence difference, especially when difference involves a hidden identity. Like the instructors and interns in our program who failed to engage Karen in a dialogue after she had come out at the workshop, the teacher believes that by not mentioning homosexuality in the classroom he is treating everyone equally. Such a view ignores the oppression of invisibility faced by members of all minorities, but especially lesbians and gay men, whose survival strategies are based on hiding and disclosure.

WHAT I LEARNED FROM KAREN

Karen's account of the diversity workshop and the survey prompts me to think about how we can mentor our lesbian and gay teacher educators with out violating their safety. Her story teaches me that our first and most important step should be to break the silence around sexuality and sexual orientation in our teacher education programs without jeopardizing the safety of our lesbian and gay student teachers. Teacher education programs have begun to support their racial and ethnic minority students by helping them connect with minority faculty and establishing small groups where minority preservice teachers can find and support one another. We need to see what insights these programs offer us as allies to our gay teacher education students, so they will no longer face a choice between invisibility (hiding who they are) or hyper-visibility (standing alone in a roomful of peers). One of the most hopeful developments in this regard has been the proliferation of chapters of GLSEN (the Gay, Lesbian and Straight Education Network) around the country, not only in big cities like New York and San Francisco but in such less likely places as Fayetteville, Arkansas, and Sioux Falls, South Dakota.

Although I no longer work in the graduate teacher education program, I still help out with the annual diversity workshop and lead similar workshops for undergraduates. As an "ice-breaker," I like to use an exercise I learned from the National Coalition Building Institute (www.ncbi.org), a diversity leadership organization that often works in schools. In this exercise, called "up-downs," people are invited to "stand and be welcomed" (rather than crossing a line) on the basis of various identities: family order, ethnic and religious heritage, gender, and so forth. As those who identify with a particular category rise, the rest of the participants welcome them with applause. Afterwards, participants discuss how it felt to be welcomed for different kinds of identities (ethnic, racial, religious, socioeconomic), how it felt to be the only one standing for a particular category, and how it felt to discover others in the room who shared their identities.

For years, I have puzzled over how to welcome lesbian and gay students in this exercise. Do I invite lesbian, gay, bisexual, or transgendered (lgbt) people to stand and be welcomed, forcing them to choose between coming out (which may well feel unsafe in the context of a teacher education workshop) or hiding? Or do I ignore the sexual orientation category altogether and perpetuate the invisibility surrounding sexual minority identities?

Since Karen shared her story with me, I have found a solution that avoids both the invisibility and the hyper-visibility that she found so painful. I begin this part of the exercise by reminding participants that a teacher may feel completely proud of being lesbian or gay but still not feel safe coming out in a professional setting. Then I invite anyone with lgbt relatives or close friends to stand and be welcomed along with those who are themselves lgbt. Since I am the parent of a lesbian daughter, this gives me the opportunity to come out as well. As people begin to stand (and they always do), no one knows who are the gay people and who are the allies. For that brief moment, we, the allies, and they, our gay and lesbian colleagues, are neither invisible nor hyper-visible, but standing together.

REFERENCES

Butler, K. L. 1994. *Prospective teachers' knowledge, attitudes and behavior regarding gay men and lesbians.* (Tech. Rep. No. 143.) Kent, Ohio: Kent State University.

Geller, W. 1990. Students and educators: Attitudes on gay and lesbian matters. Unpublished paper.

Kissen, R. 1996. *The last closet: The real lives of lesbian and gay teachers.* Portsmouth, N.H.: Heinemann.

Mainey, D., and R. Cain. 1997. Preservice elementary teachers' attitudes toward gay and lesbian parenting. *Journal of School Health* 67 (6): 236–42.

Rofes, E. 1995. Queers, education schools, and sex panic. Paper presented at the meeting of the American Educational Research Association, April, San Francisco, California.

Sears, J. T. 1989. Personal feelings and professional attitudes of prospective teachers toward homosexuality and homosexual studies: Research findings and curriculum recommendations. Paper presented at the meeting of the American Educational Research Association, April, San Francisco, California.

14

Heteronormativity and Common Sense in Science (Teacher) Education

Steve Fifield and Howard (Lee) Swain

QUEER RELATIONS OF IDENTITY AND KNOWLEDGE

Teachers' self-understandings are woven into the sense they make of academic subjects and into what they invite their students to know and become. In this chapter we draw on our experiences as a science teacher educator (Steve) and a student teacher in biology (Lee) to illustrate how personal identities and understandings of science intersect, are shaped by, and can reshape the cultural norms that regulate who it is proper to be and what it is proper to know in science (teacher) education. We apply perspectives from queer theory (Jagose 1996; Pinar 1998) and cultural studies (Levinson et al. 1996; Tierney 1997) to argue that cultural norms of (hetero)sexuality mediate constructions of identity and knowledge in classrooms.

Perspectives from queer theory unsettle normal ways of thinking, what Apple (2000, xix) calls "hegemonic common-sense," about identity, knowledge, and sexuality. For us, "queer" denotes perspectives from which one's sense of self, what one knows and can do, and what one finds thinkable are mutually implicated, sensitive to changing circumstances, and evolving (Britzman 1995). Teaching and learning can then be conceptualized not as transmitting and receiving bits of knowledge but as relations with others and the world that transform and multiply identities and knowledge (Lave and Wenger 1991; Luhmann 1998; Wenger 1998). As we show, even the well-worn topics in high school biology courses are embodied and given evolving and contested meanings by authors, teachers, and students, whose bodies of knowledge shape and are reshaped by cultural norms (Levinson and Holland 1996).

Queer theory directs our gaze to cultural norms of heterosexuality that mediate the relations of identity and knowledge. The condition of heteronormativity

177

enforces "the view that institutionalized heterosexuality constitutes the standard for legitimate and prescriptive sociosexual arrangements" (Ingraham 1994, 204). In light of this ambient heterosexuality (Murray 1995), our purpose in this chapter is not to bring sexuality to science (teacher) education, but to "excavate and interpret the way it already *is* sexed and, further, . . . to interpret the ways in which it is explicitly *heterosexed*" (Sumara and Davis 1998, 199, emphasis in original). In what follows we illustrate some ways that science (teacher) education is heterosexed, examine the effects of heteronormativity on identity and knowledge construction in science classrooms, and begin to ponder alternate stances that do not compel individuals or groups to "subsume their identities" (and understandings of science) "into a homogeneous mass" (Tierney 1997, 24).

STORIES FROM SCIENCE (TEACHER) EDUCATION

We begin with first-person accounts of our classroom experiences, then return to a shared voice to offer queer readings of our stories. We constructed the stories and analyses through what William Letts (in a personal communication) calls *critical conversations*. As a research practice, critical conversations are more disciplined efforts to interpret lived experience than everyday conversations, but more dialogic and collaborative than traditional research interviews. Our critical conversations were tape-recorded and transcribed, and studying those texts provoked further reflection and conversation.

Steve's Story: What Do Lgbt Issues Have to Do with a Science Education Methods Course?

I think of graduate school as the time I came out, not in a single event of (re)definition, but through an ongoing reconceptualization of myself and my understandings of the world as intersections rather than as bounded compartments. I came to see sexuality as relevant to how I know about and relate to people and things in the world. My nascent self-understandings as a *gay* scholar, cultured within a relational view of knowing and being, unsettled and complicated my teaching and research. When I began my current position as a science teacher educator, I found the intersections of knowledge, identity, and sexuality to be unexpectedly complex.

I taught a secondary science education methods course to seniors during my first semester on the job. One of my new colleagues had already developed the course and I gratefully pored over her course syllabus to start my planning. Gender equity was the central organizing theme of the existing course, which advanced a compelling and practical critique of dominant practices in science education (Bailey et al. 1997; Scantlebury 1994, 1995; Scantlebury et al. 1996). Since gender was already established in the course as a relevant dimension of science classroom diversity, I thought the stage was set to include lesbian, gay, bisexual, and transgendered (lgbt) standpoints as well. I wanted to break the silence around lgbt issues in science education.

But what would "breaking the silence" look like on my syllabus and in actual practice? What exactly do lgbt issues have to do with preparing future science teachers? Gender equity projects in science education address practices that differentially affect a large proportion of students, and are informed by an extensive research literature on girls' and women's experiences in science classrooms. In contrast, I soon realized that I could not clearly express what sexual orientation had to do with the core topics in a science education methods course, like content standards, curriculum development, lesson plans, classroom management, and assessment strategies. Because I could not convincingly relate sexual diversity to teaching science, I worried about my students' reactions to lgbt issues. I did not want to create the impression that some topics in the course served a narrow, personal agenda (there it was, *the* agenda!) at the expense of students' legitimate concerns as future science teachers. At a gut level I believed that it was right to address issues of sexuality with future science teachers, but I knew of nothing in the science education literature that would authorize my beliefs or guide my instruction. I worried about my credibility with students if I stepped beyond the boundary of official knowledge (Apple 2000) in science teacher education.

As fall semester approached, the course syllabus filled without a trace of lgbt lives or issues. I retreated to what Kevin Colleary (1999, 156) calls a "waiting for rather than creating" strategy and figured that if students raised lgbt issues, perhaps something to do with the homophobic language they were sure to hear in the schools, then I could safely address the topic. I waited, but the topic never came up. I stuck to the dominant script, played it straight, and taught about science teaching, including gender equity, in ways that did not mark sexuality as an issue. I took shelter in the social and epistemic privileges of the closet (Sedgwick 1990). It turned out that I had company in there.

Lee's Story: Teaching the Natural Way of Things

I was a student in Steve's science education methods course. During that semester I struggled with my sexuality and eventually came out to a few friends and my parents. When my mother asked me if I could handle being gay and working in schools, I assured her that I didn't plan on telling anyone, so it was not going to be an issue. In truth, I had some concerns, but I did not expect my sexuality to have much to do with teaching science.

As a student teacher in high school biology the following spring, I taught a unit on genetics. I noticed that some students would giggle and glance at each other when I used words like *phagocytosis*, *homozygous*, or *homologous*.[1] I thought it was strange that those words evoked that reaction, and I became suspicious. When you are in the closet, or just coming out, you like to feel that you have control over what people know about you. I began to think the students were on to me.

In one class activity, students paired up as hypothetical parents and flipped coins to determine the genes they would pass on to their children. There were more girls than boys in the class, so some girls were paired as parents. A few students, most of them boys, had a fit about that and said that two women cannot have a kid. I agreed that biologically it was impossible, but that the activity still demonstrated a principle of genetic inheritance. I could have addressed the underlying reasons for the students' discomfort, but I was worried about where that conversation might lead.

Throughout the unit I taught that males paired with females, as if that were what nature dictated, even though it did not feel natural to me. During such situations, the scientist in me and the "natural laws" I had learned conflicted with how I felt about myself. I had learned that homosexuality is not natural, but it felt natural to me. Teaching about the "natural" way of things forced me to consider whether I was somehow flawed or a genetic reject. I wondered whether my homosexuality was a choice instead of something I had no control over.

One day I asked my students to read a magazine article (Colt 1998) that discussed genetic and environmental influences on traits like shyness, thrill-seeking, obesity, addiction, and homosexuality. We had a good discussion about most of the traits, but the students were not eager to talk about homosexuality. When I pushed for the students' views, the few who responded said they thought homosexuality must have an environmental cause. I could not ignore my personal investment in this issue and I was stung by their comments, as if they had attacked me. I believed that my sexuality was genetically based, and that I should deal positively with it rather than trying to change it. A few students added that the Bible says homosexuality is wrong, so God would not have included it in our genetic makeup. I have wrestled with this issue, too, reading and rereading the scriptures, and it is still an area of uncertainty that troubles me. I wanted to tell my students the truth about me because I felt it would help them question and clarify their understandings, but I could not bring myself to do that.

My sexuality was not an issue in most of my interactions with students, but in instances like these it was an unexpected and troubling subject. I was relieved to walk out of my classroom on the last day of student teaching.

UNCOVERING HETERONORMATIVITY IN CLASSROOMS

For most of the school year we were not out to one another and neither of us was aware of the other's story. Then near the end of spring semester we unexpectedly met at an lgbt discussion group in a church near the university. Our serendipitous meeting led to conversations in which we swapped stories, pondered their meanings, and asked questions that uncovered the relations of heteronormativity, identity, and knowledge in our lives (Redman and Mac an Ghaill 1997). The following analyses suggest some of the things we learned from our stories.

Heteronormative beliefs and practices contribute to the hegemonic common sense (Apple 2000) of science classroom practice. For instance, it is *normal* (i.e., the dominant practice) to assume that sexuality has no place as a topic of study or a relevant characteristic of students and teachers in most science classrooms. The fact that normative sexualities are promiscuously inscribed by curriculum materials and classroom interactions (Epstein and Johnson 1994; Letts 1999; Nayak and Kehily 1997), while this disciplining of sexuality and knowledge usually goes unnoticed and unexamined, epitomizes the tacit nature of heteronormative common sense. Heteronormativity was implicated in our frustrating efforts to think about ourselves, our subject matters, our students, and our teaching in new ways. Learning to think beyond heteronormative common sense, and to uncover the sedimented classroom practices that inscribe common sense, are projects that go hand-in-hand.

HETERONORMATIVITY AND PEDAGOGICAL IMAGINATION

Steve could not articulate what lgbt issues had to do with a methods course for future science teachers, and he feared that raising these issues would place his credibility and authority at risk. He carried and enacted the commonsense notion that homosexuality is not a topic for polite, public discussion. This widespread assumption rests on images of lgbt people as sexually deviant and out of place in the public sphere, from which one's private life and sexuality ought to be excluded. Of course, this cultural norm utterly fails to account for the prior and ubiquitous presence of (hetero)sexuality in everyday life, including life in school and university classrooms (Epstein 1994; Letts and Sears 2000). Heteronormativity effectively strips from lgbt persons dimensions of lived experience that might otherwise enrich classroom cultures. This is an example of how conceptions of sexual identity intersect with what counts as knowledge (Tierney 1997). Steve's pedagogical imagination was impoverished by heteronormative common sense, which offered no substantive points of contact between science teacher education and lgbt lives, experiences, and standpoints. He thought that raising lgbt issues in the course would put his credibility at risk because, according to heteronormative common sense, lgbt issues *don't make sense* in science teacher education.

THE AMBIGUITIES OF KNOWING SELF AND SCIENCE

Lee also wrestled with the interpretive dead ends of heteronormative common sense. He did not expect his sexuality to have much to do with teaching science, but his sexuality was an issue thanks to the heterosexism of the biological sciences (Fausto-Sterling 2000; Schiebinger 1993) and of popular culture as it played out in his classroom. Behind his classroom door he discovered an ambiguous terrain in which he was a knowing *subject*, and an *object* of knowledge in cultural (and scientific) norms that defined him in ways inconsistent with his own feelings. In Lee's classroom, heterosexuality was normalized in seemingly innocuous ways, such as students' tittering over terms like *homozygous* and *phagocytosis*. To hold his tenuous position in the classroom closet he tried to ignore these everyday manifestations of heteronormativity. The boundaries of acceptable sexuality (Steinberg et al. 1997) were further inscribed when students objected to all-female pairs in a lesson on the transmission of genes. A few students went beyond reading heterosexuality into mere secular nature by insisting that God would not have created genes for homosexuality. That heteronormativity served to discipline both nature and God speaks to its pervasive influence on commonsense notions of what is normal, natural, and right.

Lee himself carried heteronormative baggage in his understandings of biology, even while his feelings conflicted with what he had learned about the "laws" of biology. Lee had been taught that homosexuality was unnatural and that in nature males pair with females. Was he a genetic reject for experiencing his sexuality as a natural feeling? To make sense of himself and of biology, he tried to reconcile his identities as a *knower of* and a *known about*. As a knowing *subject*, he resisted claims that homosexuality was due to environmental influences or was a matter of choice, and looked to genetics to naturalize his sexuality and to justify his decision to deal positively with it. As an *object* of the biological knowledge that he had learned and was teaching, his sexuality was usually absent, and so unnatural by default, or a minor curiosity due to its deviance from the norm. The tension between his subject and object positions remained when he considered his understanding of and relationship to God. He could not find unambiguous affirmation of his sexuality in the Bible, although he understood *all* of who he was as a part of God's creation. Neither science nor religion offered a resolution of the conflict Lee faced between his feelings and the official knowledge he taught in his biology course.

LESSONS FOR SCIENCE (TEACHER) EDUCATION

Heteronormativity bridles the diversity and quality of ideas and identities that circulate in classrooms (Leck 1999). Our stories illustrate how heteronormativity leads to uncritical stances toward disempowering cultural norms and practices. The lessons we offered our students reproduced problematic norms that ought to have been excavated and criticized.

Queer readings of our stories begin to uncover the relevance of lgbt issues and queer standpoints in science (teacher) education (Nobles and Letts 2000). Sexualities, normative and otherwise, are not and cannot be neatly relegated to students' and teachers' private lives. Ambient heterosexuality makes sexuality a ubiquitous public presence. Future teachers ought to examine the commonsense notions of sexuality, identity, and knowledge that circulate in the heterosexually charged atmosphere of schools, and consider what they can do to foster more affirming learning environments for their students and colleagues (Harris 1997; Sears and Williams 1997). Our stories also demonstrate how sexuality intersects the relations that construct and authorize academic knowledge in classrooms. Future science teachers need to think seriously about how constructions of sex, gender, and sexuality shape, and are shaped by, their understandings of science, teaching, and learning (Epstein 1994; Letts 1999; Steinberg et al. 1997).

QUEER COMPANION MEANINGS

The concept of curriculum *companion meanings* sheds more light on how heteronormativity is communicated in a curriculum, and how a queered science curriculum might foster more critical and humane understandings of science and self. Roberts and Ostman (1998) describe companion meanings as follows:

> Science textbooks, teachers, and classrooms teach a lot more than the scientific meaning of concepts, principles, laws, and theories. Most of the extras are taught implicitly, often by what is *not* stated. Students are taught about power and authority, for example. They are taught what knowledge, and what kind of knowledge, is worth knowing and whether they can master it. They are taught how to regard themselves in relation to both natural and technologically devised

objects and events, and with what demeanor to regard those very objects and events. (ix, emphasis in original)

The messages that "function as both context and subtext" (Roberts and Ostman 1998, ix) in a curriculum, whether they are deliberately inserted or unmarked elements of the cultural background, are companion meanings.

What could it mean to cultivate *queer* companion meanings? Queer companion meanings in science (teacher) education would expose and resist heteronormative and other problematic cultural norms of knowing and being. With these norms in clear view and exposed to critique, science education would explore how certain claims and practices come to be defined as scientific; how boundaries between science and other ways of knowing are drawn and redrawn, by whom, and why; the implications of these processes of knowledge production for students' understandings of themselves and the world; and the possibilities for transforming science and one's self by drawing from diverse standpoints, experiences, and interests (Barton 1998; Tierney 1997). Companion meanings in a queer science curriculum might include that knowledge is created in relations, not contained in books; qualities like "normal" and "natural" are read into nature, not reflections of it; and unity and diversity in the world need not be reduced to norms and deviations. We envision a queer science (teacher) education as open-ended, unpredictable, resistant to rationalizing accountability schemes, more about divergence than convergence, and more about production than transmission. When science teachers (of any sexuality) enact queer sensibilities they broaden what is acceptable to think and become in their classrooms (Tierney 1997) and open the curriculum to diverse identifications for recognition and re-cognition by students (Britzman 1995; Sumara and Davis 1998).

CODA: WHAT HAPPENED NEXT?

We conclude with descriptions of where we have come and gone since the events described in this chapter.

Lee

There was more to my experiences as a student teacher than we describe here. I had as many good days as bad ones, so I would not say that I was "scared away" from teaching. But the events we discuss and others like them strongly influenced my thinking following student teaching. I wanted a work environment where I could freely express myself to co-workers, an environment that high school teaching did not seem to offer.

I also began to question the nature of science, the field I had studied and been devoted to for many years. I was initially attracted to science because it seemed to be based on facts, logical processes, and predictable outcomes. I was intrigued by the mysteries of science and excited by the search for unwavering knowledge. I thought I could be secure in the truth and value of the facts, content, and skills I learned and would someday teach to my students. After student teaching, I began to see science as a social construction that is not isolated from the outside world. The scientific "facts" I taught about were not as reliable as I once thought. I felt like a hypocrite when the subject matter I taught to students questioned, devalued, and denied the credibility of my sexual orientation. I briefly pursued a master's degree in science education, hoping to augment my teaching skills while I sorted through the issues of coming out. But my experiences at the university as a resident assistant and residence hall director drew my interest more than secondary science education.

I am now enrolled in a graduate program in student affairs and higher education administration, and I work as an intern in an lgbt student services office. In this setting cultural diversity is valued and it is much easier to be out in the workplace. I enjoy working with students as they learn to critically examine what they have been taught about themselves and others. I am still fascinated by biology and I sometimes tutor students in the sciences. But given the current realities of high school teaching, a career in undergraduate student affairs is more appealing.

Steve

Visions of education are easier to sketch as text on a page than to realize in classroom practices. In my work with future science teachers I continue to explore how to frame equity and multicultural perspectives on science in ways that recognize lgbt lives and challenge hegemonic common sense. The year after Lee's experiences, I invited a panel of undergraduates from our campus lgbt student organization to speak in my student teaching seminar. The panelists discussed basic concepts about gender, sexuality, and homophobia, and shared stories of their experiences as gay, lesbian, and bisexual youth. One of the student teachers that semester, who identified as bisexual, joined the panel to share stories with her peers. Most of the student teachers seemed to appreciate what they heard, but several of them complained that they had already taken a multicultural education course and that the seminar was supposed to be about how to teach science. This is the sort of reaction I used to fear, precisely because it brings to the fore the nature of my relationships with students and their judgments of my teaching. Lately, however, I have come to embrace students' resistance to transgressions of hegemonic common sense as the seeds of reflection, critique, and reformulation. Both opportunities and challenges emerge when comfortable thinking is unsettled.

Two aspects of the lgbt student panel strike me as particularly pedagogically significant and vexing. First, as an isolated event, an lgbt panel presentation is an "add lgbt and stir" approach to multicultural science education (Letts and Fifield 2000; chapter 9). Although we need to hear more from and about lgbt students and teachers in science education, it is important to resist the urge to treat lgbt and other diversity identifiers as fixed categories that mark particular bodies and lives. Dennis Carlson (1998) is concerned by the tendency in multicultural education to reduce identity "to neat categories that can be represented in terms of identifiable lifestyles, images and beliefs" (111). By following such a prescription, he fears, "multiculturalism may have the ironic effect of reinforcing inequalities by making the Other more visible as the Other" (Carlson 1998, 114). To better appreciate lgbt lives and queer perspectives in science (teacher) education, we should engage understandings of cultural diversity and personal identities as unfixed, multidimensional, historically and spatially contingent, and awash in power relations (Kincheloe and Steinberg 1997).

Second, my reliance on the lgbt panel raises questions about my subject position as a (gay) science teacher educator. I have come out to several students individually, but never to an entire class. Although a good deal of literature in lgbt pedagogy treats coming out to students as the means to an authentic voice and empowerment for teachers and students, I am intrigued by the pedagogical possibilities of embracing multiple, ambiguous classroom identities. As Susan Talburt (2000) reminds us, coming out in the classroom consists of many ongoing and situated acts that can be read in different and contested ways. Coming out in the classroom is no guarantee that students will interpret one's voice and identity as one intends, nor does it *necessarily* serve the educational goal of "encouraging alternative forms of thought and practice" (Talburt 2000, 130). Coming out entails *being* placed and read by others, as well as *claiming* a place and a voice for one's self. I used the lgbt panel presentation to invite students to implicate *themselves* in heteronormative practices and to envision alternative ways to understand the relations of students, teachers, and the science curriculum. But what privileges do I exercise and what opportunities do I forfeit when I attempt to fade into the background? I used the bodies of the panelists rather than my own; their pleasure, pain, and identities were at work and at risk in my classroom, while I sat among the "us" and listened to the "others." In what ways do I sustain regressive classroom practices when I limit my transgressions to novel curriculum *topics* in the absence of radically embodied *pedagogies* (hooks 1994)?

The problem and promise of embodied pedagogies return us to the interwoven and evolving relations of identity and knowledge. Heteronormativity limits who students and teachers can be and what they can know. As Gillian Spraggs (1994) said so nicely, what teachers offer students, and what students make of those gifts, is enriched by the freedom to create knowledges and identities that exceed the normal:

> Successful teaching in any subject is a kind of performance art. As with all artists, your basic material is yourself and your experience: what you have learned and tested and explored. It is an interpretive art; you are offering your students ways of setting about the task of interpreting and reinventing the world they find around them. To hide what you have learned, about yourself, about possible ways of living, in contexts where it is relevant to what students wish to know, need to know—that feels deeply irresponsible. (181)

NOTES

We dedicate this chapter to the memory of Dr. Steven James Rakow, a friend, scholar, and teacher who is dearly missed. We would like to thank Nancy Brickhouse, Christian Calaguas, Zoubeida Dagher, Danielle Ford, William Letts, Steve Rosenberg, Kathryn Scantlebury, and Betty Wier for helpful feedback on earlier drafts of this chapter. Steve thanks Kit for coming out East.

1. *Phagocytosis* is a process by which cells ingest materials. An organism is genetically *homozygous* if it has two identical copies of a particular gene. The chromosomes of sexually-reproducing organisms typically occur in *homologous* pairs.

REFERENCES

Apple, M. 2000. *Official knowledge: Democratic education in a conservative age.* 2d ed. New York: Routledge.

Bailey, B. L., K. Scantlebury, and W. J. Letts IV. 1997. It's not my style: Using disclaimers to ignore gender issues in science. *Journal of Teacher Education* 48 (1): 29–36.

Barton, A. C. 1998. *Feminist science education.* New York: Teachers College Press.

Britzman, D. 1995. Is there a queer pedagogy? Or, stop reading straight. *Educational Theory* 45 (2): 151–65.

Carlson, D. 1998. Who am I? Gay identity and a democratic politics of the self. In *Queer theory in education*, edited by W. F. Pinar, 107–19. Mahwah, N.J.: Lawrence Erlbaum.

Colleary, K. 1999. How teachers understand gay and lesbian content in the elementary social studies curriculum. In *Queering Elementary Education: Advancing the dialogue about sexualities and schooling*, edited by W. J. Letts and J. T. Sears, 151–61. Lanham, Md.: Rowman & Littlefield.

Colt, G. H. 1998. Were you born that way? *Life* 21 (4, April): 38–42, 44, 46, 48–49.

Epstein, D., ed. 1994. *Challenging lesbian and gay inequalities in education*. Buckingham, UK: Open University Press.

Epstein, D., and R. Johnson. 1994. On the straight and the narrow: The heterosexual presumption, homophobias and schools. In *Challenging lesbian and gay inequalities in education*, edited by D. Epstein, 197–230. Buckingham, UK: Open University Press.

Fausto-Sterling, A. 2000. *Sexing the body: Gender politics and the construction of sexuality*. New York: Basic Books.

Harris, M. B. 1997. *School experiences of gay and lesbian youth: The invisible minority*. New York: Harrington Park Press.

hooks, b. 1994. *Teaching to transgress: Education as the practice of freedom*. New York: Routledge.

Ingraham, C. 1994. The heterosexual imagery: Feminist sociology and theories of gender. *Sociological Theory* 12 (2): 203–19.

Jagose, A. 1996. *Queer theory: An introduction*. New York: New York University Press.

Kincheloe, J. L., and S. R. Steinberg. 1997. *Changing multiculturalism*. Buckingham, UK: Open University Press.

Lave, J., and E. Wenger. 1991. *Situated learning: Legitimate peripheral participation*. Cambridge, UK: Cambridge University Press.

Leck, G. M. 1999. Afterword. In *Queering elementary education: Advancing the dialogue about sexualities and schooling,* edited by W. J. Letts and J. T. Sears, 257–62. Lanham, Md.: Rowman & Littlefield.

Letts, W. J. 1999. How to make "boys" and "girls" in the classroom: The heteronormative nature of elementary-school science. In *Queering Elementary Education: Advancing the dialogue about sexualities and schooling,* edited by W. J. Letts and J. T. Sears, 97–110. Lanham, Md.: Rowman & Littlefield.

Letts, W. J., and S. Fifield. 2000. Sexualities, silence, and science teacher education. Paper presented at the meeting of the American Educational Research Association, April, New Orleans, Louisiana.

Letts, W. J., and J. T. Sears, eds. 2000. *Queering elementary education: Advancing the dialogue about sexualities and schooling.* Lanham, Md.: Rowman & Littlefield.

Levinson, B. A., and D. Holland. 1996. The cultural production of the educated person: An introduction. In *The cultural production of the educated person: Critical ethnographies of schooling and local practice,* edited by B.A. Levinson, D. E. Foley, and D. C. Holland, 1–54. Albany: State University of New York Press.

Levinson, B. A., D. E. Foley, and D. C. Holland. 1996. *The cultural production of the educated person: Critical ethnographies of schooling and local practice*. Albany: State University of New York Press.

Luhmann, S. 1998. Queering/querying pedagogy? Or, pedagogy is a pretty queer thing. In *Queer theory in education,* edited by W. F. Pinar, 141–55. Mahwah, N.J.: Lawrence Erlbaum.

Murray, A. 1995. Femme on the streets, butch in the sheets (a play on whores). In *Mapping desire: Geographies of sexualities,* edited by D. Bell and G. Valentine, 66–74. London: Routledge.

Nayak, A., and M. J. Kehily. 1997. Masculinities and schooling: Why are young men so homophobic? In *Border patrols: Policing the boundaries of heterosexuality,* edited by D. L. Steinberg, D. Epstein, and R. Johnson, 138–61. London: Cassell.

Nobles, C., and W. Letts. 2000. Queering science education? You don't say. Paper presented at the meeting of the National Association for Research in Science Teaching, April, New Orleans, Louisiana.

Pinar, W. F., ed. 1998. *Queer theory in education.* Mahwah, N.J.: Lawrence Erlbaum.

Redman, P., and M. Mac an Ghaill. 1997. Educating Peter: The making of a history man. In *Border patrols: Policing the boundaries of heterosexuality,* edited by D. L. Steinberg, D. Epstein, and R. Johnson, 162–82. London: Cassell.

Roberts, D. A., and L. Ostman. 1998. Preface. In *Problems of meaning in science curriculum,* edited by D. A. Roberts and L. Ostman, ix–xii. New York: Teachers College Press.

Scantlebury, K. 1994. Emphasizing gender issues in the undergraduate preparation of science teachers: Practicing what we preach. *Journal of Women and Minorities in Science and Engineering* 1: 153–64.

———. 1995. Challenging gender blindness in preservice secondary science teachers. *Journal of Science Teacher Education* 6: 134–42.

Scantlebury, K., E. Johnson, S. Lykens, R. Clements, S. Gleason, and R. Lewis. 1996. Beginning the cycle of equitable teaching: The pivotal role of cooperating teachers. *Research in Science Education* 26 (3): 271–82.

Schiebinger, L. 1993. *Nature's body: Gender in the making of modern science.* Boston: Beacon Press.

Sears, J. T. and W. L. Williams. 1997. *Overcoming heterosexism and homophobia: Strategies that work.* New York: Columbia University Press.

Sedgwick, E. K. 1990. *The epistemology of the closet.* Berkeley: University of California Press.

Spraggs, G. 1994. Coming out in the National Union of Teachers. In *Challenging lesbian and gay inequalities in education,* edited by D. Epstein, 179–96. Buckingham, UK: Open University Press.

Steinberg, D. L., D. Epstein, and R. Johnson, eds. 1997. *Border patrols: Policing the boundaries of heterosexuality.* London: Cassell.

Sumara, D., and B. Davis. 1998. Telling tales of surprise. In *Queer theory in education,* edited by W. F. Pinar, 197–219. Mahwah, N.J.: Lawrence Erlbaum.

Talburt, S. 2000. *Subject to identity: Knowledge, sexuality and academic practices in higher education.* Albany: State University of New York Press.

Tierney, W. G. 1997. *Academic outlaws: Queer theory and cultural studies in the academy.* Thousand Oaks, Calif.: Sage.

Wenger, E. 1998. *Communities of practice: Learning, meaning, and identity.* Cambridge, UK: Cambridge University Press.

15

"I Was Afraid He Would Label Me Gay if I Stood up for Gays": The Experience of Lesbian and Gay Elementary Education Credential Candidates at a Rural State University

Eric Rofes

For more than twenty years since I graduated from college, I have lived in urban gay neighborhoods. In Boston, I moved from Beacon Hill to the South End, then lived in Provincetown, an old fishing village and art colony on Cape Cod, now a gay tourist center. I migrated west to California in 1985, first as close as I could afford to live to West Hollywood, then to San Francisco's Castro district, often considered the nation's premier gay ghetto.

Hence many of my gay friends consider it odd, even ironic, that I now inhabit a small cottage deep in the redwoods, outside a small town of 300 residents on the North Coast of California. What can I say? The tenure-track job offer that came my way after I completed my Ph.D. came from a rural state university, 300 miles north of San Francisco, not far from the Oregon border.

I still maintain a foothold in gay community, as I spend several weekends a month and summer vacation in San Francisco, where I maintain a home (and a lover) a few yards from the intersection of 18th and Castro, seen nationally as the crossroads of the gay community. Yet as I enter my second year teaching at Humboldt State University (HSU), I recognize that my appreciation for this part of rural California has deepened, as I become accustomed to the clean air, farm land, huge redwoods, and miles of deserted beaches along the Pacific coast. Although the university town of Arcata (population 16,000) is politically progressive, environmentally pristine, and somewhat yuppified, the nearby city of Eureka (population 24,000) and the surrounding villages, towns, and hamlets have not shared in the economic boom that much of California enjoys. Humboldt County is sparsely populated, but the people who are here are primarily poor white

folk and struggling Native American people, including many former log-
ging families, whose livelihoods have disappeared over the past twenty
years, along with the lumber companies that once reigned supreme.

During my first year at HSU, I was one of four full-time professors teaching in the elementary education credential program. About 110 students took
the requisite coursework, including my foundations course, "The School and
the Student," and completed their student teaching primarily in rural and
small town schools in the area. I had been hired with a curriculum vitae containing the words "gay" and "lesbian" at least a dozen times, and the department chair, during our one-on-one interview, indicated that my work on gay
issues in schools was something they'd welcome in the department. She was
aware that teachers in K–12 schools throughout California have to deal with
homophobic hallway slurs; the bullying of gender nonconforming children
and teens; and the presence of openly gay parents, students, and faculty
members in school communities. One of her hopes was that I would serve as
a resource for lesbian, gay, and bisexual (lgb) credential students who might
face the challenge of merging their sexual identities with their new role as
teachers.

During my first year on campus, I became aware of the complex challenges
these credential candidates faced. At a reception for lgb students and faculty
during the first week of classes, I was delighted to see one of my students,
Gina, who seemed equally delighted to see me there. Gina told me that, while
she was comfortably out of the closet on campus and in her social life, she
was cautiously discreet in her work as a recreation administrator in a nearby
town. I couldn't imagine how, in small town Humboldt County, Gina was
able to keep her identities separate.

A few weeks later, when I casually discussed my own gay identity as I was
teaching a lesson on multicultural education, I received an e-mail from Buzz,
one of my students, who expressed elation at finally having an openly gay
professor and seized the opportunity to come out to me. Yet because Buzz
was considering seeking jobs in schools in the local area, he did not want his
identity as a gay man to become widely known among HSU faculty or credential students. Again, Buzz was openly gay among his friends and had been
a member of the HSU gay student group during his undergraduate years, but
the move toward becoming an elementary teacher necessitated a reconsider-
ing of how to manage his sexual identity.

Of the 110 students, only Gina and Buzz came out to me before the very
end of the term. After classes had ended, two other women came out privately
to me, one as lesbian and one as bisexual. Yet as I went through the year with
Gina and Buzz, I began to feel that the lack of formal or informal support
mechanisms within our credential program left lgb students vulnerable to an

extra heap of stress on top of an already demanding credential year, and might play a role in some students' decision to drop out before receiving a credential or to never apply for jobs in the field. As our year together came to a close, I surveyed Gina and Buzz about the issues that emerged for them during their time in our program.

"I'M TOTALLY FRIGHTENED ABOUT COMING OUT IN MY FIRST JOB"

Gina entered our credential program as a thirty-eight-year-old woman who had been in Humboldt County for six years. She had worked for a number of years as an administrator for parks and recreation for a small rural town. Prior to coming to the area, Gina had lived in San Francisco—in the same neighborhood in which my partner and I live. Originally from the Los Angeles area, at the time I met Gina she seemed strong and secure in her lesbian identity and was an articulate advocate for social justice issues.

In the survey, Gina noted that her experience in the credential program "simply mirrored real life, where I feel somewhat like an outsider." She went on: "Most of my classmates were very supportive and gracious, however, some were taken aback." Gina came out to her mentor teacher during the fall semester, and, on the survey, indicated that she did so, "because I knew he was cool." At the same time, she insisted, "I will not come out to my spring master teacher, as she seems a little more conservative. I didn't come out to any students and don't plan on doing so."

Gina felt the credential program could have been strengthened for her by allowing "more discussion on the issue of gay teachers in public schools." She explained:

> The only courses that dealt with gay issues were your class and also multicultural education. We read a clip on gay issues in schools in that course and watched *It's Elementary* and had a good discussion afterward. It wasn't necessarily helpful but it turned out to be very emotional for me. The video was hard to watch. I felt condemned and abnormal.

She noted, "I would have liked to know more about where people stand on this issue, and what the Humboldt County climate is like on gay issues." At the same time, she felt supported by my presence as an openly gay instructor, and wrote, "It felt most helpful to have you as a really strong, confident gay instructor. I thought it was great how comfortable you were discussing issues and coming out to the class. It made me feel less alone, less different."

When asked about suggestions to improve our credential program's support for lgb students, Gina wrote:

> I envision all classes addressing the issue openly and embracing all student teacher candidates. They should make a point of welcoming gay/straight/bisexual students from the very beginning. All classes should address the issue in one way or another. They should acknowledge how scary a teaching job can be for lgb people in this society.

Another question on the survey asked, "Can you relate one story of an incident where you felt your sexual identity had an impact on your work with kids this year?" Gina responded:

> There was one incident where an eighth-grade boy called someone a "fag" and I really wanted to reprimand him but I chickened out because I was too afraid that he would label me gay if I stood up for gays. I felt lousy afterward for not voicing my opinion and not feeling strong enough to do it.

Gina's fears about reprimanding the boy surfaced again when she discussed feelings about her potential teaching career. "I'm totally frightened about coming out in my first teaching job," Gina wrote. "I fear retribution from parents mostly. I will probably keep it quiet and only tell people that I know I can trust."

After graduating from our credential program, Gina did not seek full-time teaching jobs in the area. Instead, she spent her first year working in local recreation programs and serving as a substitute teacher in local schools. When I checked in with her one year after completing the program and inquired about whether she was applying for full-time teaching positions, Gina told me, "Teaching is less of a focus now. I think I have finally decided *not* to teach but to continue to substitute to earn extra money. I don't feel that teaching will allow me to fully be myself, and that is very important to me." She went on to explain, "I don't want to hide who I am and I know that I will have to, to some extent. . . . I don't want to have to hide my true sexuality."

"I DID NOT WANT SOMEONE TO FIND OUT WHO COULD HINDER MY PROGRESS IN THE PROGRAM"

Buzz is younger than Gina, entering our credential program directly from his undergraduate years, at age twenty-two. He grew up in a small town near Sacramento, and began to take on a gay identity during his college years. Although a member of HSU's gay student group during that time, Buzz does not see himself as an activist or a political person. His greatest interest, on arriving in the program, was to find a job as a first grade teacher.

When Buzz responded to the survey, he had been in the credential program for about eight months and lamented that

> I know only one other person [in the program] who is gay besides myself. This has been challenging because I am afraid of what people might think of a gay person becoming a teacher. I think a lot of my fears of being out in the program stem from stereotypes that I have heard, such as all gay people being child molesters. I was very careful about who I shared my sexuality with because I did not want someone to find out who could hinder my progress in the program.

Buzz cited only one course during the credential year that addressed gay issues, the multicultural foundations class. (Apparently he was absent from my class during our discussions of gay issues.) Buzz expressed concern that gay issues were "one of the last things we talked about in class, and it was only given one class period." At the time, Buzz recalls being "upset" because the students were working on group projects at the time and the professor limited student discussion of their projects to show a video on gay issues and then lead a discussion. Still, Buzz was "very glad that at least one person covered the topic."

Buzz recalled the class:

> I feel the professor dealt with the topic in a very respectful manner. The video we watched gave us many examples of schools educating their students about homophobia and families other than the traditional family. The professor gave us phone numbers and addresses of places which could provide us with the information we might need as future teachers to get materials on gay issues. We also talked in class about what advice you would give to a student teacher wanting to come out to a panel who was interviewing for a position. The discussion gave me a lot of insight about how future teachers felt about homosexuality. I did not hear one negative comment the whole time, which made me feel good.

In Buzz's fall placement in a first grade classroom at a middle class school, he quickly developed friendly relationships with many of the staff. As Buzz explained on the survey:

> One particular day the school secretary asked me if I had a girlfriend. I told her that I did not, but I did not feel it was necessary to tell her why I did not have a girlfriend. She immediately tried to hook me up with the other secretary's daughter. From that day on, every time I saw her, she asked me if I had given this person a call yet. The secretary would say things such as "she is really pretty" and "she has a good job." I told her that I did not have time for a girl-

friend because the program keeps me so busy. As much as I wanted to tell her I was gay to get her off my back, I was afraid that it would be a problem with me working at the school and that it could cause me to be asked to leave.

Buzz's spring placement was in a fifth/sixth grade class in a working class neighborhood of Eureka, the closest thing to an urban center in the county. One day, while he was working with a small group of students, a girl told Buzz that a boy in the class—Bobby—had been saying things about Buzz. Buzz noted, "As soon as she said this, I knew what he was saying." He prodded the girl a bit and she told him that Bobby was telling other students that Buzz was gay. Buzz explains:

I told my master teacher that this child was saying things about me and the three of us were soon in the hall having a discussion. The teacher told Bobby that we had heard some rumors being spread about me. When I told him what I heard, he denied it and said that he meant that I was gay as in "happy." The teacher told him that she did not buy it. She talked to him about why he was saying this and how he would feel if someone were saying it about him. Then she looked at Bobby and said, "he is NOT gay." At this point I cringed, because I am gay, and I felt like I had indirectly lied to him. My reasoning behind telling her was to get the rumor to stop. Though I feel this boy just happened to be a good guesser, or maybe he picked up on some of my nurturing qualities, which make anyone a candidate for being gay, I don't think this was backed with any knowledge of my sexuality. I worried that this rumor would get home to a parent and that I would find myself in the principal's office discussing it. At this point in my life I feel that I would not deny the fact that I am gay if I were asked point blank.

Clearly this incident produced a great deal of stress for Buzz. Not only did he have to deal with being the focus of a highly charged rumor circulating among his students, but he faced an ethical dilemma about whether to tell his mentor teacher that she was incorrect in asserting that he is not gay. Buzz had to weigh his supportive relationship with the teacher against the fact that her written recommendation would be key to his job application process in the coming months.

In his responses to the survey, Buzz reflected on the impact of his gay identity on his teaching career:

I feel that being gay might affect my teaching career in many ways. One thing I think of is having to not tell the truth about my personal life, such as having to lie about what I did on the weekend, or to just not tell the whole story. I wonder how many years I will have to teach before I could bring someone I was dating to a staff party or other extra-curricular event without fear of losing my job.

I wonder how I will know if it is safe or not to tell certain members of the staff about my sexuality. I wonder what the reaction would be if I were ever found out by a parent and how they would feel about their child having a gay teacher. I wonder what the children would think if I ever came out to the class.

Buzz landed a teaching position a month or so after filling out this survey and before completing the credential program. He is now teaching in a fourth grade classroom in a suburban district outside of San Francisco. I checked in with Buzz after winter vacation to get an update on how his first year of teaching was going and how he was dealing with issues related to identity management. I learned that Buzz had a class of twenty-five students and that he was feeling most successful with classroom management and lesson planning. He said he was working to improve in the areas of developing students' critical thinking and promoting fairness and respect, especially related to racism and stereotypes.

When I asked him whether he had come out to anyone at the school; whether the school dealt with gay issues at all; and whether he had found himself in any identity management predicaments with students, parents, fellow teachers, or the principal, he told me:

When I first started at this school I did not think I would have the courage to come out to anyone. It seemed like a place where people kept to themselves and didn't speak much of family or outside interests. As the time went on I was feeling the pressure of keeping my private life out of the picture completely. I told one of the teachers at my grade level that I was gay, and she seemed to take it all right. She had confided in me about certain aspects of her life which she did not want to make public, so I considered it a fair trade. We have worked closely together since then and I feel my honesty has helped our friendship.

Buzz also made a pleasant discovery after being on the job for just a little while. He explained, "I also found out that one of the teachers I work with is also gay, but it took me a few months to approach the subject. He introduced me to his partner and we have been out a few times. It is a wonderful feeling to know that I am not the only person who is gay at the school, and also great to have some support from someone who has been in my shoes."

When I contacted Buzz at the end of his first year as a teacher, he remained committed to the profession and told me, "I have had a rather difficult year, having been put in charge of numerous problem students. Even with this, I still love my job and could see myself doing this for the rest of my life." Part of Buzz's contentment with teaching involves his decision to seek employment in the San Francisco Bay area. He reflected, "I wanted to live in a place where gay people were generally more accepted than in other locations. To this day, I know I made the right decision. Many of the people with whom I work that I told my secret to, are very accepting."

CREATING TEACHER PREPARATION
PROGRAMS THAT TRULY SUPPORT LGB CANDIDATES

Gina and Buzz had two distinct experiences in our program, but together, they served as catalysts for my rethinking of both my role as an openly gay professor in a teacher preparation program and my perspectives on the obligations teacher education programs have toward their lgb students. Through my work with Gina and Buzz, first as their professor and then as the university supervisor for their spring field placements, I came to believe that credential programs must do more to support the success of their lgb students than simply hire an openly gay professor. Regardless of whether gay professors are on their faculty, credential programs need to offer formal support services, bring about policy changes in local districts, and conduct anti-homophobia education with all faculty and staff members within the university, along with superintendents, principals, faculty members, and parents in the local district schools.

Gina and Buzz's survey responses did not only trigger my pragmatic, activist impulses—they brought out a powerful emotional response. Confronting the contradictions and distresses of my students inspired similar feelings in me. How can I be an openly gay professor and allow such conditions to continue? Don't I have a responsibility to ensure that students preparing to become teachers face neither interpersonal discrimination nor barriers to employment based on sexual orientation? Ultimately, I felt disheartened by the huge work still ahead; after twenty-five years as a gay activist I was confronting mountains that still needed to be moved. Part of my frustration involved the realization that even as an openly gay professor who feels that his own identity struggle has reached a place of peace, there are continuing complications, confusions, and contradictions. When I hear my own lgb students' anxieties and fears, I see myself a quarter century ago. When will this struggle end?

Once I became fully aware of the conflicts facing lgb candidates, I organized a special support evening aimed at bringing these folks together (they were isolated from one another and most were unaware of other lgb candidates) and introduced them to local lgb educators. Organizing this event in April, with barely a month left in the program, proved to be a challenge. Not only was this an especially busy time for the students, but most students had determined months ago that they were best off keeping their identities quiet. If coaxing students to the meeting was difficult, the greater challenge was identifying and contacting local lgb educators and convincing them to meet with the lgb credential students. I did my best to network widely to find out where the local gay educators worked, but, because most of them are closeted, I could only convince three lesbian educators to meet with the candidates.

In May, I took on the leadership of the elementary education credential program and acknowledged to myself that I felt a special obligation to lgb students that extended beyond simply being openly gay as a professor. Over the summer, I talked with colleagues in other credential programs, contacted my just-credentialed lgb students, and thought deeply about the way to proceed. This year I have instituted three formal additions to our department's work with credential students in any of our four credential programs (elementary, secondary, special education, administrative):

First, I planned and organized a meeting for lgb credential candidates at the start of the semester. This was announced at the opening meetings of our programs and signs were posted throughout the department. Over a dozen students in three of our four credential programs contacted me (there are about 210 credential students in the programs), and eight attended our first meeting. We formed a monthly support group, called the Supper Club, and determined that we'd meet regularly, informally, over dinner to swap stories and lend support.

Second, I organized and will teach an elective course this spring titled "Gay and Lesbian Issues in Schools." Although I am uncertain whether credential students will have the time or inclination to take an extra course given their already-intense workloads, I am hoping that the students with the greatest need for work in this area will at least be able to drop in to occasional classes. The course will also be open to undergraduate students—many of whom are considering entering a fifth-year credential program after getting their bachelor's—as well as master's students and folks from local schools.

Third, I met with my department chair and strategized about ways to effect policy changes in local districts. We both agreed that we could face a difficult dilemma. Whereas our university does not allow us to discriminate against students on the basis of sexual orientation, many of the local districts do not have parallel policies. What would have happened if Buzz had been asked directly by his fourth grade student if he was gay and he had answered honestly? What would our department's policy be if a school or a district tried to bar openly lgb student teachers from fieldwork opportunities? Would we screen candidates on the basis of sexual orientation and send the gay ones to selected sites? Would we refuse to send any additional student teachers to the district?

These seem to be critical questions during a time when even rural schools are confronting gay issues at an accelerating rate. At an anti-homophobia training I facilitated recently for local educators, a local high school teacher discussed a gay male senior who brought a male date to last year's prom and another situation in which he had to break up two girls who were smooching in the hallway and were late for class. An administrator from an isolated rural school discussed her difficulties locating credentialled teachers for her two schools and her fears of parental concerns if she wooed a local unemployed lesbian teacher to come to work for her district. A basketball coach discussed his handling of a conflict that arose when a star player's cheerleader girlfriend discovered her beau was having an affair with a male soccer player.

As my department chair prepares to raise the matter with local educational leaders, the constraints of being a rural state university become clear. We do not have the luxury of a surplus of field placements, as most urban districts have. If we eliminated districts that discriminate against lgb student teachers from inclusion on our list of field placements, we might not have enough placements to run our program. Likewise, it is unclear how local lgb citizens would feel about our department championing this matter. Many local closeted teachers seem to prefer that things remain unstated and unorganized. Urban schools situated in cities with organized gay communities have had to face gay issues head-on when gay political groups screen candidates for school boards on a range of gay-related matters.

As the focus of gay rights battles shifts from the urban gay enclaves I've lived in for twenty years to rural towns like the one in which I am now situated, I am sure the stark contrasts between urban schools and rural schools will create an entire new range of challenges, activist strategies, and, eventually, successes. Rural schools, for the most part, have rarely faced gay activists or others making demands that schools address homophobia and create antidiscrimination policies. At the same time, there are support programs structured on the gay-straight alliance model in three of our area high schools. An openly lesbian professor sits on a local school board. Eureka is home to our county's gay community center, where a support group for lgb youth meets weekly. Progress on gay issues in schools has started to take place, even in isolated, rural parts of our nation. Success will come when we fully welcome lgb students into our teacher preparation programs, support their struggles to manage their sexual identity along with their teacher identity, and ensure that employment discrimination is fully ended in our nation. These are daunting but necessary tasks as we look to the future.

16

Teacher Educators and the Multicultural Closet: The Impact of Gay and Lesbian Content on an Undergraduate Teacher Education Seminar

James R. King and Roger Brindley

Current calls for multicultural education and other forms of diversity within education culture often stop short of the gay and lesbian ghetto. Although educating our students about diversity currently occupies a healthy position in most undergraduate teacher education programs, little writing on the issue of gay and lesbian inclusion has appeared in the professional literature (cf. Letts and Sears 2000). This chapter examines the failure of multicultural education to include sexual orientation, and more specifically, teachers' interaction with students who are gay, or who come from a gay or lesbian home life. From our perspectives, there appears little direction for professors who intend to explore gay and lesbian lives in professional education contexts. The two authors of this chapter are professors of elementary education. The first, King, taught the seminar that is examined in this chapter, and is the "I" who appears throughout it. The second author, Brindley, was a professional confidante during the seminar and subsequently translated the events of the seminar into relationships with teacher education literature.

The present emphasis on multicultural education in teacher preparation programs emanates from an increasingly diverse society, where the vast majority of teacher candidates are white, middle class, monolingual, and heterosexual females (Ladson-Billings 1995; Scott 1995). This imbalance has caused enormous tension for teacher educators, many of whom work on the assumption that to understand the "whole child" each teacher must respect the life experiences and worldview that the child brings to the classroom. If we accept that learners construct their own knowledge within sociocultural contexts (Cobb 1994), then it is vital for teachers to help children situate their own learning in personally meaningful and relevant ways. This philosophical perspective has driven the present multicultural reform in teacher education programs.

The very essence of multicultural education is political. Powerful initiatives have focused on ethnic and racial disparities and the role of education in addressing these inequalities. The work of Banks, McLaren, and Sleeter, among others, reveals a progression from gender bias and equal opportunity within school culture and the wider society, to the role of socioeconomics in the success or failure of the school child, and to the implications for speakers of English as a second and third language. Yet rarely, if ever, has sexual orientation been discussed in the multicultural teacher education literature.

At the same time that multicultural education must object to racism, sexism, and other forms of social intolerance, the multicultural curriculum in our schools continues to focus on holidays and heroes (Banks 1994). In west central Florida in the year 2000, the elementary school multicultural curriculum essentially remains Columbus, Thanksgiving, Martin Luther King, and St. Patrick, or a curriculum of "fun, food, and festivals" (Brice-Heath 2000; Sleeter 1994). This, of course, simply confirms that knowledge is not neutral. The multicultural curriculum is a mirror of the power and social relationships within the larger society (Minnich 1990), and truth is relative to the cultural context and the operative power in the institution (Giroux 1983; McLaren 1989). This phenomenon certainly holds true in teacher education. If teacher educators accept the construct of multiple perspectives, then they must also accept the partiality of knowledge. We each take different meanings based on the "positionality" of our knowledge (McGee-Banks 2000). In light of this sociopolitical milieu, those advocating "equal time" for gay and lesbian perspectives in teacher education invariably find themselves on the outside looking in.

Access is sadly only part of the dilemma. Prospective educators enter programs predisposed toward personal theories of "good" teaching and "good" teachers based on their own life experiences (Bird et al. 1993; Holt-Reynolds 1991), and without having considered issues of cultural inequality (Xu 2000). Yet our preservice teachers *are* insiders, having spent well over twelve years in the educational system where "the reality of their everyday lives continues largely unaffected, as may their beliefs" (Pajares 1992, 232). Teacher educators who want their students to earnestly question their preexisting beliefs must create opportunities for cognitive dissonance (Cochran-Smith and Lytle 1990). Raising the cultural sensitivity of preservice teachers regarding the sexual orientations of their students and their students' families is a considerable challenge (Deering and Stanutz 1995), but culturally relevant pedagogy should be "designed to problematize teaching and encourage teachers to ask about the nature of the student-teacher relationship, the curriculum, schooling and society" (Ladson-Billings 1995, 483).

The purpose of this study was to explore the impact of including gay and lesbian content, theme, and materials in a weekly undergraduate seminar. This intention itself constituted a study of what is meant by "gay and lesbian" and how these constructs might be represented to elementary education majors. These twin questions formed the basis of a semester inquiry. Although both authors share the responsibility for this report, much of the narrative of the study is reported in the first person to reflect the first author's experience.

The students who participated in this study were all junior-level elementary education majors at the University of South Florida, a large, urban, Carnegie I, state university. They were on a team, randomly assembled from entrants into elementary education. By virtue of the team structure, this group of thirty students (twenty-eight female, two male) took all their program course work as an intact group and would continue to do so until their final internship, five semesters later. As the faculty mentor for this team, I taught the weekly seminar that accompanied their first field placement, the Level I internship.

ACTIVITIES

I chose a queer perspective as a thematic approach for the team's weekly seminar. This meant a conscious agenda to understand the world of the classroom, including its students' and teachers' lives, as inclusive of gay and lesbian sexualities. The specific activities used to bring gay and lesbian content into the seminar were constructed with several characteristics in mind. The first was the consistency of the activity with elementary education culture, such as the projected experience that the students and the professor imagine that they will have in classrooms with children. A consistent use of these projected experiences comes to constitute a set of "normal" experiences that the undergraduates are accustomed to having as students in methods courses. A second characteristic for selecting particular activity frames was to represent certain "desirable" perspectives on gay and lesbian lives. This intention requires a certain essentializing of what is meant by gay and lesbian lives, similar to any other reduction of cultural themes used as classroom content. It is an agenda ripe for self-interrogation, which occurs later in this chapter. A third aspect of the chosen activities was a staging for comfort. Activities I perceived as "less threatening" were introduced earlier. Finally, the activities were designed to have a "feed forward" effect. That is, experiences and data from previous activities were available as a base of understanding for subsequent activities. The activities are described as they were ordered in the study.

Activity 1: Parent Conference with Lesbian Couple

I had not announced that we would be discussing gay and lesbian issues prior to introducing a mini-case of a parent conference with the two moms of a troubled child. The students in the seminar reported that they would not change their plans for the conference upon realizing that the parents were a lesbian couple. The focus should remain the child. However, nine students expressed reservations that they did not have the counseling expertise to intervene in the family issues that were part of the vignette, and which might have been affecting the troubled student's school work. I wondered if the same reservations would have been present if a heterosexual couple were having relationship struggles. What if the couple were not married? When we examined the different configurations for "couple" as parents of our students, we found some hesitance to "take on" the teacher's role in relation to gay- or lesbian-headed families. Students reported their discomfort, lack of preparation, and lack of experience in working with same-sex couples in parent-teacher conferences. I took this to mean that if a teacher "is not qualified" to talk about adult relationships, then she certainly can't talk about adult gay relationships. Furthermore, the students maintained that their responses would be the same if the student Jason were instead Janice.

In this first activity, I had chosen to focus on issues that affected the children my undergrads would have as students. I figured that the sexuality of parents would be more palatable to my students if it were included as part of a student-centered problem. My undergraduates agreed with my thinking. Yet we, as authors and also teachers, remain troubled by the very belief that I had planned for and hoped to capture. One student wrote: "Their sexual preference has nothing to do with how you teach their child." We now wonder about the clean separation, about the parts of Jason's life that now have no place in the classroom. Students' responses ranged from "Do not talk about relationships. Drop or change the subject" to "They both showed up—they care!" The separation here could be the same distancing that occurred when the team members agreed that they were not trained as family therapists and therefore were not qualified to talk through some of the family issues that were affecting Jason's classroom behavior.

Activity 2: Politically Active Lesbian Colleague

A second mini-case dealt with a teacher who was planning to teach a gay pride unit to her fifth graders. The question to the team was, would/should they help her in efforts to gain permission to teach the unit? Five students in the seminar stated that they would help; eleven explicitly said that they would not. The resistant comments came in two themes: It is okay to be gay, but not to teach about it (N=3), and sexual orientation is not an okay topic for this age (N=8). Other students (N=7) suggested that any decision would depend on factors at the time of the decision. One student wrote, "I would not sign the letter because to me that means that I support the gay issue. This does not mean that I hate gays. I just do not accept what they believe." I wrote in my notes, "Hate the sin, love the sinner." In contrast, another student wrote:

> If no one stood up for women's rights, I would probably be an uneducated, knocked up "sweetie pie." I was great friends with a gay guy and I would support him in *anything* he did. He opened my eyes to a world I was always told was wrong. He taught me just because it's different don't mean it's wrong. Besides kids are more understanding than adults, so children (5th graders) should be aware of the differences in people. That way they don't become a narrow minded adult.

Another student inadvertently brought up the pervasive heterosexual norm. "I don't feel that sexual orientation should be any part of the curriculum in elementary school, no matter homosexual or heterosexual." Of course, the point of bringing up orientation is to introduce the very notion that difference from heterosexuality is a fact in our students' lives, that that difference is simply okay. As teachers we have a professional responsibility to construct that understanding within our students. For me, this was a clear case of teaching for diversity within classrooms.

Activity 3: Children's Literature

On the third meeting of the seminar, I read *Heather Has Two Mommies* (Newman 1989), *Daddy's Roommate* (Willhoite 1990), and *The Library* (Stewart 1995). I had chosen the first two books because of notoriety stemming from their propensity to suffer censorship, not necessarily for their literary merit. The third book seemed to me to be a subtextual portrayal of a lesbian relationship between older women. With this third book, I wanted to make the point that introduction of gay and lesbian themes could be accomplished more subtly. Inadvertently, I added a dimension to the seminar that would follow throughout the study, that of *indirect representation*. I provided each student with an evaluation form based on a 5-point Likert scale for appropriateness, quality, and usefulness of the three books. The results of the students' post-listening and post-viewing evaluations are presented in the following table:

Students' (N=29) Mean Ratings for Three Children's Books

	Appropriateness	Quality	Use
Heather	2.51	2.79	1.69
Daddy's	3.62	4.28	3.07
Library	4.34	4.79	4.38

Of those students who chose to write commentary, fourteen thought *Heather* had too much detail, was too graphic, and was too inclusive and technical on information about reproductive anatomy and processes. Four students thought colored pictures would be better. The students had few reactions to *Daddy's*. Four students liked the pictures; three thought the relationships were positive; and two thought the approach was a good one, that it was "gentle on students' minds." Seven students maintained that *Library* was not a lesbian story. Five students liked it because it was not blatant, and three students critiqued its stereotypic depiction of spinsters. When asked if they preferred a direct approach (*Heather, Daddy*) or an indirect approach (*Library*), eighteen of the thirty students chose the indirect approach. Two students preferred the more direct approach. Two students wouldn't use any of the materials because of bias regarding "the lifestyle" and "fear of the parents."

Activity 4: Lessons from the Matthew Shepard Tragedy

Matthew Shepard's murder has afforded diverse groups opportunities to take positions regarding his life and death. Yet this very access may also include judgments that do not accept individuals' rights to their own sexual lives. In this activity, the material facts of the Matthew Shepard story are brought into imagined classroom scenarios. The basic underlying question in the activity is, "How would you conduct such classroom talk?" As background information, I also distributed photocopies of the *Miami Herald*'s coverage on two consecutive days, as well as the Gay, Lesbian, and Straight Education Network's (GLSEN) online teaching suggestions for classroom discussions that might be conducted about the Shepard tragedy.

In their written responses and in an intense class discussion, the students agreed that the issue should be discussed but differed in the approaches they would choose. Most of the students in the seminar agreed that talking with their students about Shepard's torture and murder was legitimate. But they would wait until their students brought it up. Comments that revealed self-preservation ("getting into trouble") as well as concern for their students' welfare ("begin with current events they've heard about") were part of the seminar discussion. I learned that it is not possible to know my students' motivations for what they plan without extended talk with them as individuals. It was humbling to relearn for myself something that I was intending to teach to them: the significance of the individual student. More internally, this caused me to wonder to what degree my own sexual orientation "set me up" to view my students' formulations as not good enough. Similarly, to what degree did my status as the "out gay professor" set me up to feel defensive?

Another perspective sheds light on the undergraduates' thinking about including the Shepard case:

> As far as violence of any type is concerned, I feel it is an issue that should and could be addressed. If the discussion with Matthew Shepard turns to his being gay, I would stop the discussion. I strongly believe this topic [his being gay] does not belong in elementary school. It always involves the discussion of sex and I don't want to ever be placed in that position. That is a topic (sex) that we place ourselves in danger of discussing.

Most students focused on their moral outrage at the inhumanity of the crime and disgust at hate crimes, rather than on Shepard's sexuality. Contrast this perspective with those that emerge from the following response:

> I would first tell the students that it is not right in God's eyes to be gay. However, God loves everyone for who he or she is and no one should be murdered over being gay.

In this response, Shepard's sexual orientation will be part of the classroom discussion, but to what end? And how does a teacher say the foregoing and still show compassion for the child? The authors realize and understand that for some people, including some of these students, variation in sexual orientation is understood through a lens of religious prohibition. As such, same-sex events, be they tragedy or comedy, will be colored for their future students with the prohibition. So a discussion of Matthew Shepard might more likely focus on "the crime" and less likely on "the life." However, we find the use of a religious dodge problematic for at least two reasons. First, including one's personal version of religious valuing as part of teaching is simply not professional. Second, it occurred to me that the use of "the religious" might be a disingenuous hedge against dealing with the central issues of homophobia and gay bashing.

Activity 5: Students' Responses to the Shepard Scenario

The next activity was based on the responses that the team had written in the previous week's class on Matthew Shepard's murder. I selected representative quotes for several of the themes that had emerged in the responses. These were typed and presented to the students. Students were asked to provide a written reaction to each of the quotes and then to meet in a small group to discuss the quotes and their reactions, and to synthesize what the small group had learned from the activity. Each small group synthesized their learning on chart paper and shared it with the other class members. Four of the six quotes elicited a range of divergent responses, either agreeing with the quote, reacting oppositely, or taking on the parts that they could agree with and dismissing the parts they couldn't use. The two exceptions, with largely unanimous responses, were quotes two and three. Quote number two that was originally presented to the class was:

> Yes, I do feel we should convene such talk. First, I would tell the students that it's not right in God's eyes to be gay. However, God loves everyone for who he or she is and no one should be murdered over being gay.

Everyone who chose to respond to quote number two (N=12), did so in the same way, in effect saying that they would not bring their religious beliefs into the classroom. I also believe in the separation of church and state. Yet part of me wanted my students to take on the substance of quote number two. My personal need was to see the illogic of quote number two undone in class. Instead, they all used what seemed to us like a safer gambit of "no religion in the classroom." The other quote with a consistent response set was number three, which follows:

> I would explore the violent aspects of this tragedy, but not the sexual aspects. Sexual preference in the classroom does not need to be discussed at this level.

Students were very comfortable with this reasoning. Many used short, affirmative statements to signal their agreement, such as "I feel exactly this way," "Yes, sexual preference does not belong in class—except health," and, "I agree because violence, not sex, needs to be addressed at the elementary school age." One student wrote what I interpreted as a substantively different response:

> Sexual preference needs to be discussed at every level. That is what caused the violence. People at any age should be accepting of everyone, no matter what their differences are. You can talk about sexual preference without talking about sex.

For the most part, the students on the team were more comfortable when they considered talking with their future students about violence than talking about what they perceived as sex or religion.

A TIME OF INDECISION

The reflexive analysis of the students' comments was completed by mid-semester, but during the week that followed several students asked if we (first author and the team) were going to do anything in seminar "besides the gay stuff." I was hurt. I felt as though the "interesting" and "controversial" approach I had taken to teach about diversity was misunderstood. My students, I thought, had only seen a repetitive, self-serving fixation on my part with my own sexuality.

I talked with a colleague who was also teaching this team, but for a different course. My colleague, Jenifer, explained it this way:

> Well, I think that the students get sick of hearing the "gay stuff." They don't want to be force fed. Just like you probably get sick of hearing my arguments against "process writing." Just like I get sick of political advertisements. Just like we are all sick of Monica Lewinsky. People will listen for awhile, then they say, "OK. Let's change the subject." It's not that they don't get it, or that they are against it. They just don't love it as much as you do.

From my perspective, Jenifer's cautions are about how direct I can be when I teach from an agenda. With a direct approach, I can be seen as teaching myself. The intent to purposefully include gay and lesbian lives as a way to operationalize difference and diversity can also be read by students as self-promotion (King and Schneider 2000). Accordingly, I changed the direction of the course to a less direct one. We began to focus on time management, discipline, parent involvement, things that the students were asking for. And with each, I wondered how to make the application for our work (my work) in the first half of the semester.

TEACHERS ARE FILTERS OR CONDUITS

"Gay," "lesbian," "homosexuality," and, more broadly, "difference" were in part defined by the activities and artifacts I introduced into the seminar. What a teacher chooses (or does not choose), why the choice was made, who the teacher is perceived to be while choosing, all become part of the learning. Although at times I am paralyzed by reflecting on these complexities, I do not think such reflection is hopeless or futile. Re-viewing what I thought I was doing, what my students thought I was doing, and what we thought about each other while we learned together are all part of the lesson. My choices are not unlike those that my students made and will make.

I first noticed the filtering I was doing when, as part of the seminar, some of my students began contributing their experiences and stories about gay and lesbian friends and acquaintances. I monitored what I thought was permissible content about gay and lesbian lives brought in through my students' stories. I wanted no information to disrupt or threaten the image I was presenting of myself as the gay professor. This was the point at which I began to reflect on what my definitions of "gay and lesbian" were, and how I represented them to my students as exemplars. A second filter, then, is the "gay professor" I constructed for them. I intended to be casual (rather than formal), to be understated (rather than flamboyant), to be approachable and friendly. What is obvious now is that I was doing the same kind of monitoring of my own person as of what I brought into class. I was simply not aware that I was doing so. This monitoring is not unlike the representation of gay and lesbian identities that the media elects to portray every year as exemplars from the annual gay pride march. Although one can accuse the media of hyperbole, sensationalism, and synecdoche in their formulations of gay = drag queens, and lesbian = dykes on bikes, my monitoring was a similar act. The valency of the monitoring does not change the censuring it engenders. As an "out" and somewhat objectified "token" on my campus, I had experienced this uncomfortable self-awareness before. The added dimension in this case was my position as mentor to my team.

TEACHERS ARE PEOPLE IN TEACHER EDUCATION

In choosing how I wanted to be seen by my students, I carefully constructed an assimilationist view of my life as an "out gay man" and as a "gay professor." I brought my partner, Richard, into class with my (favorable) stories. I invited my students to call into my home life with the mention that if Richard answered the phone, they could leave a message. The significance of this strategy is revealed in its banality. It only becomes strategic in my foregrounding of mine as a "gay household." I purposefully represented us as Ozzie and Ozzie (as contrasted with Ozzie and Harriet, and always sans young Ricky!). I contrasted what I believed to be risky teaching (homosexuality) with unusually rich feedback, conversation, availability, and support during my observations of their classroom teaching with elementary students. I repeatedly appealed to the emerging notion of team building and reminded the students that we would all be together for the next level of internship one year ahead.

THE WIDER IMPLICATIONS FOR TEACHER EDUCATION

The preservice teachers' responses to the gay and lesbian content of the team seminar reveal a great deal about how and what they perceive and presume. Although other themes emerged from their verbal and written comments, three have immediate repercussions for teacher educators.

Power and Privilege

The unique culture of each team of preservice teachers needs to be recognized. In this situation, a group of first semester, junior-year undergraduates in elementary education who had just come together as a team were asked to discuss highly emotive concepts that spoke directly to their personal belief systems. Little wonder that many appeared hesitant to respond earnestly or to show their individual identities within the group culture. As soon as instructors make their opinions on any topic known, they are asking the student who wishes to disagree or give another perspective to take a huge leap of faith. If teacher educators want students to engage their personal beliefs and speak their minds, they must consciously create the right conditions in their classrooms. Students are well aware of who assigns their course grade, and failure to allow for unconditional and supportive discourse will simply result in students "playing the college game" (Bird et al. 1993, 266) and saying what they believe the instructor wants to hear.

In this particular study, power is compounded by the fact that I was sharing deeply held personal beliefs. Despite my efforts to create a caring and secure classroom environment, I *am* gay, and so my comments *were* personal. As such, I took the students' responses personally and was hurt by them. Further, the positionality of my knowledge was problematic. Mine was a privileged political act, and my students knew it. In much the same way that the objectivity and intent of an African American instructor speaking to issues of institutional racial bias in America today can be questioned by his or her students, so the perspectives and intentions of a gay male discussing sexual orientation can be second guessed, or worse, dismissed.

The Professional Obligation of the Teacher

Some of the comments of the team were disturbing to the authors, particularly as they reflected attitudes we see in the wider preservice teacher community.

The team members were able to make neat and tidy separations between their own cultural experiences and experiences of which they had little or no knowledge. We tell preservice teachers that they must get to know each child they teach as an individual. They are exhorted to teach the "whole child" and to assist children as they learn new concepts. They are encouraged to plan for personally meaningful and relevant curriculum delivery. Despite this, the team conversations show preservice teachers interweaving their professional obligation to children with their personal beliefs. So we hear of their intentions to tell children from gay and lesbian home lives that "It's not right in God's eyes to be gay," or of their plan to simply avoid the subject altogether. What will these preservice teachers do when they hear two school children yelling "fag" or "homo" or "dyke" at each other? Will they turn a blind eye? Few on the team seemed to realize that prohibiting gay and lesbian information may undermine the child's relationship with his or her homosexual parent(s). Using a personal opinion may place the teacher directly in conflict with the people the child loves and depends upon for nurturing and care. At least some of the team members failed to analyze where their professional obligations lie in this situation. How do we make gay and lesbian studies relevant and meaningful to the vast majority of our preservice teachers?

Perhaps one way to address these questions would be to explode the myths that emerged from this team. Despite a large body of research that children begin to notice differences in each other and start to build classificatory categories before preschool, one student suggested that young students won't create stereotypes until later years. There also seems to be a simplification of sexual orientation to the physical act of sex. Nowhere do these preservice teachers discuss concepts of caring, love, nurturing, sharing, monogamy, and so forth in their constructions of gays and lesbians. Elsewhere in the student discussions, a student asserted that he wouldn't focus on the treatment of gays and lesbians to highlight man's inhumanity. Rather he would consider the Holocaust. Clearly this student doesn't know of the hundreds of thousands of gays and lesbians murdered before and during World War II by the Nazis. But then why should he? If teachers and teacher educators elect to ignore or dismiss the heinous maltreatment of gays, then these students will never know. The message is simple. We have to actively help preservice teachers to embrace multiple perspectives and to appreciate that their professional obligation to children supersedes their personal opinions.

Fear

This final theme was apparent each time the students tried to situate the gay and lesbian conversation of the seminar in their future classrooms. They are

deeply concerned about the ramifications of raising, or even simply responding to, issues about sexual orientation. They fear the parents, they worry
about what their principal will say and do, and they are anxious about how
their colleagues will respond. In short, they are afraid they will lose their jobs
and possibly ruin their careers. We believe there is a message here for teacher
educators. We are doing preservice teachers a disservice if we emphasize gay
and lesbian perspectives in our coursework without giving them the tools to
apply this knowledge in their classrooms. Do we teach them how to seek
parental permission before reading *Heather Has Two Mommies*? Do we help
them refine and practice their rationale for why they include this content
when, as is inevitable, they are asked? Are we there to support them after they
graduate and need our professional guidance on these issues? Teacher educators need to realize that within our privileged world we are to some degree
safe from censorship. It is too easy to "tell" students what they ought to do
from the safety of the ivory tower. If we truly want to encourage preservice
teachers to create classrooms respectful of sexual orientation and other cultural identities, we have to assist them as they dare to step out of the shadow
of societal norms. After all, we want them to be applauded for their inclusive
approach to teaching, rather than watch them become a target for retribution
as they put their careers on the line.

REFERENCES

Banks, J. 1994. *An introduction to multicultural education.* Boston: Allyn & Bacon.
Bird, T., L. Anderson, B. Sullivan, and S. Swidler. 1993. Pedagogical balancing acts:
    Attempting to influence prospective teachers' beliefs. *Teaching & Teacher Educa-
    tion* 9 (3): 253–67.
Brice-Heath, S. 2000. Multicultural education in the 21st century: Multiple perspec-
    tives on its past, present, and future. Paper presented at the meeting of the Ameri-
    can Educational Research Association, April, New Orleans, Louisiana.
Cobb, P. 1994. Where is the mind? Constructivist and sociocultural perspectives on
    mathematical development. *Educational Researcher* 23 (7): 13–20.
Cochran-Smith, M., and S. Lytle. 1990. Research on teaching and teacher research:
    The issues that divide. *Educational Researcher* 9 (2): 2–11.
Deering, T., and A. Stanutz. 1995. Preservice field experience as a multicultural com-
    ponent of a teacher education program. *Journal of Teacher Education* 46 (5): 390–94.
Giroux, H. 1983. *Theory and resistance in education: A pedagogy for the opposition.*
    New York: Bergin & Garvey.
Holt-Reynolds, D. 1991. *The dialogues of teacher education: Entering and influenc-
    ing preservice teachers' internal conversations.* East Lansing, Mich.: National Cen-
    ter for Research on Teacher Learning.

King, J., and J. Schneider. 2000. Locating a place for gay and lesbian themes in elementary reading, writing, and talking. In *Queering elementary education: Advancing the dialogue about sexualities and schooling,* edited by W. J. Letts and J. T. Sears, 125–36. Lanham, Md.: Rowman & Littlefield.

Ladson-Billings, G. 1995. Toward a theory of culturally relevant pedagogy. *American Educational Research Journal* 32 (3): 465–91.

Letts, W. J., and J. T. Sears, eds. 2000. *Queering elementary education: Advancing the dialogue about sexualities and schooling.* Lanham, Md.: Rowman & Littlefield.

McGee-Banks, C. 2000. Multicultural education in the 21st century: Multiple perspectives on its past, present, and future. Paper presented at the meeting of the American Educational Research Association, April, New Orleans, Louisiana.

McLaren, P. 1989. *Life in schools.* New York: Longman.

Minnich, E. 1990. *Transforming knowledge.* Philadelphia: Temple University Press.

Newman, L. 1989. *Heather has two mommies.* Los Angeles: Alyson Publications.

Pajares, M. 1992. Teachers' beliefs and educational research: Cleaning up a messy construct. *Review of Educational Research* 62 (3): 307–32.

Scott, R. 1995. Reading methods courses: A multicultural perspective. In *Developing multicultural teacher education curricula,* edited by J. Larkin and C. Sleeter, 115–27. Albany: State University of New York Press.

Sleeter, C. 1994. White racism. *Multicultural Education* 1: 5–39.

Stewart, S. 1995. *The library.* New York: Farrar, Straus, Giroux.

Willhoite, M. 1990. *Daddy's roommate.* Boston: Alyson Publications.

Xu, H. 2000. Preservice teachers integrate understandings of diversity into literacy instruction: An adaptation of the ABC's model. *Journal of Teacher Education* 51 (2): 135–42.

17

Can of Worms: A Queer TA in Teacher Ed.

Karleen Pendleton Jiménez

If you can talk to me in ways that show you understand that your knowledge of me, the world, and "the Right thing to do" will always be partial, interested, and potentially oppressive to others, and if I can do the same, then we can work together on shaping and reshaping alliances for constructing circumstances in which students of difference can thrive.

—Ellsworth, "Why Doesn't This Feel Empowering?" 115

Look Karleen, I'll open up the can of worms in classrooms just like you've asked of me. But you gotta tell me what it is that I'm supposed to do once it's open.

—Rebecca Norman, a teacher candidate

I wanted to convince them by sheer will. I thought if they saw my body enough, if they heard my voice, my jokes, some of my vulnerabilities, my loves, they would have to find me an acceptable human being. There were times when I went out of my way to help students, partly because of the care I felt for them, partly because of the care I wanted them to feel for me. If they spent a year with a real live lesbian instructor and didn't end up hating her, it could just possibly mess up their homophobia on some fundamental level.

This faith came from four years of teaching at San Diego State University. For most of this time I was a lecturer in Chicana/o studies courses such as composition and speech. The bulk of my students were eighteen-year-old Chicana/os from California. I was out to my classes, I included lesbian content in the readings and discussions, and I still received consistent outstanding evaluations. Only one class out of approximately twenty ever attacked me for my sexuality. Their attacks appeared in my written evaluations and in an angry silence I confronted each time I walked in to teach the course. Even

215

then, in my worst case scenario, two thirds of the class gave me excellent comments, which I am hoping also means that they enjoyed learning in my classroom. I believed I could take this success over to York University in Toronto—a far more politically liberal university in a far more politically liberal city, over to students who did not share my Chicana/o heritage,[1] over to fifth-year plus university students, over to a change in teaching status (from lecturer to teaching assistant), and over to teacher education courses, without much rethinking of my style.

My TAship was with the consecutive bachelor of education program that allows university graduates to qualify as public school teachers in one year. Among the other antidiscrimination segments that dealt with racism, classism, and sexism, it was agreed that I would do some anti-homophobia work with the class of approximately ninety students.

During the first week of classes I conducted a fishbowl exercise.[2] I will say that on the surface approximately 90 percent of the students took in the activity with no evidence of hate or even anger. Another twenty or thirty personally offered their thanks for how much they learned, for the massive ways in which it had moved their thinking on the subject. Some confessed to having had little or no knowledge at all beforehand and relished the opportunity to learn. One reacted with visible anger. Other specific anti-homophobia[3] practices were discussed in one session near the end of the year that featured two queer[4] guest teachers, the showing of *It's Elementary*, and a group of students who were asked to present on the topic and facilitate discussion. In addition, because there were at least three vocal gay and lesbian identified students, the topic was brought up from time to time in relation to other issues in pedagogy. Finally, twelve volunteers on the last day of class agreed to take part in a focus group on the topic of anti-homophobia for the immediate purpose of aiding me with this chapter. I did not ask them specifically what my influence on their lives had been; that would have been unfair. I did ask them more general questions about their capabilities of teaching anti-homophobia and what they felt about the topic as a whole.

When I asked the participants of this focus group if they saw challenges distinct to working with homophobia in teacher education programs, one teacher candidate started chanting, "The children, The children!" I think she got it right. Because elementary and secondary school teachers are in fact legally in charge of children, the most difficult societal barrier is convincing people that we will not harm their children (Khayatt 1992, 8). It is this distinction that makes anti-homophobia work in teacher education specifically treacherous. Learning about homophobia in a teacher education program would constitute what Deborah Britzman (1998) terms *difficult knowledge*. There are tremendous emotional stakes in learning about hate: hate directed at some members of the class, hate directed at oneself, hate directed by oneself. There is also the dangerous possibility of the loss of privilege. Heterosexuals might not be so valued if homosexuals were not hated:

> [H]ow can we grapple with the stakes of the learning when the learning is made from attempts at identification with what can only be called *difficult knowledge*? The term of learning acknowledges that studying the experiences and the traumatic residuals of genocide, ethnic hatred, aggression, and forms of state-sanctioned—and hence legal—social violence requires educators to think carefully about their own theories of learning and how the stuff of such difficult knowledge becomes pedagogical. This exploration needs to do more than confront the difficulties of learning from another's painful encounter with victimization, aggression, and the desire to live on one's own terms. It also must be willing to risk approaching the internal conflicts which the learner brings to learning. Internal conflicts may be coarsened, denied, and defended against the time when the learning cannot make sense of violence, aggression, or even the desire for what Melanie Klein calls the "making of reparation." (Britzman 1998, 117)

There is no formula for fixing homophobia, for learning difficult knowledge. The only constant I held to was this "risk [of] approaching the internal conflicts which the learner brings to the learning." I had not yet read Britzman to know this. I sensed it, knowing how long it took me to come to terms with the fact of my queerness, and how long it subsequently took my brother. For a year and a half I wrote in journals about how much I hated myself; my brother seemed to give up hating only after a close family member died. In either case, time was essential in returning to love. I always share this with students. They are aghast that a lesbian could be homophobic. Even another instructor noted that this was one of the things I said that moved him most on the subject.

The bodies that house our perspectives are primary. The color, size, desires, gender, and sex of our bodies place them into distinct relationships with homophobia. These characteristics influence our fears. They inform how each of us would not only learn about homophobia but also how we might continue on to teach about it. This attention to our bodies while teaching is not only difficult in contemplating homophobia but difficult generally. As bell hooks (1994) notes in her essay, "Eros, Eroticism, and the Pedagogical Process," "To call attention to the body is to betray the legacy of repression and denial that has been handed down to us by our professional elders" (191).

I used my body as a text in our classroom.[5] I presented myself as a lesbian the first week of teaching as part of a homophobia exercise. I referred to having a significant girlfriend in my life. I shared anecdotes about our young children. One student described my presentation as that of a "wholesome" lesbian.

I have a clean-cut boy haircut. I wear Doc Martin boots, jeans, men's dress shirts, and blazers to teach. Most people would recognize me as a butch lesbian stereotype. Often people mistake me for a young boy. I identify as a Chicana lesbian, but I am perceived as white and masculine. These can be privileges, because while many people fear butches, even despise us for exposing the whole lot of queers, I sincerely believe that if the group of people I am dealing with at any given time doesn't actually want to kill me, they will unconsciously provide me more privilege than my more feminine, browner colleagues. They will recognize me as a white, masculine figure above all and offer me that particular kind of "respect."[6] What this means is that although students might still be harboring homophobia for these queers out in the world, they believe that I am someone who should have a wife at home taking care of me. I do not have any hard facts to support these claims, only my sense of how I read reactions. I realize that the idea of my students hating queers while respecting me is a contradiction. I use the authority these characteristics provide me, as they grant more legitimacy to what I say. If I were more feminine and could more easily pass as a heterosexual, I might strategize in a different way. Perhaps I would not come out so abruptly, or then again maybe I would feel the need to bring up queer issues more often. Maybe the sexism off-balances the homophobia or vice versa. My point is that students will respond to each distinct characteristic of our bodies as instructors. I do not think it is possible or even desirable to seek out the most privileged social position but rather to be conscious of our individual sources of power and vulnerability and to use them as productively as possible.

I presented myself as if to say, this is of course what my gender expression is, this is of course who I desire, and can't we all see the naturalness of the whole thing. I brought my feminine girlfriend to social engagements and felt the students' eyes on us while we danced. I wondered if they were as struck as I was when I first watched two lesbians dance together a decade ago. I brought our five-year-old child to the potluck on the last day and heard a widespread, "ooh," as we entered the room. What did they think when they saw their instructor, an obvious queer, with her child on her lap, whispering away with him as if this were an everyday sort of activity? It was an everyday activity for me and him. It's just that it is not an everyday image for most of them. I cannot think of one public image of a queer with a child. Again I am reminded of the first time I saw a lesbian friend taking care of her niece and sensed the awe of it. I remember wondering if the earth would crack open, or at the least, a bunch of swat team soldiers would burst into the room at any second and separate them. Some students were moved by the image of my body and his body in ways I could never reproduce in a lecture.

Finally, I attended the graduation and congratulated and hugged each and every student with my queer Chicana body. I loved them throughout the year with this body. I do not know if my physicality and care had anything to do with being Chicana. I do know that I learned to love and I learned my manner for expressing it from a Chicana mother and community. I am not suggesting that all teachers should go off and hang out with a Chicano community, or find some little kid to put on your lap, or go out dancing, or whatever; what I do suggest is to use your body, your interests, your specific ways of caring as strategically as possible.

I also took advantage of my position as a TA. First, it would be difficult to fire me. I belong to the strongest TA union in the country. We are virtually guaranteed teaching contracts along with our studies. The most anyone could probably have done would have been to move me to another site. A TAship also meant that while I did not have control over our classroom, I also did not have ultimate responsibility. If somebody had complained to the administration about our teaching strategies, the professors would have been brought into the office, not me.

In my Chicana/o studies classes, I would keep questioning a student's homophobic statements until the logic fell over onto itself, because the only genuine truth in homophobia is that people are scared. Since most people are not willing to admit that the issue is as simple as fear, they attempt to argue with concepts that ultimately fold. Even the Bible and nature are too full of contradictions to keep up a strong argument. This arguing takes tremendous patience and time and experience, none of which was available in our particular bachelor of education program. I had had a lot more control in my previous composition courses, partly because my task there was to simply create environments in which good writing was being produced, and controversy can be a great way to do this. In teacher education courses, there seem to be a million more things to accomplish in a year's time.

With such limitations, labeling people or their behavior as homophobic becomes the quicker solution, but it creates an awful silence and makes you question whether you actually would rather hear that people are fearing and hating you. One thing is certain, just as Ellsworth (1992) discovered in her classroom, "Acting as if our classroom were a safe space in which democratic dialogue was possible and happening did not make it so" (107).

Because I had less direct connection with students as a TA, I had to maximize the interactions available to me. If I could not lecture very often, then I could find them in my conversations with their papers. I spent dozens of early mornings under a blanket on the couch with my coffee on the floor next to me and their stack of papers lying across my chest. Grading someone's writing is often perceived as the most boring of teaching tasks; however, nearly everyone is vulnerable in their writing. When they hand in an essay, they are handing in a tender piece of themselves. If you take this piece and read and respond, you have reached under their skins and they into yours. It doesn't really matter how much you criticize their work; what matters is that you've seriously considered and valued their words. It is difficult to hate someone who has just loved your words.

One of the queer students in the focus group presents a similar strategy:

> One of the reasons that I always stay closeted in the beginning, and it's not closeted, I don't lie or hide but I don't come out right away, is because usually what happens, my strategy up until now is that somebody will like me. And when you like me, if you're going to leave me based on the fact that I'm a lesbian, you're going to have to really face the fact that you're leaving me because I'm a lesbian. So I try and lay all the foundation for a friendship so that when they go, they are only rejecting me based on my sexuality. And if they can't bear to be that blatantly discriminating, then they will actually somewhere along the way get a little bit educated.

Although the Human Rights Code of Ontario "include[s] sexual orientation as one of the factors where individuals are protected from discrimination in employment, housing and services" (cited in Khayatt 1992, 205), queer teacher candidates expressed significant fears about coming out and/or teaching homophobia. Lorna,[7] a masculine queer woman, exclaimed,

> Your original question was if we're going to teach antihomophobia. Well I'm personally quite scared to teach it, especially for the first couple years of teaching, when we're on probation. But in my last placement I started talking. I read this book called *Discrimination* and we started talking about discrimination. We didn't get too specific. I'm committed to doing that, but not at the risk of losing my job. And I might find after a year of not being able to do that, that I don't want to actually do this job. Because if I can't be myself and stand up for my own being and the people that I love, then what kind of a job is that for me?

One of the heterosexual students immediately challenged her: "What makes you think you're going to lose your job?" Lorna responded,

> Yeah there's policy but people can find ways to get people out of things, as we know. We've seen that if somebody, if I'm too out, the way that I've been this year, you guys, there's no way in hell that I could ever be this out, not even close. I haven't been out all year in my practicum. . . . If somebody knew I was

queer and wasn't cool with it, they would find a way to get me out of teaching, and for me to lose my job. That's why I'm going to tip toe around until I have a secured position.

These fears frustrated and shocked a couple of the heterosexual students. One expressed admiration for the "strength" and the "self-love" she had always noticed in Lorna. Thee responses helped explain why Lorna felt safe to be out in our program, surrounded by peers who might in fact follow her to future jobs, but not in the school at which she imagines later working.

Several heterosexual teacher candidates in the focus group felt they were more protected and therefore in some sense obligated to teach anti-homophobia. Sean, a heterosexual married man, fclt it was important not to identify his sexuality. He decided he would remove his wedding ring while teaching and refer to his "wife" as his "partner," so that his students could not be sure about his orientation.

Sean had already begun teaching anti-homophobia as a teacher candidate, but noted that he could only do it when the host teacher was out of the classroom and he was alone with the students. Another heterosexual teacher candidate acknowledged that she taught anti-homophobia to her students while her host teacher was there, but that it was the only lesson shc delivered, "where I was shaking because I was breaking the silence." She associated some of this fear with the fact that homophobic name calling was the only kind of name calling allowed in the class. This meant that while in the past anything from "poopoohead" to racial slurs to "stupid" would have been mixed in with "fag," now, because these other slurs were no longer tolerated, everybody was only calling each other "fag."

When I asked what there was to be afraid of, several teacher candidates mentioned that it was more generally "the fear of sex." Although it is not necessary to discuss sex in anti-homophobia education, there was a feeling that the general public would assume that this was what was happening. Various comments followed this theme: "It's the fear of talking about sex," "The average person doesn't want to talk about sex and they definitely think that it's not appropriate to talk to kids about it," "If we start talking about that [sex], our very culture and our very society will start to fall apart."

Sharon, a lesbian teacher candidate also fearful of teaching anti-homophobia, spoke of how hegemonic conditions played out in another crucial aspect of a teacher's life—the staff room:

[I]n the staff room, trying my darndest to be really professional, there's, I can't remember. There was like an awards ceremony. There was something on TV, and there was a discussion about somebody like Britney Spears' blouse or something. And it's men and women having this conversation, and they're talking about her breasts and they're talking about her nipples and they're talking about how she looks. And then the conversation is sort of going to what other people are wearing. It's bringing everybody's conversation down to the breasts of all the staff, which was all fine, it was really a fine conversation, like there's nothing—I moved slowly back out of the conversation, because there was no way in hell that I was going to make a comment that might make a reference to one of my colleague's breasts, to even be looking at her breasts or commenting on my own. Even though everyone else is, men and women and this is really an important point, coed within a straight frame. And then have them later find out, because I'm assuming that they'll find out I'm a lesbian, I had no idea at this point I was going to stay closeted the entire time.

Commenting on all of the female teachers' breasts in a staff room is probably illegal, and at the very least sexist and uncomfortable. However, Sharon focuses on the fear of homophobic attacks. No matter how well I could instruct teacher candidates to incorporate anti-homophobia into their curriculum, staff rooms would still threaten their confidence in their work. Another paper should be devoted to strategies of anti-homophobia in the staff room.

What is fair to assume is that if queer teacher candidates could be out comfortably in their schools, they might feel as if they had more choices in terms of their own anti-homophobia classroom teaching. As teacher education faculty, we cannot decide whether our queer students should be out or not, but we can suggest that being out is a possibility. And for those who want to be out, we can suggest strategies, such as subtle conversations to discover allies on the staff who can provide support before they make grander announcements.

Near the end of the discussion, I asked how the program could be improved, and the students revisited their fears about open explorations of homophobia:

I'm disappointed with the turn out [at this focus group]. The people most comfortable are here, and the ones who really need it aren't here. In breaking through fear, in vocalizing, you are silencing. You really have to listen. You have to be super patient. You might have to shut up sometimes, you might. You know, there's times I've had to listen to things that I didn't agree with this year, because I knew that sometimes saying something meant that they would close their mouths and they might not open them again. And it doesn't mean that their attitudes changed, it just means that they weren't heard which is much more frightening.

This is the first time in my education that I have felt that this is queer positive space where my voice could be heard as an out lesbian, but it was at the expense of people who could have really benefited and moved.

The teacher candidates also offered multiple strategies for strengthening the program's anti-homophobia component in general:

Student: I think it should be mandatory that we have to teach it in our blocks. We should have been forced to deal with all the issues. This program failed in this way. It taught us here, but then it left it. It didn't make us bring it into the classroom.
Karleen: It failed specifically with homophobia?
Student: With all the issues I would say, I would say most of us encountered "the nod."[8]
We haven't learned how to build alliances or make allies cuz that's something we'll really have to do especially in the school if people are going to deal with antihomophobia education. We have to build allies. We have to have allies within the school and outside the school in order to succeed. And I think this is one area in the program. I haven't been able to build relationships.
You need some tools to teach queer stuff. You need some information, they didn't give us that. I mean even to address the question of when kids say fags. We're unequipped to do it.

Despite the fact that students felt ill-prepared to teach anti-homophobia pedagogy, I asked them to come up with lesson plans for various grade levels. I gave them approximately fifteen minutes to think of ideas and then presented them to the focus group. They worked in pairs and then confidently presented their strategies, just as they had presented hundreds of lesson plans in every subject throughout the year.

We were all very tired of teaching, writing papers, grading papers, and thinking, on the last day of class when we held this focus group. As other students were eating at a potluck party in the auditorium, we carried our plates into a quiet, sunny classroom at the end of the hall. I promised them that I would not take more than an hour of their time. They refused to stop talking even as we passed the two-hour mark. The tape recording saves the breaks of laughter when we all fell over in our chairs, the voices cracking in nervousness when they confessed to feelings that scared them, the edge of anger or frustration at the end of a sentence, and several beautiful admissions between students of how much admiration or respect they had developed for each other throughout the course of the year. I did not know until months later when I was transcribing, that they had taken my recorder after the session ended and for several minutes, whispered playful and loving words to me. I laughed and cried when I heard them, knowing that while many students from that program might never utter a queer word in their classrooms, these twelve responded to me, to my body, and to a shared understanding that anti-homophobia pedagogy is significant to their lives.

NOTES

1. Although it is outside the scope of this paper, I did find that no longer sharing the oppressions and joys of being Chicana/os with my students immediately created more emotional distance. Although I did identify myself as Chicana and at times incorporated my understandings of race and culture from this context, they did not, in any kind of visible way, respond to this piece of me. Perhaps this absence could be interpreted as a response. I find that most Canadians I encounter have no understanding of what a Chicana is.

2. This exercise is an adapted version of an exercise taught to me by members of the Lesbian Gay Bisexual Transgender Student Union at San Diego State University in 1994. We often conducted this exercise in classrooms at SDSU and in the San Diego community. The story goes that some group at the University of California at Santa Cruz created the exercise and named it a Cluh (Coalition for Learning and Undermining Homophobia) panel. In this particular case, I asked for twenty volunteers to sit in an inner circle, with the approximately sixty-five other students circling us. The volunteers were asked to identify as gay or lesbian for a half hour and take part in a mock gay and lesbian support group for the teacher education program. I played the role of the support group facilitator and made up questions and stories about their lives that would create a theatrical feeling that each student was actually going through the various struggles and successes of gay and lesbian students in the program. Following this session, the twenty volunteers could ask me and one out gay student, who was willing, any question they wanted about our lives as a gay man and lesbian. We also stated that we would inform them if we felt that a question was too personal for us to answer.

3. I define *anti-homophobia* as those knowledges and practices that counter and complicate homophobia.

4. I define *queer* as all those who have a sexuality other than heterosexuality. I realize that the term is contentious, and that some of the people referred to might not self-identify with this term, but I felt it would be more of a problem to ask each person what his or her current specific sexuality was.

5. This idea was mentioned to me by Lara Doan, a fellow doctoral student at York University, in the fall of 1999. She believes it is sometimes useful to draw attention to her own body, the body of the instructor, as a tool in teaching.

6. At San Diego State University where I worked as a lecturer, various more feminine colleagues spoke about how some male students became verbally aggressive, using specifically misogynistic terms in their classrooms, which to date has never happened to me. I often had the same students as they did, and spoke about similar feminist issues.

7. All of the names attached to direct student quotes are a mixture of real names and pseudonyms depending on the preference of the participant.

8. The "nod" was a concept that one of the student groups developed in the course. Briefly, it referred to the way in which their host-teachers or other faculty had an unconscious expectation of them to nod in agreement after some type of oppressive statement (sexist, racist, classist, anti-immigrant, homophobic, etc.) was made by that person. They found that resisting such statements could be achieved by refusing to nod in agreement.

REFERENCES

Britzman, D. 1998. *Lost subjects, contested objects: Toward a psychoanalytic inquiry of learning.* Albany: State University of New York Press.

Ellsworth, E. 1992. Why doesn't this feel empowering? Working through the repressive myths of critical pedagogy. In *Feminisms and critical pedagogy*, edited by C. Luke and J. Gore, 90–119. New York: Routledge.

Haraway, D. J. 1991. *Simians, cyborgs, and women: The reinvention of nature.* New York: Routledge.

hooks, b. 1994. *Teaching to transgress: Education as the practice of freedom.* New York: Routledge.

Khayatt, M. D. 1992. *Lesbian teachers: An invisible presence.* Albany: State University of New York Press.

18

I'm Every Woman: Multiple Identities as Part of the Diversity Curriculum

Karen Glasgow

One of the main reasons I became an administrator was to provide teacher support. As a teacher, and now as an administrator, I have always felt that in a school environment I'd have the power to change the invisibility of sexual minority people as well as of people of color and those of mixed ancestry.

I remember as a child running from my classroom to the front of my school one day, anxious to ask my mother a question. I ran up to her, asking, "Mommy are you white?" Her answer was "Where'd you hear that?" It was the turbulent sixties, when racism was overt, and she feared that someone at school had said something derogatory to me or about my family. My response was simple: "One of the kids at school asked me why I was Negro and my mom was white." My mom smiled and seemed to relax a bit. "Yes I am white and therefore you're part too. You're also part Negro like daddy. You see mommy and daddy love each other and wanted to share that love with children so we had your sister and you, and we love you!"

I was six years old, and I still remember that day. I was satisfied with my mother's answer and all was right with the world. At least all was right until I looked for images of myself and my family everywhere at P.S. 41, my New York school, and found none. My parents reinforced my identities as good, right, and beautiful, but society didn't—not on TV, in magazines, not in the textbooks I read or the books I checked out of the school library. To add to my biracial identity, my mom was Jewish and therefore so am I. Jews of European descent weren't seen or discussed, let alone Black Jews of mixed parentage.

Actually I was lucky. My parents brought our identities into our everyday lives through Black dolls, books about interracial friendships, and museum exhibits that spoke about the Holocaust. My parents were extremely political, having spent their youth fighting in the Civil Rights movement and exposing their children to the same fight. Among their friends were many interracial couples as well as people from around the world. I had images everywhere except in school. I recognized that, and though I felt secure and comfortable in who I was, I wasn't so sure others felt the same way.

As an elementary school student I was aware that I had crushes on my girl-friends. In junior high school I was smitten with my favorite female friends, and by high school I was in love with two classmates who were also friends of mine. There was a name for who I was and what I was feeling, but it wasn't spoken about and there were no books, movies, texts, or teachers that I could go to, to discuss how I felt. I knew it was "wrong," but I couldn't change how I felt. It was as difficult discovering I was gay as it was being Black. Being Black was visible while my sexual identity wasn't, but the confusion, fear, and need to talk to someone, anyone, were overwhelming. I spent my high school years constantly monitoring what I said and how I looked at other fe-males. I tried to engage in discussions that centered on who the cutest boys were. It was a painful time. There were no discussions about homosexuality except for the occasional negative ones. It was in school that I discovered my sexual identity. Sexuality is such a huge part of the school culture. For those of us who knew we weren't heterosexuals, there was an added burden not to be out, to fit in, and to try to be someone we weren't. I was a straight "A" stu-dent, so school wasn't a problem, but the social pressure of dating and acting straight was.

I have grown into a healthy well-rounded adult, who embraces her multi-ple identities, but I run into opposition and ignorance daily, and unfortunately that still occurs most often in our schools.

My theory has always been, take care of the teachers and they'll take care of the children. When children's developmental needs are met they learn, grow, develop self-esteem, and have a healthy school experience. Then why are "fag tag" and "Gaylord" common games and names used on elementary school playgrounds daily? Why are queer middle and high school students dropping out of school at disproportionately higher rates than their peers and committing suicide at the same disproportionate rate? What's missing? In this chapter I explore the notion that something is not being provided to teachers and therefore not being taught to children.

Recently I was watching a story on *20/20* introducing the "first wave of children raised by gay and lesbian couples." What I found most interesting was not that these children were all well adjusted and very comfortable with their families but that the first place, and one of the only places, where they encountered teasing, ridicule, and alienation was at school. That spoke volumes to me about what we aren't teaching in our local schools and universities. We are not teaching teachers in teacher education programs or providing professional development on K–12 school sites about the needs of sexual minority children, their families, and others such as staff and community members. The need for this education is so great because its absence affects the learning environment and threatens self-esteem and safety.

Teachers must take responsibility for their students' safety as well as their academic achievement. When fundamental parts of a child's life are overlooked, the child suffers. As a youngster, I grew up in school environments that were silent about differences. We discussed the Civil Rights movement and surface issues of racial segregation and conflict, as was common in the sixties and seventies, but we never discussed my family or me. I was the product of an interracial couple, with my mother white and Jewish and my father African American and Protestant. Not only did I never hear about families like mine, but I never saw my type of family reflected in our school's library books or curricular material. Now, as an adult, I am also a lesbian and I still do not see images that mirror who I am in school materials. My first suggestion for educating teachers is to help them understand the importance of curricular materials that represent all diversities. That includes but is not limited to library resources, text books, videos, and bulletin board displays that show people of color, biracial people, gay and lesbian people, and people with disabilities. If you are fortunate enough to have access to a person like me, who encompasses multiple identities (Black, biracial, Jewish, lesbian, and a fat woman), you can invite those people to address your students directly about their experiences. As an administrator at an urban elementary school, I am aware of the gay and lesbian families on my campus who never hear discussions about their lives or communities. We have over 5,000 books in our school library, but I have not found one with a story about a gay family or person. I am reminded of the not so long ago days when you would never find Blacks in the literature used in teacher education programs or in schools; when you did they were always portrayed negatively. That portrayal had a profound effect on my self-esteem and on how I viewed the worth of Blacks in our society. The same is true for our sexual minority children and parents.

Another important reason for educating teachers about sexual minorities is to empower them to create and maintain a safe learning environment in which all persons feel accepted and respected. Suggestion number two is that teachers learn about district, state, and federal guidelines as well as the education codes as they relate to talking and teaching about homosexuality. Children who are gay or simply perceived as such are targeted daily on our K–12 campuses. What often starts as cruel teasing and occasional fighting in the primary grades can escalate to severe physical harm and even death at the high school level. I personally have watched teachers stand by as children yell "fag" at one another. Would they do the same if they heard a racial slur? Probably not, for they have been educated about racism, yet educating about sexually diverse populations is the final frontier, untouchable. So much is involved when we say and do nothing. It's a powerful message in itself, one that gives silent permission for abuse and the total disregard for an entire population.

Currently an enormous struggle is unfolding between me and the parent representative for our school. I work in the Los Angeles Unified School District, where we have policies banning discrimination based on sexual orientation and where as a part of our curriculum we celebrate a variety of months that highlight disenfranchised groups such as Asian Pacific Islanders (celebrated in May) and Gay and Lesbian Awareness (celebrated in June). It all began in September. I was a brand new principal having my first meeting with the four parents who are members of the schools' leadership councils. I had posted a signup sheet for teachers listing all of the committees available for their participation. I listed the regular holidays, such as winter show and Halloween, but I also listed the months that we recognize according to our district mandates. Among these was June's Gay and Lesbian Awareness month. One parent representative pointed to it and said, "What is this?" I gave an explanation. Her response was, "We're going to do this for a whole month?" I said, "No, I wouldn't know what to do for a month and I doubt if anyone else would either." "Well I never heard of this month!" she said. I gave her a copy of the district bulletin explaining what, why, and when we were to recognize Gay and Lesbian Awareness month. Then I spent the next three hours listening to some of the most derogatory and inflammatory words about "them" and how "they aren't normal." Thankfully the three other parents spoke out against much of what she said while I sat back, until finally I said, "Sandy, I'm a lesbian and I'm only telling you this to bring home the point that you never know whom you're speaking with, and as a school employed parent representative you must make sure you represent all of our families so that everyone feels welcome and respected at our school."

Coming out as the school principal was very difficult. I felt very vulnerable at a time when I was working so hard to build relationships and show my abilities. I had to expose a part of me that could work against the very things I was trying to do. Unfortunately this issue has accelerated all year long, to the point where this parent has now passed out "student exemption forms" with a cover letter to all of our parents, telling them that if they sign this form, the school will have to honor it and we will not be allowed "to teach, instruct, advise, counsel, discuss, test, question, examine, survey or in any way provide data, information or images" to their children about any aspect of "homosexuality, lesbianism, bisexuality, transgender, or transsexual issues." The form also states that this prohibition will pertain to

> classroom instruction, presentations, school approved displays on campus, reading assignments, books, magazines, newspapers, or other written or printed material, photographs, movies, films, slides, filmstrips, DVDs, CDs, video or audio tapes, CD-ROMS, computer programs, field trips, assemblies, theatrical performances, individual or group assigned activities or extracurricular activities.

Eleven groups including the Pro-Family Law Center and the Christian Coalition signed this letter.

What makes this even more difficult is that I have been trying not to do as much as I could do because I am gay. I don't want my parents, staff, or supervisors to think that I am reacting from a personal place, that I have an agenda, so I have been extremely careful. I am working with my superintendent and an attorney from our district to be sure that I am following policy when I respond to this parent's actions, but I feel that if this were a racial incident, swifter and more aggressive measures would be applied to stop her. This has been a powerful experience for me. In a district that speaks liberally and appears relatively progressive, we are not very advanced in the way we handle sexual minority issues.

As June grows nearer, our parent representative is escalating her efforts. The irony of all of this is that her daughter is in the same class as a child with lesbian parents. Recently I asked her how she thinks those parents felt when they received her parent exemption form. My staff and many of my parents have been very supportive of me and that helps so much. Unfortunately there are parents who support this person because of misrepresentations she has put forth. This will take a long time to undo.

Teachers need to know how to cite policies to defend their classroom curriculum and the discussions they provoke. Most of my teachers support the district's policy on teaching against homophobia. Unfortunately they really do not know what policies protect them while teaching these issues, especially when challenged by parents who assert their rights to exempt their children from this part of the curriculum. This mother has created the very discussion she does not want at school through her petitioning, but unfortunately because of misrepresentations and untruths, the discussions have been negative. If teachers had been armed with information and resources before stepping into the classroom, they would have been able to be proactive.

Suggestion number three is to teach teachers how to have age appropriate discussions about children with gay and lesbian families. Many teachers will have children in their classrooms from these families. In my school one of my kindergarten teachers has a child in her class with two moms. In this particular teacher's classroom the common discussion about "Who are the members of your family?" came up. One student said the members of his family were his two sisters and his two moms. The discussion continued, with many of his kinder-classmates saying that he couldn't have two moms. The teacher was rather uncomfortable with this talk and wasn't sure what to say. Being an extraordinary professional she finally said, "Well John does have two mothers and that's okay." She then redirected the conversation altogether. It would have been easier, more comfortable, and more appropriate if the teacher had already possessed the skills to use that teachable moment with a discussion on different kinds of families. The discussion could then have been followed by either a book such as *Asha's Mums* or the video *That's a Family* (Chasnoff and Cohen 2000), which highlights twelve diverse families including three gay and lesbian ones and is narrated by the children from those families.

What happens when your school has "Open House" or "Back to School Night" and one of your students shows up with his two dads? No matter how one feels personally about these issues, for a teacher there is the responsibility to support all children equally and to engage their families in the education of their children. This means that discussions about sexually diverse families must occur in teacher education programs and at K–12 schools. They should be as normal as the discussions of multiculturalism are becoming.

Over half of all high school graduates will have heard their *teachers* use the words "faggot" or "dyke" (GLSEN 2001). Teachers are only people with their own perceptions and beliefs. They are also supposed to be lifelong learners. They should be educated about sexual minorities and their families before they become responsible for children's education.

In conclusion, when teachers take on the responsibility of educating our children, that education must include twenty-first-century issues about sexual minorities. The only way they can engage their students in meaningful dialogues about differences and diversity is to include discussions of sexual minority children and their families.

Teachers need to be made aware of relevant state and district policies already in place to support them in teaching about homosexuality. They need anti-homophobia training as part of their teacher education curriculum. Queer issues in education should be viewed as a subject worthy of academic inquiry. Teacher education programs should promote community linkages, and teachers can help create awareness within their communities. Teachers must know what resources are available to help with their teaching, and they must be taught what are acceptable and age-appropriate discussions they can have with their students.

When school environments become places where all children and staff feel valued, respected, and safe, then we will see all children learning and developing lifelong skills of acceptance devoid of prejudice and hate. It all begins with their first introduction to formal education, their classroom teachers, and the lessons they will learn from them.

REFERENCES

Chasnoff, D., director/producer, and H. S. Cohen, producer. 2000. *That's a family.* [Video.] (Available from Women's Educational Media, 2180 Bryant St., Suite 203, San Francisco, CA 94110, and distributed by New Day Films, Hohokus, NJ.)

Elwin, R., and M. Paulse. 1990. *Asha's mums.* Toronto: Women's Press.

GLSEN. 2001. Press releases. Available: <www.glsen.org>.

19

Campus Dyke Meets Teacher Education: A Marriage Made in Social Justice Heaven

Ronni Sanlo

I wanted to say that hearing you speak has really changed my perspective on homosexuality. I will admit that I never agreed with it, but at the same time I never understood it. I have never heard anyone talk about their personal experience, and now I feel guilty for disagreeing with something I know nothing about. I admire you for sharing with us and I'm sure I'll never forget the way I felt after that lecture.

—A female Asian student

As the director of the UCLA Lesbian Gay Bisexual Transgender (LGBT) Campus Resource Center, I am a proud homocrat: a gay-for-pay. My staff and I provide services in the areas of advocacy, information, education, referral, crisis intervention, and research, as well as support and acceptance for and about lesbian, gay, bisexual, and transgendered (lgbt) students, faculty, and staff and their issues. The Center is one of about thirty-five in the country with full-time professional staff. Not only do we serve the entire campus community on issues related to lgbt people, we also serve those, especially students, who may have gay parents or family members, roommates, or friends.

In addition to directing the LGBT Center, I teach a required course called "Social Justice and Cultural Diversity in American Education" in the UCLA master's level Teacher Education Program (TEP). The TEP is part of a larger entity within UCLA's Graduate School of Education and Information Studies called Center X, which is founded on conceptual principles that include a social justice orientation and a commitment to the integration of research-based theory and practice. The TEP seeks to give teachers the commitment, capacity, and resilience to promote social justice, caring, and instructional equity in low-income, urban schools. Our students serve

populations traditionally underserved by high-quality educational programs, especially those that are racially, culturally, and linguistically diverse (www.centerx.gseis.ucla.edu/tep/home.htm).

Our TEP students do their novice and resident teaching in the worst schools
in Los Angeles. Although the foundational emphasis of my course—and the TEP
as an educational entity—is on race and class, other issues such as religion, ethnicity, gender, ability, and language also receive our full attention. Lesbian, gay,
bisexual, and transgendered issues are also deeply infused into the course.

This chapter describes the way that I attempt to create a socially just classroom in which all people, viewpoints, and issues are welcome, and how lgbt
issues are an integral part of the course design. I show how my students reflect on their discomfort, and how they say they plan to use the information
in their classrooms. Although I enter the classroom in my dominant identity
as a white person, I also share my subordinate identities as a woman, as a
Jewish person, as an older person, and, especially, as a lesbian. The purpose
of this chapter is to share my experiences in a graduate teacher education
course that broadens students' horizons and expands their abilities to work in
classrooms as social justice educators.

THE TEACHER EDUCATION PROGRAM

You've challenged me in many ways. I take pride in my undergraduate
coursework at UCSD as an Ethnic Studies major. However, I must admit that
although the "invisible minority" was addressed in our curriculum, I now realize that there is room for more information to transfer through the coursework. It is humbling to know that in our desire to represent marginalized
voices we fail or neglect to address the myriad of ways in which the marginalization of the gay community persists throughout our society.

—A female Asian student

HOW I BECAME A BIG DYKE ON CAMPUS

I think gays and lesbians have it very tough, because they have to deal with the
conflict of whether or not to "come out of the closet." I can only imagine the internal pain inflicted in dealing with this debate, in addition to the discrimination
faced if open about it. I ask myself if I am bisexual sometimes, and part of me
feels like I am, while other parts of me tell me I'm not. Since I do not want to
face discrimination and the judgments of my friends and family, I sort of sweep
any thoughts of bisexuality under the carpet.

—A white male student

Although I knew I was a lesbian by the time I was eleven years old, I did not come out until I was thirty-one. When I finally acknowledged my sexual identity, I was married, living in Central Florida, and the mother of two precious young children. When I came out, two years after Anita Bryant attempted to "save" Miami from the lgbt community in 1977, I lost custody of my three-year-old son and six-year-old daughter to my ex-husband. The Florida court system said that because I was a lesbian I provided nothing to show that it was in the best interests of my children for me to have custody of them. When I came out, I was naïve about laws pertaining to lesbian and gay people, and because I knew no other lesbian or gay people yet, I had no support system to guide and advise me. On the day the custody decree was final, I made a silent, solemn promise to my children that I would do everything in my power for the rest of my life to try to make this world a better place for other lesbian and gay people. (This was prior to my awareness of people who were bisexual and transgendered.) The rage that roiled inside me as a result of such a traumatic loss propelled me into public service, first as the executive director of the Florida Lesbian and Gay Civil Rights Task Force, then later as an AIDS epidemiologist for Northeast Florida. Between paying jobs, I founded or co-founded numerous gay-related organizations in both Central and Northeast Florida. A word about paying jobs: I had many because I was constantly fired for doing my activist work on company time with company resources. Closed-minded, I thought, but understandable.

During my tenure with the Florida AIDS program, I obtained advanced degrees from the University of North Florida (UNF), a master's in education with a focus on counseling and sexual identity, and a doctorate in educational leadership and organizational development with a research cognate in sexual orientation issues in education. In addition to working as an adjunct instructor at UNF, I helped initiate the lgbt student organization on campus and facilitated a lesbian/bisexual women's support group.

One afternoon I visited Shirley Webb, the UNF Women's Center director. In her usual busy style, Shirley waved a piece of paper in my direction. "Hey, Ronni, glad you stopped by. Here's your next job!" The paper was a fax, an advertisement for the position of director of the Lesbian and Gay Center (Bisexual and Transgender were added later) at the University of Michigan. I was astounded to see a real job that would pay me to do work for which I had been repeatedly fired! Although Ann Arbor, Michigan, was much farther north—and much colder—than my beloved Florida, I applied for the job that had my name on it. Three months later I packed my car and moved north.

As I immersed myself in my work and in my students, I finally began to learn about diversity far beyond my own white, Jewish, Miami Beach upbringing. As I learned more about being *other* in the areas of sexual orientation and gender identity, I began to struggle, to my surprise, with the concepts of *otherness* about race, gender, age, ability, and class. I began to understand the intersections, how the *isms* feed off one another, and that as long as those who are *other* are fighting among themselves, the power structure remains in place and unchallenged. I began to broaden the scope of my work in the context of my little world of lgbt students.

As my horizons expanded, so did the opportunity to do this work more fully. I was recruited by UCLA to direct and build their lgbt center and moved to Los Angeles in September 1997.

THE MARRIAGE OF THE TEACHER
EDUCATION PROGRAM AND THE BIG DYKE

You helped me realize that perceptions can be just as powerful as intentions, while words can be just as disparaging as overt actions.

—An Asian male student

In February 1998, Dr. Sharon Ritchie, a professor in the UCLA TEP, invited me to facilitate a retreat for her cluster of about twenty-five students to provide information about lgbt issues in education. Although I wanted to teach the students about lgbt issues in education, I also wanted the experience to be more than that for those students who would be teachers in the public school system in Los Angeles. I decided to try to expand students' understanding of *other* by focusing on self. I used a method adopted by Theresa Brett for the leadership training program at the University of Michigan, aimed at encouraging students to provide information about themselves based on their invisible identities. Invisible identities are those unseen identities that we all have, that are part of who we are, and that inform the way we do our work and move through the world. Invisible identities could be race, bi- or multiple races, religion, disability, socioeconomic status, sexual orientation, gender identity, survivorship of abuse or neglect, or anything else that affects and defines who a person might be. That particular workshop was profound not only for those student participants but for Dr. Ritchie and me as well. Based on that facilitation, Dr. Ritchie recommended to the chair of the TEP that I be considered as one of the instructors for the required social justice course. I was thrilled with the invitation and accepted the offer to teach this course as part of a four-faculty, four-section team.

I attended the national Social Justice Training Institute, developed and facilitated by Maura Cullen, Kathy Obear, Vernon Wall, and Jamie Washington, and began to explore more deeply the multiple identities I bring to the classroom. Always the consummate lesbian seeking to educate educators and change-agents about lgbt issues in education and especially higher education, I present my lesbian identity in as powerful and useful a manner as possible. My other identities certainly inform my work—especially as a Jewish woman and as a grandmother. But I rarely enter the classroom with a thought about my dominant, most visible identity: my whiteness. It is my white skin that students see first, then my gender, then perhaps my age range. The power I bring to the classroom, however, is in the form of a white professor who speaks out for *other*. Because of my work, it is nearly impossible for me to be closeted whether in the classroom or any other setting. I can no longer—vocationally, ethically, or otherwise—pass for anything other than what I am—a white dyke Jewish grandmother!

TO COME OUT IN THE CLASSROOM?

I was raised in a fairly rural part of [another country] where I did not meet anyone who openly identified as homosexual until I went to college. It is not something that most members of my family would be open about and the subject has never really been discussed. However, my father let me know that just like it was not OK to date Black men, it was not OK to be homosexual. I don't think that I ever shared either of my parents' biases, but sometimes I am scared that they are a part of me. I think this contributes to why I feel self-conscious and uncomfortable in certain situations.

—A white female student

I first struggled with coming out in a classroom in 1992. I was teaching my first course—"Lifestyles and Social Issues"—at the University of North Florida. It was an undergraduate course that offered glimpses into a multitude of definitions of family. I deliberately chose not to come out to my students, fearing that they would think I was pushing a personal political agenda, that I was "recruiting," that I was using my power as a professor to play with their minds. I feared that they would not be able to hear my words or take me seriously beyond my revelation. In other words, I had every negative fear based on my internalized homophobia coupled with my fear of being rejected by people I had never met.

We eventually got around to talking about same-sex families, and I invited speakers from the gay community to share their stories with my class. Privately I told the speakers I was not out to the class, and they agreed to collude with me, to maintain my secret. One of the speakers, in his enthusiastic sharing of his story, brought copies of the local gay newspaper for the class. The issue he brought was the one that covered the 1993 National Lesbian and Gay March on Washington, with many photos of my partner and me splattered throughout. I was horrified! Although my class overall was quite forgiving, I felt completely fraudulent, unethical, and, frankly, sad that I made choices based on what I thought my students would think about me as a person and a professor. I was second-guessing the thoughts and feelings of other human beings. I felt terrible that I had not been honest, and I apologized. I also made the commitment to never leave any piece of myself at the classroom door again.

When I was invited to teach the TEP course, the invitation was extended knowing that I would bring my lesbian identity into the classroom. I needed to find ways to be fully present with all of my identities that would both validate and honor the invisible identities of my students by modeling my sense of pride in my own identities and by showing my trust in my students in working together to create a safe, welcoming classroom. I felt that the best way for them to learn to be social justice educators was to actively, consciously be one for them.

> Thank you for sharing your story with us in class. It really touched my heart and it made me realize how important it is to educate the world about these issues in hope that we can prevent hate crimes from recurring.
>
> —A white female student

SHARING STORIES, PROVIDING VOICE

The course I teach—which occurs in the fall quarter each year—is one of the foundational courses on which the TEP is built and one of the first courses students take. UCLA operates on the ten-week quarter system, so October 11— National Coming Out Day, one of the major lgbt holidays—occurs during the second week of school each fall. During that week I show the video *It's Elementary: Talking about Gay Issues in Schools* (Chasnoff and Cohen 1996). The film not only provides glimpses of what happens when educators address lesbian and gay issues with students in age-appropriate ways, it also offers excellent examples of pedagogy in a variety of grades and school settings. I ask my students to view the video with an eye not only on content but also on pedagogy: the skills and styles used by the teachers to talk about a difficult topic.

There is always active discussion following the video, and always a myriad of questions. It is during this time that I provide information about lgbt youth in school settings, including laws that do and do not protect lgbt students. I engage students through activities and exercises so that they say the words— lesbian, gay, bisexual, transgender, queer, dyke, faggot—and understand the definitions and the historical loading these words carry. And then I tell them about myself, bring myself into the room as a story teller, modeling appropriateness and tenderness while personalizing my words for my students.

Your story and the video made me realize how important it is as a teacher to provide a safe place for children to be open and comfortable with their identities.

—A Latina student

Through their journals, my students reflect on class discussion and share pieces of their personal stories as well as confessions. However, before students can talk effectively and openly in the classroom about lgbt or any other issues—and their feelings about these issues—they must experience several things: a sense of safety in the classroom, respect for their own and others' opinions, and a trust in me as their professor.

Following is the actual syllabus for my class, with comments from the students for some of the sessions. As we follow the curriculum, students learn about themselves, about others, and about how to create a socially just class. The activities help students personalize the concepts of social justice and provide them with the ways of seeing their students beyond the faces the students present. In addition to the activities, we talk each week about the theories identified in the readings, and how those theories inform the work we do.

Week One. Course Introduction, Boundaries, and Identities: Social Justice in Action
Introduction of the course; introduction to one another

Activities: Use of concentric circles to get students to meet and chat with one another individually using guided questions. Questions are determined based on the makeup of the group and are based on experiences and visible identities. Discussion of invisible identities in small and large groups follows, and we make a paper "quilt" based on the identities of those present. An excellent resource for these and other activities is *Teaching for Diversity and Social Justice* by Adams, Bell, and Griffin (1997).

Journal Prompt: Reflection on the day: Did you feel included? Did you feel censored? Did you feel silenced? Do you think you silenced anyone? Were information and sharing put forth in a way you could hear them? Were ideas put forth in a way that turned you off? Are you satisfied with the way you communicated who you are? Is there anything you'd like to share now that you deliberately did not share with the group?

I must admit that my knowledge of "diversity" issues usually [has] to do with race, ethnicity, or gender and not as much [with] sexual orientation. I realize now that is something that I've overlooked in the past, and it's good to be educated about it now. I like how you pointed out that it is an "invisible minority" but an important minority because just as other children from diverse cultures have needs, so do children from whatever sexual orientation.

—A white female student

Week Two. Pedagogy: Social Justice and Difficult Issues in the Classroom

Video: It's Elementary: Talking about Gay Issues in Schools. (Deborah Chasnoff, director/producer; Helen Cohen, producer).1996. (Available from Women's Educational Media, 2180 Bryant St., Suite 203, San Francisco, CA 94110, and distributed by New Day Films, Hohokus, NJ.)

Guest Speaker: Gail Rolf, director of Project 10, a program of the Los Angeles Unified School District

Class Discussion: In small groups, then larger groups, discuss what you know about people who are different from yourself and how you learned what you know.

Journal Prompt: What if you woke up in the morning and discovered you were lesbian or gay. How would your life be different than it is right now?

Assignment for the week: Interview someone who brings a particular understanding about Los Angeles's political, economic, and social life, and share his or her ideas in light of the readings.

Readings:
Carnoy, M., and H. Levin. 1985. Social conflict and the structure of education. In *Schooling and work in the democratic state,* 1–6. Stanford, Calif.: Stanford University Press.

Kluger, R. 1975. Text of the *Brown* decision. In *Simple justice: The history of Brown v. Board of Education and Black America's struggle for equality,* 779–85. New York: Vintage.
Tyack, D. 1993. Constructing difference: Historical reflections on schooling and social diversity. *Teachers College Record 95* (1): 8–34.

I am very comfortable around gays and lesbians. I find I can relate to gay and bisexual men because I reject the idea that being a man is limited to certain stereotypical rules. Sometimes I need to show my feelings and vulnerabilities. I know first hand too that some people find this freedom threatening. In one incident in high school I was so close to being beat up by a guy who had me against a car saying, "Why are you acting like such a faggot?" Still, after I heard your story I asked myself, "Do I cherish the gays and lesbians in my life enough? Do I take their courage for granted?" Many are on the frontlines in the battle for the freedom of all of us. Or do I sometimes secretly think, "I'm glad I'm not gay." Why do I feel the need to assert this? Because I have been called effeminate various times throughout my life? It's important for me to be aware of these thoughts that originate from fear of being ostracized.

—A white male student

Week Three. Resource Inequity and Segregation

Video: Eyes on the Prize: Fighting Back, 1957–1962. (H. Hampton and J. Vecchione, producers).

Class Discussion: From the video and the readings and from the week's assignment. [I've discovered that this video is so powerful, so intense, that it takes time for students to process and recover.]

Journal Prompt: Reflect on today's session. How has the Civil Rights movement affected your family and your community?

Readings:
Anyon, J. 1997. *Ghetto schooling: A political economy of urban educational reform*, chapters 1, 2, 5, 8. New York: Teachers College Press.
Bigelow, B. 1998. The human lives behind the labels: The global sweatshop, Nike and the race to the bottom. In *Teaching for social justice*, edited by W. Ayers, 21–38. New York: The New Press.
Kohl, H. 1993. The myth of "Rosa Parks the tired." Teaching about Rosa Parks and the Montgomery bus boycott. *Multicultural Education* 1 (2): 6–10.
Madhubuti, H. 1993. *Why LA happened: Implications of the 1992 Los Angeles rebellion*, 274–78. Chicago: Third World Press.
Ong, P., and E. Blumenberg. 1996. Income and racial inequality in Los Angeles. In *The city: Los Angeles and urban theory at the end of the twentieth century*, edited by A. Scott and E. Soja, 311–35. Los Angeles: University of California Press.

Week Four. Exclusion and Hostile Environment

Video: The Fire This Time: Why Los Angeles Burned. 1994. (R. Holland, director). Rhino Home Video.

Class Discussion: Why is the will to exclude (and segregate) so powerful within American education? How are social barriers—lines of distinction and separation—maintained in schools today? How and when are these lines questioned?

Journal Prompt: Reflect on today's discussion. How do your identities— seen and unseen—play a role in the construction of social barriers in school?

continued

continued

Readings:

Sanchez, G. 1993. *Becoming Mexican American: Ethnicity, culture and identity in Chicano Los Angeles 1900–1945,* 87–107. New York: Oxford University Press.

Sanlo, R. 1999. Lesbian and gay educators: Documenting their existence. In *Unheard voices: The effects of silence on lesbian and gay educators,* edited by R. Sanlo, 5–13. Westport, Conn.: Greenwood Press.

Wollenberg, C. 1976. "Yellow Peril" in the schools. In *All deliberate speed: Segregation and exclusion in California schools 1855–1975,* 48–81. Los Angeles: University of California Press.

Week Five. Deficit Models of Pedagogy.

Small Group Discussion: Internalized Oppression: In what ways do you feel oppressed? What do you hate hearing about your group? What do you love about being part of your group? What do you never want to hear people say about your group? [Groups could be based on race/ethnicity, age, socioeconomics, sexual or gender identities, survivorship, body image, ability, whatever gets identified in the classroom.]

Class Activity: On one side of a 5-by-8-inch card write all the ways in which you've been silenced in your life and by whom. On the other side list those whom you've silenced.

Journal Prompt: Reflect on today's session. What are the ways that you encounter silence?

Assignment: In your classes [the students are observing classes in the Los Angeles school system], notice how the teacher silences students. Notice who gets silenced and how.

Readings:

Freire, P. 1921, 1998. Eighth letter: Cultural identity and education. In *Teachers as cultural workers: Letters to those who dare teach,* 69–74. Boulder, Colo.: Westview.

Ogbu, J. U. 1992. Understanding cultural diversity and learning. *Educational Researcher* 21 (8): 5–14.

Valdes, G. 1996. *Con respeto: Bridging the distances between culturally diverse families and schools,* chapters 1, 2, 7, 8, and 9. New York: Teachers College Press.

I pondered one of your questions for days. "Did anyone in this class ever feel 'abnormal'"?" Nearly everyone in the class raised their hands. I was so surprised to see so many people felt the same way as me, which also makes [me] realize that my "future" students might also experience the same feeling. And, how important it is for me to be aware of it and provide my support, besides focusing on their academic progress.

—A Korean female student

Week Six. Cultural Dissonance.

Discussion of assignment; discussion of readings using scenarios from the readings. Students must take pro/con sides as educators, students, parents, elected school board officials, the mayor, and newspaper reporters.

Journal Prompt: According to Valdez and/or Ogbu, what does it mean for teachers to create a respectful relationship with families from different socio-economic, cultural, and linguistic backgrounds?

Readings:
Levin, H. 1999. High stakes testing and economic productivity. In *The civil rights project.* Cambridge, Mass.: Harvard University.
Madaus, G., and M. Clarke. 1999. The adverse impact of high stakes testing on minority students: Evidence from 100 years of data. In *The civil rights project.* Cambridge, Mass.: Harvard University.
McNeil, L., and A. Valenzuela. 1998. The harmful impact of the TAAS system of testing in Texas: Beneath the accountability rhetoric. In *The civil rights project.* Cambridge, Mass.: Harvard University.
Oakes, J., and M. Lipton. 1999. *Teaching to change the world,* 220–33. Boston: McGraw-Hill College Press.
Oakes, J., J. Rogers, M. Lipton, and E. Morrell. Forthcoming. The social construction of college access: Confronting the technical, cultural, and political barriers to low income students of color. In *Extending our reach: Strategies for increasing access to college,* edited by W. G. Tierney and L. S. Haggedorn. Albany: State University of New York Press.
Reed, A. 1995. Intellectual brown shirts. In *The bell curve debate: History, documents, opinions,* edited by R. Jacoby and N. Glauberman, 263–68. New York: Times Books.

The bottom line for me, the main concern, is that we do not harm other people just because they are different from us or just because we don't agree with them.

—A white female student

*Week Seve*n. Testing and Sorting.

Discussion from readings; small group scenarios: What is the impetus behind the testing regime, and what is its impact on the culture of learning?

Journal Prompt: What has been your personal experience of testing, and how was it relevant for you from a cultural perspective?

Readings:
Activist forum I: Awakening justice. 1998. In *Teaching for social justice,* edited by W. Ayers, 48–55. New York: The New Press.
Bartolomé, L. I. 1994. Beyond the methods fetish: Toward a humanizing pedagogy. *Harvard Educational Review* 64 (2): 173–94.
Delpit, L. 1988. The silenced dialogue: Power and pedagogy in educating other people's children. *Harvard Education Review* 58 (3): 280–98.
Freire, P. 1921, 1998. Sixth letter: On the relationship between the educator and the learners, and Seventh letter: From talking to learners to talking to them and with them; From listening to learners to being heard by them. In *Teachers as cultural workers: Letters to those who dare teach,* 55–68. Boulder, Colo.: Westview.
McLaren, P. 1989. Preface. In *Life in schools: An introduction to critical pedagogy in the foundations of education,* xiii–xvii. New York: Longman.

Week Eight. Toward a Critical and Culturally Relevant Pedagogy

Discussion from readings. Describe yourself as a social justice educator. What is social justice in the classroom? How do you know what it is and how do you know when you've become a social justice educator?

Readings:
Activist forum V: Racing justice. 1998. In *Teaching for social justice,* edited by W. Ayers, 288–94. New York: The Free Press.
Ayers, W. 1998. Forward: Popular education. Teaching for social justice. In *Teaching for social justice,* edited by W. Ayers, xvii–xxv. New York: The Free Press.
Dewey, J. 1981. United, we shall stand. In *John Dewey: The later works, 1925–1951,* edited by Jo Ann Boydston, 339–82. Carbondale: Southern Illinois University Press.
Freire, P. 1921, 1998. Fifth letter: The first day of school. In *Teachers as cultural workers: Letters to those who dare teach,* 47–53. Boulder, Colo.: Westview.
hooks, b. 1994. Embracing change: Teaching in a multicultural world. In *Teaching to transgress: Education as the practice of freedom,* 35–44. New York: Routledge.
Kohl, H. 1998. Afterword: Some reflections on teaching for social justice. In *Teaching for social justice,* edited by W. Ayers, 285–87. Boulder, Colo.: Westview.

Participating in the last two lectures forced me to look deep inside myself. I really appreciate your sharing your personal experiences. That was my first day attending the class and I had awesome realizations. Not all good ones though. Like most people, I like to think of myself as open-minded and good at heart. But hearing and participating in those two lectures made my flaws stand out to me in giant neon bold print.

—A Latino student

Week Nine. Teachers as Transformative Intellectuals.

Small Group Discussion and Individual Action Plan: As a teacher, what do you plan to do to disrupt the reproduction of inequality in the school system?

I remembered when I first came to the United States, I cannot understand a word that my teacher was trying to tell me, but I understand that my teacher really cared about me. Thus, I think before I begin to give a lecture about how important it is to respect each other, I am going to model for them how I show my respect to others.

—A Chinese female student

Week Ten. Ending the Course.

Small and Large Group Sharing: How will you use the information you learned in this class to create a socially just classroom environment? How has this course affected you? How would it have been better for you? What do you think should be added or deleted?

In the Asian community to be anything but straight is a disgrace to the family name (and many people may argue this is how it is for anybody). But specifically in the Asian culture, it is not customary for people to air their "dirty laundry" or deviate from the "norm." My own personal life growing up demonstrates to me that I had to try to assimilate to the best of my ability while not causing any problems. I could not even imagine myself confronting my parents about my sexual identity when I don't even talk to them about boys that I am interested in. As an educator who plans to be in a predominately Asian community I want to be sensitive and aware of the issues that my students may have to encounter by themselves in family structures that prefer silence over communication.

—An Asian female student

THE END, OR THE BEGINNING?

It is truly a privilege to teach people to be teachers. By infusing lgbt issues and my own personal story into the curriculum, I hope I normalize not only lgbt issues but all aspects of social justice for them, model it for them, and encourage them to do the same when they have their own classrooms. I have no doubt that my students will change the ways in which teachers and administrators approach every issue in the school system, finally making schools safe for every student regardless and inclusive of sexual/gender identity.

> You made me deal with a lot of issues and a lot of being honest and real with myself. I tend to think that most people have biases even if they say they do not, myself included. So you challenged us to do some real self examining before we get into the classrooms.
>
> —An Asian male student

REFERENCE

Adams, M., L. A. Bell, and P. Griffin, eds. 1997. *Teaching for diversity and social justice.* New York: Routledge.

Afterword: A Word about *Getting Ready for Benjamin* from His Mommies

Michelle Hoffner-Brodsky and Denise Hoffner-Brodsky

Since *Getting Ready for Benjamin* is named for our son, we thought it only fitting that we put in our two cents about what it will take to prepare teachers to create a school system that is truly ready for Benjamin. Before Benjamin was even born, we worried about how his future teachers would treat him and whether they would honor his family. Now that he is only a few years away from school, our concerns are becoming more real. Benjamin has two moms. Will his teachers be prepared to welcome him and create a safe place in which to celebrate his family?

From our first contact with Benjamin's teachers, we will either be made to feel at ease or ostracized, included or invisible. Will they treat us both as his parents and recognize us as a family? Or will they marginalize us with well-intentioned but misguided statements, such as "Oh yes, we have all different kinds of families—divorced parents, drug addicted parents, alcoholic parents and gay parents." (Yes, a very popular daycare provider in our community said this to us.) When talking to another daycare provider recently, we explained that Benjamin has two moms and that we wanted to make sure that the provider was comfortable with that. The response we were met with was: "That won't be a problem since we focus on the individual child, not their family." We knew immediately that this would not be an environment that would approach our son's education holistically. We don't want Benjamin's family to be ignored, we want it to be celebrated. Moreover, heterosexism obscures the fact that children's families are brought up in the classroom all the time.

When Benjamin is in the classroom, we want his teachers to refer with respect to his family. We hope they remember not to make assumptions about his or any child's family constellation. When talking to Benjamin, we want them to refer to "your mommies." When other children make comments or ask questions about Benjamin's parents, we want the teachers to use this as a teachable moment to explain that there are all kinds of families, that some children have a mommy and a daddy, some children have a grandma, some children have two daddies, or an auntie, or two mommies. We want Benjamin's teachers to see it as their duty to interrupt any kind of ignorance or hate speech in the classroom, including homophobic comments.

This is easier said than done. Teachers have to think on their feet, and when thinking on one's feet, often what comes out of one's mouth is what a person is familiar with. "Did your mommy and daddy go on a date for Valentine's Day?" might seem like a harmless enough question. But not only does it exclude children who do not have a mommy and a daddy, it sends the child a message about what the teacher thinks is normal.

Denise remembers many times during physical education class when her teachers laughed right along with her classmates who were making homophobic remarks because they had to be paired up with a member of the same sex for a partner dance when there was not an even number of boys and girls. If she tries, she can still feel a pit in the bottom of her stomach caused by both the behavior of her classmates and the complicity of her teachers. Certainly, those teachers meant no harm and probably had no idea of the negative impact they were having. They were only acting unconsciously. Just as we are working to be conscious parents, we ask that Benjamin's teachers approach teaching with the utmost consciousness.

We want those who are preparing Benjamin's teachers to make them aware on Mother's Day and Father's Day that not all children have "nuclear families" and to help them encourage children to celebrate the families they do have. We want the books and materials in Benjamin's classrooms to represent a diversity of children. We want him to be able to see his own image reflected in stories, songs, and games. We don't want him to learn from his environment that he is abnormal, "different," or that there is anything wrong with his family. Nor do we want him to feel invisible. Years ago when Michelle was teaching high school English, the students had to write a research paper on an oppressed minority. Michelle suggested many different groups to the class, and included "gay and lesbian people" on the list. Because she had already named the group and written it on the board, it became safe for two of the students to choose this topic for their papers. One of those students later ended up coming out to Michelle.

Preparing teachers to make the learning environment welcoming for Benjamin requires not only teaching them how to create a supportive classroom setting but encouraging them to help build a school community that embraces diversity. We recognize that this is no easy task because it requires teacher educators and classroom teachers to step outside their comfort zones. In some school districts this will involve more than personal growth. In identifying as an ally, an educator may find himself or herself subject to some of the same prejudices faced by lesbian, gay, bisexual, and transgendered (lgbt) people and their families. This may be risky at times, but it's the right thing to do. We hope that Benjamin's teachers will see it as their responsibility to educate their colleagues, to interrupt homophobic comments heard in the teacher's room, and to help the staff and administration make sure that the school is home to all families. His teachers can make it clear that they are safe, supportive people by hanging posters in their classrooms, putting rainbow stickers on their doors, acting as advisors to gay-straight alliances, and using inclusive language.

We hope that Benjamin's teachers will be encouraged to advocate for lgbt rights and celebrate diversity outside the classroom as well. This could include anything from interrupting homophobic remarks heard in line at the grocery store to marching in a pride parade. Acting as an ally in this way helps make not only the classroom safe for Benjamin, but the world.

To summarize what is most important to us, we have devised a top ten list to assist teacher educators as they help future teachers in getting ready for Benjamin.

TOP TEN LIST FOR HOW TO GET READY FOR BENJAMIN

1. Use language that includes all kinds of families.
2. If asking kids questions about their families in the classroom, don't skip the child of gay parents out of your own discomfort.
3. Educate yourself about lgbt families and lgbt culture.
4. If you're not sure about something, ask the parents, even if you're worried that you'll seem clueless.
5. Interrupt homophobic language and behavior. Use it as an opportunity to teach.
6. Seek out books, posters, and other learning materials that reflect familial diversity.
7. Affirmatively identify yourself as an ally to lgbt people and their friends and families.
8. Question your students' (and your own) heterosexist assumptions.
9. Seek out opportunities to challenge your colleagues to join you in creating an inclusive school environment.
10. Love our children for who they are.

We hope that these suggestions will help educators as they are getting ready for Benjamin. He might just be in your classroom!

Index

About the Contributors

Tim Bedford grew up in Leicester, England, and is a graduate of Churchill College, Cambridge University. He has taught in high schools in the United Kingdom, Kenya, and Japan and currently teaches at Oulun Lyseon Lukio in Oulu and Oulu University Department of Education, Finland. He directs the European Union supported Gay and Lesbian Educational Equity (GLEE) Project to create a network of schools providing safe and affirming learning environments for lesbian, gay, bisexual, and transgendered students and staff.

Deborah P. Berrill is an associate professor with the Faculty of Education, Queen's University, Canada. She is interested in teaching for social justice, and her research explores issues of identity and community, with a focus on the sites of gender and science, gender and teachers/teacher candidates, and literacy. She has published books and papers in Canada, the United States, and the United Kingdom and conducts much of her present work on masculinities with her colleague Wayne Martino of Australia.

Roger Brindley is an assistant professor of elementary education at the University of South Florida, where he teaches qualitative research methods, teacher education, and constructivist theory.

Kevin P. Colleary teaches elementary social studies methods at Hunter College, City University of New York. His teaching and research interests intersect around incorporating sexual diversity into the elementary social studies curriculum, helping preservice and in-service teachers understand their role in perpetuating justice, and teacher awareness of the connections between sexual diversity issues and civil rights in the classroom and beyond.

Steve Fifield is an assistant professor in the Department of Biological Sciences and the School of Education at the University of Delaware. His research in science education examines students' and teachers' beliefs and practices, personal identity, and how meanings of science are produced in curricula and classrooms. He teaches courses in introductory biology and secondary science education.

Michael Gard is a lecturer in physical education, dance, and the sociocultural foundations of sport and physical activity at Charles Sturt University, where he is also a member of the Centre for Cultural Research into Risk. He has written and published on gender, sexuality, the human body, and the shortcomings of biological explanations of human behavior. Michael has recently also completed a major piece of qualitative research into the involvement of men in ballet and contemporary dance.

Karen Glasgow holds a Ph.D. in urban leadership and is a principal of an elementary school in Los Angeles. She is an adjunct professor at both Claremont Graduate University and California State University Los Angeles in the Department of Education. Her interests include diversity issues and racial transitions in urban neighborhoods.

Michelle Hoffner-Brodsky and **Denise Hoffner-Brodsky** are having an amazing time raising Benjamin and his baby brother Julian. Denise works as an environmental justice attorney and regards herself as a garden variety activist who is addicted to the written word. Michelle is an educator who has taught children in the classroom, educated community members on the effects of domestic violence on children, and worked as a bilingual advocate in the deaf community. They live in Davis, California, with Benjamin and Julian and their two cats, Sasha and Chantal.

James R. King is a professor of reading education at the University of South Florida in Tampa, where he teaches in literacy and qualitative research methods.

Rita M. Kissen is an associate professor of teacher education and women's studies at the University of Southern Maine. She is the author of *The Last Closet: The Real Lives of Lesbian and Gay Teachers* (Heinemann, 1996), as well as articles on teaching for social justice. She is a co-founder and past president of the Southern Maine chapter of GLSEN, the Gay, Lesbian and Straight Education Network.

Paula Kluth is an assistant professor in the Department of Teaching and Leadership at Syracuse University. She is a former special educator who has served as a classroom teacher and consulting teacher. She has taught in and engages in research in both elementary and secondary schools. Her professional and research interests center on including students with significant disabilities in inclusive classrooms and designing curricular adaptations for learners with and without disabilities.

Will Letts is the associate director of the Centre for Cultural Research into Risk at Charles Sturt University, Bathurst, Australia, where he teaches science methods and sociology of education. He is currently engaged in research examining the extent to which lesbian, gay, bisexual, and transgendered teachers and administrators are "at risk" at work. His research interests lie in the cultural studies of science and science education, especially with respect to sexuality, gender, and indigenous knowledges.

Arthur Lipkin is a research associate at the Harvard Graduate School of Education, a senior trainer for the Massachusetts Safe Schools Program for Gay and Lesbian Students, and the author of *Understanding Homosexuality, Changing Schools* (Westview, 1999). He taught English for twenty years at the Cambridge Rindge & Latin School and was a founder, with Lawrence Kohlberg, of the Cluster School Program.

Delores D. Liston is an associate professor of curriculum and foundations at Georgia Southern University. Her research and teaching interests focus on the application of philosophical, ethical, and feminist understandings to education. She received her Ph.D. from the University of North Carolina at Greensboro. She recently authored a book, *Joy as Metaphor of Convergence: A Phenomenological and Aesthetic Investigation of Social and Educational Change* (Hampton Press, forthcoming).

Wayne Martino was formerly a high school teacher and now lectures in the School of Education, Murdoch University, Perth, Western Australia. He is the co-author of two forthcoming books, *Boys' Stuff: Boys Talk about What Really Matters* (Allen & Unwin) and *So What's a Boy? Addressing Issues of Masculinity and Schooling* (Open University Press). His current research with Deborah Berrill explores the impact of masculinities and sexuality on the lives of male teacher candidates and male teachers in Canada and Australia.

Cris Mayo is assistant professor in the School of Education at the University of Delaware, where she teaches multicultural education and gender studies.

Her research interests include sexuality education, queer studies, anti-bias education, and philosophy of education.

Michael J. Middleton is an assistant professor in the Department of Education at the University of New Hampshire. He was a high school mathematics teacher prior to completing a Ph.D. in education and psychology at the University of Michigan. His research interests include motivation and learning environments, school transitions, and teacher education at the middle and high school levels.

Jane A. Page is professor and department chair of Curriculum, Foundations, and Research at Georgia Southern University. She is also founder and co-chair of the Gay, Lesbian, & Straight Education Network of Southeast Georgia. She is the author of numerous articles and book chapters related to diversity issues. Her current research focus is homophobia in the schools. In addition to her work at Georgia Southern, Page is enrolled in ministerial studies at Meadville Lombard Theological School.

Karleen Pendleton Jiménez is a writer, teacher, and doctoral student in education at York University. She is a member of Lengua Latina, a writing group for Latinas in Toronto. She is also the author of the children's book, *Are You a Boy or a Girl?* (Green Dragon Press, 2000).

Karen Phillips resides in Portland, Maine, with her partner and dog. As a migrant teacher at Portland High School, Karen enjoys working with predominantly immigrant and refugee students. Working with such a diverse population has led her to further explore her identity as a Japanese American along with issues of bicultural identity. The need to provide a voice for underrepresented or nonrepresented groups in society remains an integral part of Karen's personal and professional life.

Eric Rofes is assistant professor of education at Humboldt State University in Arcata, California. A former sixth-grade and middle school teacher, he is the author of nine books, including *Socrates, Plato, & Guys Like Me: Confessions of a Gay School Teacher* (Alyson, 1985).

Ronni Sanlo is the director of the UCLA Lesbian Gay Bisexual Transgender Campus Resource Center and a lecturer in the UCLA Graduate School of Education. She earned her degrees from the University of Florida and the University of North Florida. Her research area is sexual orientation issues in education and higher education. Ronni is the editor of *Working with LGBT*

College Students: A Handbook for Faculty and Administrators (Greenwood Press, 1998).

Mara Sapon-Shevin is professor of education at Syracuse University. Her areas of interest include anti-racist pedagogy, teacher education reform, and teaching for social justice. Her most recent book is *Because We Can Change the World: A Practical Guide to Building Cooperative, Inclusive Classroom Communities* (Allyn & Bacon, 1998). Mara attributes her strong commitment to creating schools and societies that expand definitions and possibilities for gender and sexual definition to the powerful example set by her two daughters.

Genét Simone lives in Boulder, Colorado, where she is finishing her doctorate in teacher education. She teaches at Naropa University and also works for the Institute for Social and Emotional Learning. Genét co-edited an issue of *Education and Urban Society* (Corwin Press, 2000) on sexual orientation and published a chapter about the personal growth of preservice teachers in *Unfolding BodyMind: Exploring Possibility Through Education* (Holistic Education Press, 2001). Her most recent publication appeared in *Educational Leadership* (September 2001).

"Starr" is the pseudonym of an educator who grew up in the Northeastern United States, where she was very active in her high school agriculture program and the Future Farmers of America. She attended an Ivy League university first as a biology major, then as a graduate student earning her MAT. She currently teaches high school agriculture near her hometown.

Diana Straut is an assistant professor in the School of Education at Syracuse University. Among the courses that she teaches is "Social Studies Methods for Elementary School Teachers." Her interests include understanding how elementary school teachers manage complex and controversial topics with elementary school children.

Howard (Lee) Swain is a graduate student in the Department of Administration, Leadership and Technology at New York University. He is a graduate assistant in the NYU Office of Lesbian, Gay, Bisexual and Transgender Student Services (www.nyu.edu/lgbt), where he coordinates programs on sexual orientation and gender identification.

Allison J. Young is an assistant professor in the College of Education at Western Michigan University in Kalamazoo, Michigan. Her research interests involve motivational beliefs and self-regulated learning in the social contexts of secondary and postsecondary schooling and epistemological beliefs and their relation to curriculum. Her most recent work centers on representations of gays and lesbians in education, particularly as these issues intersect with the context of teacher education programs.